studies in jazz

The Institute of Jazz Studies
Rutgers—The State University of New Jersey
General Editors: Dan Morgenstern and Edward Berger

1. BENNY CARTER: A Life in American Music, *by Morroe Berger, Edward Berger, and James Patrick, 2 vols., 1982*
2. ART TATUM: A Guide to His Recorded Music, *by Arnold Laubich and Ray Spencer, 1982*
3. ERROLL GARNER: The Most Happy Piano, *by James M. Doran, 1985*
4. JAMES P. JOHNSON: A Case of Mistaken Identity, *by Scott E. Brown;* Discography 1917–1950, *by Robert Hilbert, 1986*
5. PEE WEE ERWIN: This Horn for Hire, *as told to Warren W. Vaché Sr., 1987*
6. BENNY GOODMAN: Listen to His Legacy, *by D. Russell Connor, 1988*
7. ELLINGTONIA: The Recorded Music of Duke Ellington and His Sidemen, *by W. E. Timner, 1988; 4th ed., 1996*
8. THE GLENN MILLER ARMY AIR FORCE BAND: Sustineo Alas / I Sustain the Wings, *by Edward F. Polic;* Foreword *by George T. Simon, 1989*
9. SWING LEGACY, *by Chip Deffaa, 1989*
10. REMINISCING IN TEMPO: The Life and Times of a Jazz Hustler, *by Teddy Reig, with Edward Berger, 1990*
11. IN THE MAINSTREAM: 18 Portraits in Jazz, *by Chip Deffaa, 1992*
12. BUDDY DeFRANCO: A Biographical Portrait and Discography, *by John Kuehn and Arne Astrup, 1993*
13. PEE WEE SPEAKS: A Discography of Pee Wee Russell, *by Robert Hilbert, with David Niven, 1992*
14. SYLVESTER AHOLA: The Gloucester Gabriel, *by Dick Hill, 1993*
15. THE POLICE CARD DISCORD, *by Maxwell T. Cohen, 1993*
16. TRADITIONALISTS AND REVIVALISTS IN JAZZ, *by Chip Deffaa, 1993*
17. BASSICALLY SPEAKING: An Oral History of George Duvivier, *by Edward Berger;* Musical Analysis *by David Chevan, 1993*
18. TRAM: The Frank Trumbauer Story, *by Philip R. Evans and Larry F. Kiner, with William Trumbauer, 1994*
19. TOMMY DORSEY: On the Side, *by Robert L. Stockdale, 1995*
20. JOHN COLTRANE: A Discography and Musical Biography, *by Yasuhiro Fujioka, with Lewis Porter and Yoh-ichi Hamada, 1995*
21. RED HEAD: A Chronological Survey of "Red" Nichols and His Five Pennies, *by Stephen M. Stroff, 1996*
22. THE RED NICHOLS STORY: After Intermission 1942–1965, *by Philip R. Evans, Stanley Hester, Stephen Hester, and Linda Evans, 1997*

23. BENNY GOODMAN: Wrappin' It Up, *by D. Russell Connor, 1996*
24. CHARLIE PARKER AND THEMATIC IMPROVISATION, *by Henry Martin, 1996*
25. BACK BEATS AND RIM SHOTS: The Johnny Blowers Story, *by Warren W. Vaché Sr., 1997*
26. DUKE ELLINGTON: A Listener's Guide, *by Eddie Lambert, 1998*
27. SERGE CHALOFF: A Musical Biography and Discography, *by Vladimir Simosko, 1998*
28. HOT JAZZ: From Harlem to Storyville, *by David Griffiths, 1998*
29. ARTIE SHAW: A Musical Biography and Discography, *by Vladimir Simosko, 2000*
30. JIMMY DORSEY: A Study in Contrasts, *by Robert L. Stockdale, 1998*
31. STRIDE!: Fats, Jimmy, Lion, Lamb and All the Other Ticklers, *by John L. Fell and Terkild Vinding, 1999*
32. GIANT STRIDES: The Legacy of Dick Wellstood, *by Edward N. Meyer, 1999*
33. JAZZ GENTRY: Aristocrats of the Music World, *by Warren W. Vaché Sr., 1999*
34. THE UNSUNG SONGWRITERS: America's Masters of Melody, *by Warren W. Vaché Sr., 2000*
35. THE MUSICAL WORLD OF J. J. JOHNSON, *by Joshua Berrett and Louis G. Bourgois III, 1999*
36. THE LADIES WHO SING WITH THE BAND, *by Betty Bennett, 2000*
37. AN UNSUNG CAT: The Life and Music of Warne Marsh, *by Safford Chamberlain, 2000*
38. JAZZ IN NEW ORLEANS: The Postwar Years Through 1970, *by Charles Suhor, 2001*
39. THE YOUNG LOUIS ARMSTRONG ON RECORDS: A Critical Survey of the Early Recordings, 1923–1928, *by Edward Brooks, 2002*
40. BENNY CARTER: A Life in American Music, Second Edition, *by Morroe Berger, Edward Berger, and James Patrick, 2 vols., 2002*
41. CHORD CHANGES ON THE CHALKBOARD: How Public School Teachers Shaped Jazz and the Music of New Orleans, *by Al Kennedy,* Foreword *by Ellis Marsalis Jr., 2002*
42. CONTEMPORARY CAT: Terence Blanchard with Special Guests, *by Anthony Magro, 2002*
43. PAUL WHITEMAN: Pioneer in American Music, Volume I: 1890–1930, *by Don Rayno, 2003*
44. GOOD VIBES: A Life in Jazz, *by Terry Gibbs with Cary Ginell, 2003*
45. TOM TALBERT—HIS LIFE AND TIMES: Voices from a Vanished World of Jazz, *by Bruce Talbot, 2004*
46. SITTIN' IN WITH CHRIS GRIFFIN: A Reminiscence of Radio and Recording's Golden Years, *by Warren W. Vaché, 2005*

47. FIFTIES JAZZ TALK: An Oral Retrospective, *by Gordon Jack, 2004*
48. FLORENCE MILLS: Harlem Jazz Queen, *by Bill Egan, 2004*
49. SWING ERA SCRAPBOOK: The Teenage Diaries and Radio Logs of Bob Inman, 1936–1938, *by Ken Vail, 2005*
50. FATS WALLER ON THE AIR: The Radio Broadcasts and Discography, *by Stephen Taylor, 2006*
51. ALL OF ME: The Complete Discography of Louis Armstrong, *by Jos Willems, 2006*
52. MUSIC AND THE CREATIVE SPIRIT: Innovators in Jazz, Improvisation, and the Avant Garde, *by Lloyd Peterson, 2006*
53. THE STORY OF FAKE BOOKS: Bootlegging Songs to Musicians, *by Barry Kernfeld, 2006*
54. ELLINGTONIA: The Recorded Music of Duke Ellington and His Sidemen, 5th edition, *by W. E. Timner, 2007*
55. JAZZ FICTION: A History and Comprehensive Reader's Guide, *by David Rife, 2007*
56. MISSION IMPOSSIBLE: My Life In Music, *by Lalo Schifrin, edited by Richard H. Palmer, 2008*
57. THE CONTRADICTIONS OF JAZZ, *by Paul Rinzler, 2008*
58. EARLY TWENTIETH-CENTURY BRASS IDIOMS: Art, Jazz, and Other Popular Traditions, *edited by Howard T. Weiner, 2008*
59. THE MUSIC AND LIFE OF THEODORE "FATS" NAVARRO: Infatuation, *by Leif Bo Petersen and Theo Rehak, 2009*
60. WHERE THE DARK AND THE LIGHT FOLKS MEET: Race and the Mythology, Politics, and Business of Jazz, *by Randall Sandke, 2010*
61. JAZZ BOOKS IN THE 1990S: An Annotated Bibliography, *by Janice Leslie Hochstat Greenberg, 2010*

Jazz Books in the 1990s

An Annotated Bibliography

Janice Leslie Hochstat Greenberg

Studies in Jazz, No. 61

The Scarecrow Press, Inc.
Lanham • Toronto • Plymouth, UK
2010

Published by Scarecrow Press, Inc.
A wholly owned subsidiary of The Rowman & Littlefield Publishing Group, Inc.
4501 Forbes Boulevard, Suite 200, Lanham, Maryland 20706
http://www.scarecrowpress.com

Estover Road, Plymouth PL6 7PY, United Kingdom

Copyright © 2010 by Janice Leslie Hochstat Greenberg

All rights reserved. No part of this book may be reproduced in any form or by any electronic or mechanical means, including information storage and retrieval systems, without written permission from the publisher, except by a reviewer who may quote passages in a review.

British Library Cataloguing in Publication Information Available

Library of Congress Cataloging-in-Publication Data

Hochstat-Greenberg, Janice Leslie.
  Jazz books in the 1990s : an annotated bibliography / Janice Leslie Hochstat Greenberg.
    p. cm. — (Studies in jazz ; no. 61)
  Includes bibliographical references and indexes.
  ISBN 978-0-8108-6985-1 (pbk. : alk. paper) — ISBN 978-0-8108-6986-8 (ebook)
  1. Jazz—Bibliography. I. Title.
  ML128.J3H63 2010
  016.78165—dc22
                                                                             2009051072

∞™ The paper used in this publication meets the minimum requirements of American National Standard for Information Sciences—Permanence of Paper for Printed Library Materials, ANSI/NISO Z39.48-1992.

Printed in the United States of America.

Dedication

To my husband, Maury
My mom, Evelyn, and late dad, Irving
My friend, colleague, and mentor, the late Thelma Tate
My friend, mentor, and editor, Ed Berger
My goddaughter, Rachel
My friend, Kelsey

This book is for you
and
because of you.

JLG

Contents

Series Foreword		xi
Introduction and Methodology		xiii
Acknowledgments		xv
1	Biographies	1
	Individuals	1
	Collective Biographies	32
	Bands/Orchestras	41
	Women in Jazz	43
2	History	45
	General History	45
	Eras & Styles	48
	Institutions	53
	Media	53
	Recordings	53
3	Individual Instruments	55
	Bass Guitar	55
	Drums	55
	Guitar	56
	Piano	57
	Saxophone	57
	Trombone	58
4	Essays and Criticism	59

5	Musicology	71
	Musical Theory/Improvisation	71
	Jazz and Race	72
6	Regional Studies	75
	Africa—South Africa	75
	Australia	76
	Europe	76
	North America	78
7	Discographies	89
	Artists/Groups	89
	Comprehensive	150
	Geographical	150
	Recording Companies	151
8	Record Guides	155
9	Pictorial	159
	Photography	159
	Album Covers	162
	Posters	163
10	Reference Works	165
	Bibliographies	165
	Dictionaries and Encyclopedias	166
11	Miscellaneous	169
	Conference Proceedings	169
	Other	170

Indexes	
Subject	173
Author	189
Title	199
About the Author	211

Series Foreword

The past two decades have seen a tremendous growth in the literature of jazz. One reason is the acceptance of jazz within the academy and the nation's major cultural institutions. Whereas most of the significant early works in the field were the province of amateur (in the best sense of the word) scholars, journalists, and enthusiasts, a significant portion of the current literature comes from academically trained scholars. At the Institute of Jazz Studies, we have witnessed this growth graphically as our book collection has expanded from a few bays to completely filling a stack area that seemed spacious only a few years ago. In addition to our own *Studies in Jazz*, university presses, such as Michigan, Illinois, Oxford, L.S.U., and Chicago, have longstanding jazz series. At the other end of the spectrum, self-published works have also burgeoned, particularly in the discographical field, as have Internet-based publications.

Jazz bibliography has not kept pace with this rapid growth. Early pioneering efforts, such as Alan Merriam's *Bibliography of Jazz* (1954), set the stage for the *International Jazz Bibliography* (1969, with supplements to 1973) by Carl Gregor, Herzog zu Mecklenburg. Gregor's admirable work was followed by several less successful attempts at comprehensive jazz bibliography, as well as some fine specialized works. It became increasingly clear that a new jazz bibliography was sorely needed. It also became clear that no single volume could contain the enormous output of jazz books over the past three decades.

Janice Greenberg has leaped into the breach with this first volume of a projected decade-by-decade examination of the jazz literature. My colleagues and I at the Institute of Jazz Studies witnessed firsthand the dedication and tenacity Janice brought to this project as she relentlessly pursued every lead in a venture where "the devil is in the details." Dan Morgenstern, my series co-editor, once wrote an article in *Down Beat* with the title "Discography: The Thankless Science." Surely, bibliography is an equally thankless task. This volume is an important first step that will benefit jazz researchers for years to come.

Ed Berger
Series Editor

Introduction and Methodology

The purpose of this bibliography is to provide the reader with as comprehensive a listing as possible of the adult nonfiction books on jazz published in English from 1990 through 1999. Reprinted volumes are included only if they contain new material, such as an updated introduction. Works of fiction, poetry, children's literature, and jazz instruction are not included. The books listed in this volume were published not only in the United States, Canada, Australia, New Zealand, and the United Kingdom, but also in Finland, the Netherlands, Japan, and India, among other countries. Some listed books are written primarily in another language but have English portions. Although the scope of this work is books published in the 1990s, the subject matter extends back to jazz's earliest history.

In 1991, on a visit to the Institute of Jazz Studies at Rutgers University in Newark, New Jersey, I was intrigued to learn that no comprehensive, reasonably current jazz bibliography existed. The last thorough listing of jazz books was the Duke of Mecklenburg's *International Jazz Bibliography: Jazz Books from 1919 to 1968*, with supplements extending only to 1973.

In late 2001, when this book was conceived, the 1990s sounded like a good place to start. Some of my colleagues estimated this bibliography would have 300 volumes. Then I found more and more books—more than 700 in all. Although it did not seem so in the beginning, the search has so far proven to be endless. The biggest chapter is "Discographies," with 332 entries.

I particularly relied on the online library catalogs of Rutgers University, the Center for Black Music Research at Columbia College in Chicago, the Library of Congress, the New York Public Library, the British Library, and the national libraries of Canada, Australia, New Zealand, France, Germany, Finland, and the Netherlands. I was also fortunate to obtain a list of books in the collection of the Jazzinstitut Darmstadt, Europe's largest public research archive on jazz.

My bibliographic guide was the *Chicago Manual of Style*, 15th edition (Chicago: University of Chicago Press, 1993). If publication details were not included with the book, I tried, either through online library catalogs or the publishers, to add this information in brackets.

Each chapter is arranged by author, except for the biography, discography, and regional studies chapters.

For each entry, I indicate when a book contains a bibliography, discography, notes, indexes, musical transcriptions, illustrations, photographs, or any other additional material. In the discography chapter, the inclusion of unissued material or reissues is noted.

Each book is listed only once, even if it falls between categories. For example, William Claxton's book of Chet Baker photographs is in the biographical chapter, not the pictorial chapter. Thus the reader is encouraged to make use of the indexes for cross-referencing.

For the few cases in which I was not able to personally examine a book, "not reviewed" appears in the entry.

In writing this book I've gotten reacquainted with many of my favorite jazz musicians, and learned about many interesting musicians I had only heard of in passing. I have also discovered fascinating works by writers such as Whitney Balliett, Krin Gabbard, Gary Giddins, Eric Nisenson, Lewis Porter, Ralph J. Gleason, Paul Berliner, and Barry Kernfeld, among others. While working on this project, my admiration has grown for the musicians who create jazz, and for the writers who describe the music in its many facets.

I have enjoyed both the detective work and the process of compiling the information in this book. I hope that you, the reader, find this a useful tool for facilitating your research or simply enhancing your appreciation of jazz.

Acknowledgments

The seeds for this book were first sown by my mom, Evelyn, and late dad, Irving Hochstat. They instilled in me a love for reading and music and always encouraged me to achieve my goals, no matter what the challenges were.

The late Thelma Tate first taught me how to write an annotation back in 1991, and allowed me to write some annotations for a bibliography she was compiling. A decade later, after I had prepared several bibliographies of my own, Thelma encouraged me to submit a proposal for what eventually became this book. She simply said, "You can do it!" She also helped me organize the structure of this book. This book would not have been possible without her encouragement in its early stages.

I am very fortunate to be able to turn to Ed Berger for guidance. In matters of writing style and jazz information, he is a fount of knowledge and has a gift for making it look good on paper.

I have also learned much from Dan Morgenstern, whose love for all things jazz is highly contagious.

Renée Camus, thank you very much for your time, patience, encouragement, and firm guiding hand.

Evan Spring, your eye for detail and wonderful advice for putting the finishing touches on this book have been quite helpful.

The late Esther Smith was the first person I met at IJS, and she was always a big source of encouragement. Vincent Pelote helped me find books on jazz from other libraries. Tad Hershorn, Annie Kuebler, John Clement, and Bob Nahory spent time discussing aspects of the project with me. Joe Peterson, April Grier, and Ryan Mahoney helped patiently with my endless reference questions.

Early on in my research, Dr. Wolfram Knauer of the Jazzinstitut Darmstadt sent me a lengthy printout of all the Institute's jazz books. Gerard Bielderman and Dennis Huggard also provided valuable information. Metolius Music Company answered a number of my phone inquiries. Samuel Perryman and Larry Appelbaum of the Library of Congress and Suzanne Flandreau of the Center for Black Music Research (at Columbia College in Chicago) were of great assistance in my research. The library staffs at the New York Public Library for the Performing Arts, the John Cotton Dana Library at Rutgers-Newark, and the Mabel Smith Douglass Library, Archibald S. Alexander Library, and Blanche and Irving Laurie Music Library at Rutgers-New Brunswick, have been very generous with their time, assistance, and support. Countless other staff members at libraries around the world have been extremely helpful in my quest for information.

One of my most serendipitous visits was to the Jazz Record Mart in Chicago. The staff was very accommodating, and I was able to sit and pore over jazz books for many hours.

The consummate reference librarian, Susan Kheel, has reviewed several of my chapters (including the reference chapter) and offered invaluable advice, which I have endeavored to incorporate in this book.

Walter Dean Myers and Constance Myers have each offered priceless support and advice—from first-hand experience.

Francoise Puniello offered her support and example and I follow in her footsteps.

My sister Lauren Brenner and I have shared a love of music since we were both very young. Her encouragement has helped me immensely.

Rachel and Dan Brenner and Kelsey Goebel, your enthusiasm has helped me more than you know through this long process.

My sister-in-law Dorothy Greenberg, nephews Andrew and Justin, and niece Kim have also given me much encouragement.

My aunt Adele Feierstein, aunt Jean Glass, late aunt Rose Miller, and late uncles Bernard Feierstein and Martin Glass have provided much TLC and encouragement, not only during this project, but throughout my entire life.

My cousins Sara Miller McCune, Dorothy Furiness, and Laurie Glass have each given important feedback and support.

My REFORMISTA friends Ben Ocón, Luis Herrera, Nancy Herrera, Camila, Alire, John Ayala, Roxana Benavides, Sandra Ríos Balderrama, Ana-Elba Pavón, Jacqueline Ayala, Ingrid Betancourt, Ina Rimpau, Isabel Espinal, and Mario Gonzalez have also provided insight and support.

My professional supervisors Priscilla Gardner, Sonia Araujo, and Hussein Odeh encouraged me to tackle this project.

My supervisors in the Technical Services department, Clare Newton and Nancy Mendoza, have been very supportive.

My special friends Kathleen Krantz, John James, Yolanda Richardson, Jack James, Darryl James, David James, Tim Friel, Georgette Clark, Nancy Thomas, Robert Fabbro, Susan Stewart, Vanessa Benekin, Mary Bronner, Sam Saulsberry, Mary Quinn, Barbara Murrell, Ellen Rice, Nelly Flores, Bea Urrutia, John Butler, Michael Kaplan, Pat Mulligan, Cynthia Raysor, Tyara Tucker, Sasha Martinez,

Cynthia Harris, Troy Boatright, Robert Rivers, Cliff Waldman, Betty Turrock, Satia Orange, Laura Cooper, Carla Hayden, KG Schneider, Mark Levine, Sam and Esther Horowitz, Barbara Genco, Gail and Barry Wittman, Emilie and Ed Herzberg, Joyce Houston, Ann Marie and Bob Gobel, Shai and Ruth Richardson, Lynn Wolfcale, Kim Sauer, Bob and Naomi Blum, Barbara Stallone, Patty Jackson, Rabbi Michael Pont, Brian Jill, Evan Lillianthal, Janet and Bill Schwartz, Stuart and Joann Abraham, Phyllis Brooks, Elaine Singer, Alice Grun, Sid and Audrey Rabinowitz, Neal Brunson, Keline Adams, and Ted Brunson—and my late friends Molly Tauchner, Etta Milovsky, Grace James and Helena Robinson—have each been a great source of strength, support, and perspective.

My train friends Alby, Mark, Dr. Jay, Audrey Sanders, Tom Greco, Paul Tepperman, Karen Aguilar, Donna Lombardi, Tom Lucas, Laura Friedman Young, Yolanda Milanese, and Erica Kearns have shared in the news of my book's journey.

Last, but definitely far from least, my husband, Maury Greenberg, has been a constant source of support, often forgoing joint weekend activities over this project's eight-year span. He has also accompanied me on many research expeditions to New Brunswick and Newark and Washington, DC. I cannot thank him enough.

1
Biographies

Biographies published in the 1990s varied greatly in style and quality. They ranged from "tell-all" chronicles to detailed analyses of a musician's life and work. In addition to biographical and autobiographical narratives, the books took the form of essay collections, interviews, and anthologies of many types. Collective biographies covering two or more individuals were also popular.

I have organized the biographical section into four categories: Individuals, Collective Biographies, Bands and Orchestras, and Women in Jazz.

INDIVIDUALS

Adler, Larry (harmonica, U.S.)

1-1 Adler, Larry. *Me and My Big Mouth.* With Philip Judge. Edited by William Hall. London: Blake, 1994. 222 pp.
  Biography.
  Photographs.

Ahola, Sylvester (trumpet/singer, U.S.)

1-2 Hill, Dick. *Sylvester Ahola: The Gloucester Gabriel.* Studies in Jazz, no. 14. Foreword by Brian Rust. Metuchen, NJ: The Scarecrow Press, 1993. 219 pp.
  Ahola was a little-known but prolific musician, recording in both the United States and England during the 1920s and 1930s.
  Bibliography; discography; illustrations; indexes; photographs.

Allison, Mose (piano/singer, U.S.)

1-3 Jones, Patti. *One Man's Blues: The Life and Music of Mose Allison.* London: Quartet Books, 1995. 358 pp.
  Biography.
  Discography; index; notes; photographs.

Archey, Jimmy (trombone, U.S.)

1-4 Carr, Peter. *Jimmy Archey: The Little Giant of the Trombone.* New Orleans: Jazzology Press, 1999. 188 pp.
  Biography.
  Index; photographs.

Armstrong, Louis (trumpet/singer, U.S.)

1-5 Armstrong, Louis. *Louis Armstrong, in His Own Words: Selected Writings.* Edited and with an introduction by Thomas Brothers. Annotated index by Charles Kinzer. New York: Oxford University Press, 1999. 302 pp.
  Selection of Armstrong's writings from 1922 to 1970, mostly unpublished. Includes personal letters, autobiographical writings, essays, and periodical articles.
  Appendix; bibliographies; index.

1-6 ———. *Swing That Music.* New foreword by Dan Morgenstern. New York: Da Capo Press, 1993. 136 pp.
  Autobiography. First published in 1936 by Longmans, Green.
  Musical transcriptions; photographs.

1-7 Bergreen, Laurence. *Louis Armstrong: An Extravagant Life.* New York: Broadway Books, 1997. 364 pp.
  Biography.
  Bibliography; discography; index; notes; photographs.

1-8 Berrett, Joshua, ed. *The Louis Armstrong Companion: Eight Decades of Commentary.* New York: Schirmer Books, 1999. 299 pp.
  Collection of readings that "attempt to capture the essence of Louis Armstrong's spirit and illuminate his contributions to twentieth-century culture as musician, entertainer, civil libertarian, and human being." Includes previously published articles, interviews, and reviews as well as some of Louis's writing (letters, articles, and essays).
  Bibliography; chronology; discography; index; photographs.

1-9 Boujut, Michel. *Louis Armstrong.* Translated by Charles Penwarden. New York: Rizzoli, 1998. 143 pp.
  Photobiography. Translated from the French.
  Bibliography; discography; filmography; index; photographs.

1-10 Giddins, Gary. *Satchmo*. New York: Da Capo Press, 1998. 219 pp.
Photobiography. First published in 1992 by Anchor Books.
Bibliography; discography; photographs.

1-11 Miller, Marc H., ed. *Louis Armstrong: A Cultural Legacy*. Seattle: Queens Museum of Art, New York, in association with University of Washington Press, 1994. 248 pp.
Catalog of the Queens Museum of Art exhibition chronicling Armstrong's life. Includes five essays: "Louis Armstrong: A Cultural Legacy" and "Louis Armstrong: A Portrait Record," by Marc H. Miller; "Louis Armstrong and African-American Culture," by Richard A. Long; "Louis Armstrong and the Development and Diffusion of Jazz," by Dan Morgenstern; and "Louis Armstrong: The Films," by Donald Bogle. Includes itemization of objects on display in the exhibition.
Bibliography; illustrations; index; photographs.

1-12 Stratemann, Klaus. *Louis Armstrong on the Screen*. Copenhagen: JazzMedia, 1996. 670 pp.
Annotated listing of film and television appearances from 1924 to 1971. Appendixes include "Chronological Film List," "Louis Armstrong on TV," and "European Itineraries."
Illustrations; indexes; photographs.

1-13 Travis, Dempsey J. *The Louis Armstrong Odyssey: From Jane Alley to America's Jazz Ambassador*. Chicago: Urban Research Press, 1997. 240 pp.
Biography. Includes recollections by some of Armstrong's colleagues.
Bibliography; index; illustrations, photographs.

Asher, Don (piano, U.S.)

1-14 Asher, Don. *Notes from a Battered Grand: A Memoir*. New York: Harcourt Brace Jovanovich, 1992. 305 pp.
Autobiography.

Baker, Chet (trumpet, U.S.)

1-15 Baker, Chet. *As Though I Had Wings: The Lost Memoir*. Introduction by Carol Baker. New York: St. Martin's Press, 1997. 118 pp.
Autobiography.
Discography.

1-16 Claxton, William. *Young Chet: The Young Chet Baker Photographed by William Claxton*. Preface by Christian Caujolle. New York: teNeues Publishing Company, 1998. 110 pp.
Photographs, 1952 to 1957.

1-17 Wulff, Ingo, ed. *Chet Baker in Europe, 1975–1988.* Kiel, Germany: Nieswand, 1993. 171 pp.
   Collection of photographs, and recollections by Baker's colleagues. In German and English.
   Discography; photographs.

Baker, Kenny (trumpet, UK)

1-18 Crosby, Robert G. *Kenny Baker: The Life and Times of a Jazz Musician.* Foreword by Jack Parnell. Craigweil on Sea, UK: Evergreen Graphics, 1999. 132 pp.
   Authorized biography. Includes interviews with Baker's musical colleagues.
   Illustrations; photographs.

Bennett, Tony (singer, U.S.)

1-19 Bennett, Tony. *The Good Life.* With Will Friedwald. New York: Pocket Books, 1998. 312 pp.
   Autobiography.
   Discography; photographs.

1-20 Hoffman, Matthew. *Tony Bennett: The Best Is Yet to Come.* New York: MetroBooks, 1997. 120 pp.
   Pictorial biography.
   Bibliography; discography; index; photographs.

Berigan, Bunny (trumpet/bandleader, U.S.)

1-21 Dupuis, Robert. *Bunny Berigan: Elusive Legend of Jazz.* Baton Rouge: Louisiana State University Press, 1993. 368 pp.
   Biography.
   Bibliography; discography; index; photographs.

Blowers, Johnny (drums, U.S.)

1-22 Vaché, Warren W. Sr. *Back Beats and Rim Shots: The Johnny Blowers Story.* Studies in Jazz, no. 25. Lanham, MD: Scarecrow Press, 1997. 197 pp.
   Biography. Contains excerpts from interviews with Blowers and some of his journal entries.
   Discography; index; photographs.

Bockemuehl, Eugene (saxophone, U.S.)

1-23 Bockemuehl, Eugene. *On the Road with the Jimmy Dorsey Aggravation, 1947–1949.* San Diego: Gray Castle Press, 1996. 135 pp.

Autobiography. Focuses primarily on his experiences as a member of the Jimmy Dorsey Band, where he went by the name "Gene Bockey."
Illustrations.

Bolden, Buddy (cornet, U.S.)

1-24 Barker, Danny. *Buddy Bolden and the Last Days of Storyville.* **Edited by Alyn Shipton. London: Cassell, 1998. 164 pp.**
Oral history. Includes recollections by some of Bolden's contemporaries and tales from the Storyville district of New Orleans.
Index; photographs.

1-25 Marquis, Donald M. *In Search of Buddy Bolden: First Man of Jazz.* **Baton Rouge: Louisiana State University Press, 1993. 193 pp.**
Biography, revised edition. Chapters include "Bolden's Sidemen and Contemporaries" and "How and What He Played." First published in 1978. Appendixes.
Bibliography; illustrations; index; photographs.

Braxton, Anthony (saxophone/composer, U.S.)

1-26 Ford, Alun. *Anthony Braxton: Creative Music Continuums.* **Exeter, Devon, UK: Stride Publications, 1997. 70 pp.**
Study of Braxton's work "in reference to both the traditions of African-American music and that of European and Euro-American music."
Bibliography; diagrams; discography; notes.

1-27 Heffley, Mike. *The Music of Anthony Braxton.* **Contributions to the Study of Music and Dance, no. 43. Westport, CT: Greenwood Press, 1996. 493 pp.**
Musicological analysis of Braxton's compositions from 1968 to 1992. Appendixes.
Bibliography; discography; flowcharts; illustrations; indexes; musical transcriptions; notes; photographs; tables.

1-28 Lock, Graham, ed. *Mixtery: A Festschrift for Anthony Braxton.* **Exeter, Devon, UK: Stride Publications, 1995. 269 pp.**
Collection of essays, interviews, recollections, and letters on the occasion of Braxton's 50th birthday. Includes contributions by Val Wilmer; Jack Cooke; Bill Smith; Herman Gray and Nathaniel Mackey; Marty Ehrlich; and Richard Barrett.
Illustrations; musical transcriptions; photographs.

1-29 Radano, Ronald M. *New Musical Figurations: Anthony Braxton's Cultural Critique.* **Chicago: University of Chicago Press, 1993. 315 pp.**

Bio-musicological study. Appendixes. Portions of the text were previously published.
Diagrams; discography; figures; illustrations; indexes; musical transcriptions; photographs; schemata.

Brubeck, Dave (piano, U.S.)

1-30 Hall, Fred M. *It's About Time: The Dave Brubeck Story.* Fayetteville: University of Arkansas Press, 1996. 182 pp.
Biography.
Discography; index; photographs.

1-31 Storb, Ilse, and Klaus G. Fischer. *Dave Brubeck: Improvisations and Compositions; The Idea of Cultural Exchange.* Translated by G. Bertram Thompson. New York: P. Lang, 1994. 317 pp.
Bio-musicological study. Includes "Chronological Description of His Works—Musical Development in the Individualistic Stylistic Phases" and "Critical Evaluation and Classification."
Bibliography; chronology; diagrams; discography; figures; illustrations; musical transcriptions.

Bushell, Garvin (clarinet/saxophone/bassoon, U.S.)

1-32 Bushell, Garvin. *Jazz from the Beginning.* As told to Mark Tucker. New preface by Stanley Crouch. New York: Da Capo Press, 1998. 196 pp.
Account of Bushell's life, based on a series of interviews with jazz scholar Mark Tucker.
Discography; glossary of musicians; index; notes; photographs.

Campi, Gigi (record producer, Italy)

1-33 *Campiana: ein Stück vor dem Beat; Pierluigi Campi zum 70. Geburtstag am 15. Dezember 1998.* 2nd ed. Köln-Rheinkassel, Germany: Dohr, 1999. 81 pp.
Chiefly in German. "The Art of the Impossible," an essay by Mike Hennessey, is in English. Campi helped organize the Clarke-Boland Big Band, led by drummer Kenny Clarke and pianist Francy Boland.
Bibliography; illustrations.

Cheatham, Adolphus "Doc" (trumpet, U.S.)

1-34 Cheatham, Adolphus "Doc." *I Guess I'll Get the Papers and Go Home: The Life of Doc Cheatham.* Edited by Alyn Shipton. Recording chronology by Howard Rye. London: Cassell, 1996. 147 pp.

Autobiography.
Photographs; bibliography; discography; index.

Clooney, Rosemary (singer, U.S.)

1-35 Clooney, Rosemary. *Girl Singer: An Autobiography.* With Joan Barthel. New York: Doubleday, 1999. 336 pp.
Autobiography.
Discography; index; photographs.

Cole, Nat "King" (piano/singer/bandleader, U.S.)

1-36 Epstein, Daniel Mark. *Nat King Cole.* New York: Farrar, Straus & Giroux, 1999. 437 pp.
Biography.
Bibliography; index; notes; photographs.

Cole, Paddy (saxophone, UK)

1-37 Ryan, Tim. *Tell Roy Rogers I'm Not In: The Paddy Cole Story.* Dublin: Blackwater Press, 1995. 185 pp.
Not reviewed.
Photographs.

Coleman, Bill (trumpet, U.S.)

1-38 Coleman, Bill. *Trumpet Story.* Discography compiled by Evert (Ted) Kaleveld and Lily Coleman. London: Macmillan Press, 1990. 259 pp.
Autobiography.
Discography; filmography; index; photographs.

Coleman, Ornette (saxophone, U.S.)

1-39 Litweiler, John. *Ornette Coleman: A Harmolodic Life.* New York: William Morrow, 1992. 258 pp.
Biography. Includes a transcription of "Free," a Coleman solo from *Change of the Century* (Atlantic LP 1327), transcribed by David Wild.
Indexes; musical transcriptions; notes; photographs.

1-40 Wilson, Peter Niklas. *Ornette Coleman: His Life and Music.* Foreword by Pat Metheny. Berkeley, CA: Berkeley Hills Books, 1999. 244 pp.
Bio-musicological study. Chapters include "Prime Time for Harmolodics" and "Ornette Coleman's Influences."
Bibliography; discography; indexes.

Coltrane, John (saxophone, U.S.)

1-41 Hester, Karlton Edward. *The Melodic and Polyrhythmic Development of John Coltrane's Spontaneous Composition in a Racist Society.* Studies in the History and Interpretation of Music, vol. 54. Lewiston, ME: E. Mellen Press, 1997. 252 pp.

Scholarly examination of Coltrane's music. Explores the evolution of his spontaneous compositional styles with special emphasis on his last creative period. Includes a study of the effects of racism on Coltrane's music and an analysis of the piece "Interstellar Space." Based on Hester's Ph.D. thesis (1990).

Bibliography; discography; glossary; musical transcriptions.

1-42 Kofsky, Frank. *John Coltrane and the Jazz Revolution of the 1960s.* New York: Pathfinder Press, 1998. 500 pp.

Expanded and revised edition of Kofsky's book *Black Nationalism and the Revolution in Music.* Includes: "John Coltrane and the Black Music Revolution"; "John Coltrane and Albert Ayler"; and "Elvin Jones, John Coltrane, and the Evolution of Jazz Rhythm in the Coltrane Quartet." Also contains interviews with Coltrane, Elvin Jones, and McCoy Tyner.

Indexes; musical transcriptions; notes; photographs.

1-43 Nisenson, Eric. *Ascension: John Coltrane and His Quest.* New York: St. Martin's Press, 1993. 278 pp.

Biography. According to the author, Coltrane's quest was primarily a spiritual one. The book is about "the way Coltrane both reflected and changed the world around him."

Discography.

1-44 Porter, Lewis. *John Coltrane: His Life and Music.* Ann Arbor: University of Michigan Press, 1998. 409 pp.

Bio-musicological study. Includes analysis of Coltrane's composing and practicing habits.

Bibliography; chronology; diagrams; illustrations; index; musical transcriptions; notes; photographs.

1-45 Woideck, Carl, ed. *The John Coltrane Companion: Five Decades of Commentary.* New York: Schirmer Books, 1998. 270 pp.

Collection of articles, interviews, performance reviews, and record reviews. Contains previously published material by Ira Gitler, Martin Williams, Nat Hentoff, Peter Watrous, Stanley Crouch, Lewis Porter, David Wild, Frank Kofsky, Joe Goldberg, and Ralph J. Gleason.

Bibliography; chronology; discography; index.

Crosby, Bing (singer, U.S.)

1-46 Crosby, Bing. *Call Me Lucky: Bing Crosby's Own Story.* As told to Pete Martin. New introduction by Gary Giddins. New York: Da Capo Press, 1993. 344 pp.
Autobiography. First published in 1953 by Simon & Schuster.
Index; photographs.

Dameron, Tadd (pianist/arranger/composer, U.S.)

1-47 MacDonald, Ian. *Tadd: The Life and Legacy of Tadley Ewing Dameron.* Sheffield, UK: Jahbero Press, 1998. 133 pp.
Biography. Includes recollections by Dameron's associates and analysis of his compositions "Soulphony" and "Fontainebleau."
Discography; illustrations; index; music transcriptions; photographs.

Dankworth, John (clarinet/bandleader, UK)

1-48 Dankworth, John. *Jazz in Revolution.* London: Constable, 1998. 229 pp.
Autobiography.
Discography; filmography; index; photographs.

Davis, Joe (song publisher/record producer, U.S.)

1-49 Bastin, Bruce. *Never Sell a Copyright: Joe Davis and His Role in the New York Music Scene 1916–1978.* Chigwell, UK: Storyville, 1990. 346 pp.
Biography.
Photographs.

Davis, Miles (trumpet, U.S.)

1-50 Carner, Gary, ed. *The Miles Davis Companion: Four Decades of Commentary.* New York: Schirmer Books, 1996. 274 pp.
Collection of previously published essays, interviews, and articles about Davis. Includes "The Complete Prestige Recordings," by Dan Morgenstern; "Miles's Jazz Life," by Nat Hentoff; "Miles in England," by Benny Green; and "The Danish Connection," by Gary Giddins.
Bibliography; chronology; discography; index.

1-51 Cerchiari, Luca. *Miles Davis: da Charlie Parker al jazz modale; gli anni Quaranta e Cinquanta; discografia 1945–1959 di Jan Lohmann.* Musica del Novecento 2. Torino, Italy: Trauben, 1999. 251 pp.

Analysis in Italian of Miles Davis's improvisational technique. Discography (pp. 142–251) in English.
Bibliography; discography; photographs.

1-52 Chambers, Jack. *Milestones: The Music and Times of Miles Davis.* **New York: Da Capo Press, 1998. 416 pp.**
Biography. Originally published in 1983 by University of Toronto Press in two volumes: *Milestones 1: The Music and Times of Miles Davis to 1960* and *Milestones 2: The Music and Times of Miles Davis since 1960.* New introduction traces the last decade of his life.
Bibliography; index; notes; photographs.

1-53 Kirchner, Bill, ed. *A Miles Davis Reader.* **Washington, DC: Smithsonian Institution Press, 1997. 273 pp.**
Anthology of 24 previously published interviews, reviews, record liner notes, and critical essays about Davis as a musician. Includes "Miles Davis and the Cool Tendency," by André Hodeir; "Sheer Alchemy, for a While: Miles Davis and Gil Evans," by Max Harrison; and "The Lost Quintet," by Peter Keepnews.
Index; musical transcriptions.

1-54 Nisenson, Eric. *'Round About Midnight: A Portrait of Miles Davis.* **Updated edition. New York: Da Capo Press, 1996. 302 pp.**
Originally published in 1982, this biography includes a new preface, a new recommended listening section, and new material covering Davis's life in the 1980s.
Discography; index.

1-55 Williams, Richard. *Miles Davis: The Man in the Green Shirt.* **New York: Henry Holt, 1993. 192 pp.**
Photobiography.
Index; photographs.

Davison, Wild Bill (cornet, U.S.)

1-56 Armstrong, Doug. *Wild Bill Davison: A Celebration; An Illustrated Tribute.* **Ottawa: Leith Music, 1991. 207 pp.**
Photobiography.
Bibliography; chronology; discography; illustrations; photographs.

1-57 Willard, Hal. *The Wildest One: The Life of Wild Bill Davison.* **Monkton, MD: Avondale Press, 1996. 437 pp.**
Biography. Includes: "Condon: Front Man in More Ways than One"; "The Jazz Giants"; "Stars of Jazz." Appendixes.
Bibliography; index; notes; photographs.

Dibango, Manu (saxophone/bandleader/composer/producer, Cameroon)

1-58 Dibango, Manu. *Three Kilos of Coffee: An Autobiography.* In collaboration with Danielle Rouard. Translated by Beth G. Raps. Chicago: University of Chicago Press, 1994. 146 pp.

Autobiography. Dibango created "Afro-Music" that "joyfully blends blues, jazz, reggae, traditional European and African serenades, 'high life,' Caribbean and Arabic music." Includes "African Jazz"; "Soul Makossa"; "Honors and Dissertations."

Discography; index; photographs.

Dodds, Baby (drums, U.S.)

1-59 Dodds, Baby. *The Baby Dodds Story.* As told to Larry Gara. Revised ed. Baton Rouge: Louisiana State University Press, 1992. 105 pp.

Autobiography based on a series of interviews conducted by Larry Gara. First published in 1959.

Bibliography; discography; index; notes; photographs.

Duvivier, George (bass, U.S.)

1-60 Berger, Edward. *Bassically Speaking: An Oral History of George Duvivier.* Studies in Jazz, no. 17. Foreword by Benny Carter. Musical analysis by David Chevan. Metuchen, NJ: Scarecrow Press, 1993. 483 pp.

Biography. Consists of interviews with Duvivier conducted in 1984 as part of the Jazz Oral History Project funded by the National Endowment for the Arts. Includes "The Duvivier Style: Technical Analysis," by David Chevan.

Bibliography; discography; indexes; musical transcriptions; notes; photographs; solography.

Ellington, Duke (piano/bandleader/composer, U.S.)

1-61 Byrd, Veronica, et al., eds. *Jump for Joy: Jazz at Lincoln Center Celebrates The Ellington Centennial, 1899–1999.* [New York: Museum Press, 1999.] 159 pp.

"Official companion publication" to Ellington Centennial. Includes "Farewell to Jazz Fakers," by Duke Ellington; "What Would It Mean without You?" by Wynton Marsalis and Robert G. O'Meally; "Portraits of Ellington" and "A Number One Himself," by Stanley Crouch; "Reminiscing in Tempo," by Michael James; "Sepia Panorama," by Eugene Holley Jr.; "The Popular Ellington" and "Storiella Americana as She is Swyung," by Albert Murray; "The Hot Bach," by Richard O. Boyer; "Duke Ellington: A Brief Chronology," by Stanley Dance; "Homage to Duke Ellington on His Birthday," by Ralph Ellison; and Jazz at Lincoln Center Centennial activities.

Photographs.

1-62 Hasse, John Edward. *Beyond Category: The Life and Genius of Duke Ellington.* **New York: Simon & Schuster, 1993. 479 pp.**

Biography. "Beyond category" was a "phrase Ellington used as a term of the highest possible praise." Most chapters contain a short essay "Essential Ellington," on prominent recordings of a particular era. Includes "Ellington's Musical Sources: A Treasury of Tradition"; "Ellington's Key Musicians"; and "Ellington Songbooks and Folios."

Bibliography; discography; filmography/videography; illustrations; index; photographs.

1-63 Lambert, Eddie. *Duke Ellington: A Listener's Guide.* **Studies in Jazz, no. 26. Lanham, MD: Scarecrow Press, 1999. 374 pp.**

Chronological study of Ellington's recordings. Includes the appendixes "French RCA Integrale, Volumes 14 to 17: A Guide" and "The Ellington Musicians and the Dates They Were with the Band."

Bibliography; discography; index.

1-64 Nicholson, Stuart. *Reminiscing in Tempo: A Portrait of Duke Ellington.* **Boston: Northeastern University Press, 1999. 538 pp.**

Biography about Ellington's life and music, told through recollections by Ellington, his family, and colleagues. Includes excerpts from magazine and newspaper articles.

Discography; illustrations; index; notes; photographs.

1-65 Rattenbury, Ken. *Duke Ellington: Jazz Composer.* **New Haven, CT: Yale University Press, 1990. 327 pp.**

Musical analysis of Ellington's "approach to composition." Focuses on the influences of the blues, ragtime, and Tin Pan Alley on his music. Compositions analyzed include "Koko," "Mr. J. B. Blues," "Concerto for Cootie," "Junior Hop," and "Subtle Slough." Also includes an appendix on "Ellington's Principal Sidemen."

Bibliography; chronology; discography; illustrations; index; musical transcriptions; notes; photographs; tables.

1-66 Steed, Janna Tull. *Duke Ellington: A Spiritual Biography.* **Select discography by John Edward Hasse. New York: Crossroad Publishing, 1999. 192 pp.**

Biography with an emphasis on Ellington's spirituality as manifested in some of his work, including "Black and Tan Fantasy," *Black, Brown and Beige*, and the *Sacred Concerts*.

Bibliography; chronology; discography; illustrations; index; notes; photographs.

1-67 Stratemann, Klaus. *Duke Ellington: Day by Day and Film by Film.* **Copenhagen: JazzMedia ApS, 1992. 782 pp.**

Biography with emphasis on the films Ellington was involved in.
Bibliography; index; photographs.

1-68 Travis, Dempsey J. *The Duke Ellington Primer*. **Chicago: Urban Research Press, 1996. 202 pp.**

Biography. Includes "Ellington and Strayhorn: The Compatible Geniuses"; "Views of the Duke through the Eyes of Louis Bellson"; "Clark Terry: An Ellington University Cum Laude Grad"; "Herb Jeffries: Ellington's Forgotten Flamingo"; and "Ellington Compositions."

Bibliography; index; map; photographs.

1-69 Tucker, Mark. *Ellington: The Early Years*. **Urbana: University of Illinois Press, 1991. 343 pp.**

Bio-musicological study of Ellington up to his debut at the Cotton Club in 1927. Includes musical analysis of his earliest compositions and recordings.

Bibliography; photographs; illustrations; index; musical transcriptions; notes; photographs.

1-70 ———, ed. *The Duke Ellington Reader*. **New York: Oxford University Press, 1993. 536 pp.**

Anthology of previously published writings about Ellington. Includes magazine and newspaper articles, essays, interviews, and reviews of performances and recordings. Among the writers are R. D. Darrell, Hugues Panassié, André Hodeir, Stanley Dance, Max Harrison, Gunther Schuller, Martin Williams, Gary Giddins, Stanley Crouch, Dan Morgenstern, and Ellington himself. Among the topics covered are "*Black, Brown and Beige* (1943)"; "Selected Commentary and Criticism (1964–1993)"; and "Ellingtonians."

Indexes (general index and topical index of selections); musical transcriptions.

1-71 Vail, Ken. *Duke's Diary, Part One: The Life of Duke Ellington 1927–1950*. **Cambridge, UK: Vail Pub., 1999.**

"Month by month chronology of Ellington's life from his opening at Harlem's famous Cotton Club in December 1927 to his orchestra's extended European tour in June of 1950." Includes Ellington's club and concert engagements, film appearances and recording sessions. [Note: *Duke's Diary, Part Two: The Life of Duke Ellington 1950–1974* was published in 2002.]

Photographs.

Europe, James Reese (conductor/composer, U.S.)

1-72 Badger, Reid. *A Life in Ragtime: A Biography of James Reese Europe*. **New York: Oxford University Press, 1995. 328 pp.**

Biography. Europe helped to bring African-American music to prominence in the early twentieth century, "winning new respectability and popularity for ragtime" in New York. As bandleader for the all-black 15th Infantry Regiment ("he was the first African-American officer to lead men into combat"), Europe "took France by storm with the new sounds of jazz." Appendix: "Musical Compositions of James Reese Europe."

Discography; illustrations; index; notes; photographs.

Evans, Bill (piano, U.S.)

1-73 Pettinger, Peter. *Bill Evans: How My Heart Sings.* **New Haven, CT: Yale University Press, 1998. 346 pp.**

Biography. Includes analysis of Evans's music.

Discography; index; musical transcriptions; notes.

Ferguson, Maynard (trumpet, U.S.)

1-74 Lee, William F. *M F Horn: Maynard Ferguson's Life in Music.* **Ojai, CA: M. F. Music U.S.A., 1997. 338 pp.**

"Authorized" biography. Contains interviews with Ferguson and his band members, family, and associates. Includes "MF Band Personnel" and "MF with Other Orchestras."

Bibliography; discography; index; photographs.

Fitzgerald, Ella (singer, U.S.)

1-75 Fidelman, Geoffrey Mark. *First Lady of Song: Ella Fitzgerald for the Record.* **Secaucus, NJ: Carol Pub. Group, 1994. 379 pp.**

Biography.

Discography; index; photographs.

1-76 Nicholson, Stuart. *Ella Fitzgerald: A Biography of the First Lady of Jazz.* **Discography by Phil Schaap. New York: C. Scribner's Sons, 1994. 334 pp.**

Biography. First published in London in 1993.

Bibliography; discography; index; notes; photographs.

Franco (guitar/bandleader/composer, Democratic Republic of the Congo)

1-77 Ewens, Graeme. *Congo Colossus: The Life and Legacy of Franco & OK Jazz.* **North Walsham, UK: Buku Press, 1994. 320 pp.**

Biography. The "Grand Maître" ("Great Master") was "one of the best-known and most loved figures in post-war African culture." Includes analysis of some of his song lyrics translated into English. Appendix: "Bana OK."

Bibliography; chronology; illustrations; index; map; musical transcriptions; photographs.

Garbarek, Jan (saxophone, Norway)

1-78 Tucker, Michael. *Jan Garbarek: Deep Song.* EastNote: Hull Studies in Jazz. **Hull, UK: University of Hull Press, 1998. 390 pp.**
Biography.
Bibliography; discography; index; notes; photographs.

Getz, Stan (saxophone, U.S.)

1-79 Maggin, Donald L. *Stan Getz: A Life in Jazz.* **New York: William Morrow, 1996. 417 pp.**
Biography.
Index; notes; photographs.

Gillespie, Dizzy (trumpet, U.S.)

1-80 Shipton, Alyn. *Groovin' High: The Life of Dizzy Gillespie.* **New York: Oxford University Press, 1999. 422 pp.**
Biography. Includes "Cab Calloway and the Dawn of Bebop"; "From Earl Hines to 52nd Street"; "Billy Eckstine"; "Bird, Big Band, and Berg's"; "The Big Band Records"; and "The 1950s Big Bands."
Bibliography; index; notes; photographs.

1-81 Tanner, Lee, ed. *Dizzy: John Birks Gillespie in His 75th Year.* **Introduction by Jeff Kaliss. San Francisco: Pomegranate Artbooks, 1994. 86 pp.**
Collection of photographs of Gillespie, with quotes by Dizzy and various contemporaries. Also includes "Waiting for Dizzy," an essay by Gene Lees.
Photographs.

1-82 Vail, Ken. *Dizzy Gillespie: The Bebop Years 1936–1952.* **Lanham, MD: Scarecrow Press, 2003. 96 pp.**
Chronicle of Gillespie's life "up to his departure for France in 1952."
Chronology; illustrations; index; maps; photographs.

Goodman, Benny (clarinet/bandleader, U.S.)

1-83 Firestone, Ross. *Swing, Swing, Swing.* **New York: W. W. Norton, 1993. 522 pp.**
Biography.
Bibliography; index; photographs.

Green, Grant (guitar, U.S.)

1-84 Green, Sharony Andrews. *Grant Green: Rediscovering the Forgotten Genius of Jazz Guitar.* Foreword by Yoichi Nakao. San Francisco: Miller Freeman Books, 1999. 274 pp.

Biography written by Green's daughter-in-law. Includes interviews with his musical colleagues, family, and friends. Also includes "On Sound, Style, and Technique" and "Selected Reviews," by Tobias Jundt.

Bibliography; discography; index; photographs.

Gryce, Gigi (saxophone, U.S.)

1-85 Ward, Tyrone. *When Art Farmer Remembered Gigi Gryce: An Oral History of a Life in Jazz.* Chicago: T. Ward, 1992. 53 pp.

Interviews with trumpeter Art Farmer about Gryce (conducted on November 27, 1987, and October 28, 1988).

Bibliography; discography; photographs.

Hawkins, Coleman (saxophone, U.S.)

1-86 Chilton, John. *The Song of the Hawk: The Life and Recordings of Coleman Hawkins.* Ann Arbor: The University of Michigan Press, 1990. 429 pp.

Biography. Hawkins was called "the father of the tenor saxophone."

Bibliography; index; notes; photographs.

Heath, Ted (bandleader, UK)

1-87 Parker, Tony. *The Greatest Swing Band in the World: (The Ted Heath Story).* Oldham, UK: Hirst, Kidd & Rennie, 1993. 128 pp.

Biography with recollections by colleagues and band members.

Illustrations; photographs.

Herman, Woody (clarinet/saxophone/bandleader, U.S.)

1-88 Clancy, William D. *Woody Herman: Chronicles of the Herds.* With Audree Coke Kenton. New York: Schirmer Books, 1995. 430 pp.

Biography. Consists largely of interviews with Herman and his family, friends, and colleagues.

Bibliography; index; notes; photographs.

1-89 Herman, Woody. *The Woodchopper's Ball: The Autobiography of Woody Herman.* With Stuart Troup. New York: E. P. Dutton, 1990. 162 pp.

Autobiography. Includes recollections of friends and associates.

Index; photographs.

1-90 Kriebel, Robert C. *Blue Flame: Woody Herman's Life in Music.* **West Lafayette, IN: Purdue University Press, 1995. 288 pp.**

Biography. Appendixes include "Significant Recordings by Woody Herman" and "Major Players in the Woody Herman Band."
Discography; index; photographs.

1-91 Lees, Gene. *Leader of the Band: The Life of Woody Herman.* **New York: Oxford University Press, 1995. 414 pp.**

Biography. Appendixes include "Woody Herman Alumni" and "Chart of Hit Records" compiled by Kirk Pasich.
Bibliography; index; notes; photographs.

Heywood, Eddie (piano/composer, U.S.)

1-92 Khair, Emilie Eklin. *Passion's Piano: The Eddie Heywood Story; Based on the Private Account of Evelyn Heywood about Her Beloved Music Man, Eddie.* **Atlanta, GA: Care Pub. House, 1997. 124 pp.**

Biography. Includes a listing of Heywood's published music.
Illustrations; photographs.

Hodes, Art (piano, U.S.)

1-93 Hodes, Art, and Chadwick Hansen. *Hot Man: The Life of Art Hodes.* **Discography by Howard Rye. Urbana: University of Illinois Press, 1992. 160 pp.**

Biography.
Bibliography; discography; index; photographs.

Hopkins, Claude (piano/bandleader, U.S.)

1-94 Vaché, Warren W. Sr. *Crazy Fingers: Claude Hopkins' Life in Jazz.* **Washington, DC: Smithsonian Institution Press, 1992. 134 pp.**

Biography. Based on a journal written by Hopkins and augmented by Vaché.
Bibliography; chronology; discography; filmography; index.

Horn, Paul (saxophone, U.S.)

1-95 Horn, Paul, with Lee Underwood. *Inside Paul Horn: The Spiritual Odyssey of a Universal Traveler.* **San Francisco: Harper, 1990. 284 pp.**

Autobiography. Emphasizes Horn's musical career and his spiritual experiences with transcendental meditation.
Discography; photographs.

Hughes, Dick (piano, Australia)

1-96 Hughes, Dick. *Don't You Sing: Memories of a Catholic Boyhood.* Kenthurst, Australia: Kangaroo Press, 1994. 164 pp.
Autobiography. Not reviewed.

James, Etta (singer, U.S.)

1-97 James, Etta, and David Ritz. *Rage to Survive: The Etta James Story.* New York: Villard Books, 1995. 271 pp.
Autobiography.
Discography; index; photographs.

James, Harry (trumpet/bandleader, U.S.)

1-98 Levinson, Peter J. *Trumpet Blues: The Life of Harry James.* New York: Oxford University Press, 1999. 334 pp.
Biography.
Bibliography; index; notes; photographs.

Jarrett, Keith (piano, U.S.)

1-99 Carr, Ian. *Keith Jarrett: The Man and His Music.* London: Grafton, 1991. 237 pp.
Biography. Touches upon Jarrett's relationship with critics. Also covers his gigs with the Charles Lloyd Quartet, the Miles Davis Band, and Jan Garbarek.
Bibliography; discography; index; notes; photographs.

Johansson, Jan (piano/composer/arranger, Sweden)

1-100 Kjellberg, Erik. *Jan Johansson: A Visionary Swedish Musician; Jazz Pianist, Composer, Arranger.* Translated by Sven H. E. Borei. Stockholm: Svensk Musik, Swedish Music Information Center, 1998. 142 pp.
Bio-musicological study.
Annotated discography; illustrations; photographs.

Johnson, J. J. (trombone, U.S.)

1-101 Berrett, Joshua. *The Musical World of J. J. Johnson.* With Louis G. Bourgois. Studies in Jazz, no. 35. Lanham, MD: Scarecrow Press, 1999. 441 pp.
Bio-musicological study of Johnson, known as "the spiritual father of modern trombone." Includes "a thorough investigation of Johnson's classical roots as a writer," and interviews with Johnson, family members, and associates.

Bibliography; catalog of compositions; discography; filmography; musical transcriptions; notes.

Jones, Quincy (trumpet/arranger/producer, U.S.)

1-102 Ross, Courtney Sole, and Frankfurt Gips Balkind. *Listen Up: The Lives of Quincy Jones*. Essay by Nelson George. **New York: Warner Books, 1990. 191 pp.**

Photobiography based on the Warner Brothers motion picture *Listen Up: The Lives of Quincy Jones*.

Chronology; discography; illustrations; index; musical transcriptions; photographs.

Joplin, Scott (piano/composer, U.S.)

1-103 Berlin, Edward A. *King of Ragtime: Scott Joplin and His Era*. **New York: Oxford University Press, 1994. 334 pp.**

Bio-musicological study. Appendixes include "The Music" (alphabetical and chronological listings of Joplin's works) and "Three Songs" ("Goodbye Old Gal Goodbye"; "Snoring Sampson"; and "Lovin' Babe.")

Bibliography; illustrations; index; map; musical transcriptions; notes; photographs.

1-104 Curtis, Susan. *Dancing to a Black Man's Tune: A Life of Scott Joplin*. **Columbia: University of Missouri Press, 1994. 265 pp.**

Socio-historical biography.

Bibliography; illustrations; notes; index; photographs.

Jordan, Louis (saxophone/singer, U.S.)

1-105 Chilton, John. *Let the Good Times Roll: The Story of Louis Jordan and His Music*. **London: Quartet Books, 1992. 286 pp.**

Bio-musicological study.

Bibliography; discography; index; notes; photographs.

Jordan, Steve (guitar, U.S.)

1-106 Jordan, Steve. *Rhythm Man: Fifty Years in Jazz*. **With Tom Scanlan. Michigan American Music Series. Ann Arbor: The University of Michigan Press, 1991. 176 pp.**

Autobiography.

Discography; index; photographs.

Kenton, Stan (piano/arranger/bandleader/composer, U.S.)

1-107 Gabel, Edward F. *Stan Kenton: The Early Years, 1941–1947.* Lake Geneva, WI: Balboa Books, 1993. 120 pp.
  Chronicle of Kenton and his orchestra written by his personal assistant.
  Photographs.

Kirby, John (bass/bandleader, U.S.)

1-108 Williams, Alan. *Fall from Grace: The John Kirby Story.* Pensacola, FL: Alcoral Books, 1993. 131 pp.
  Biography of Kirby written by his grandson.
  Bibliography; chronology; discography; index; photographs.

Krupa, Gene (drums/bandleader, U.S.)

1-109 Klauber, Bruce H. *The World of Gene Krupa: That Legendary Drummin' Man.* Ventura, CA: Pathfinder Publishing, 1990. 214 pp.
  Biography. Contains portions of previously published interviews from *Metronome*, *Down Beat*, *Modern Drummer*, *Esquire*, and *Variety* magazines. Includes "Gene Krupa Collective Personnel."
  Chronology; discography; filmography; photographs.

Lamond, Don (drums, U.S.)

1-110 Harris, Kenny. *First Call Drummer Don Lamond.* Ventura, CA: Pathfinder Publishing, 1990. 142 pp.
  Biography. Includes "Not for Drummers Only," an interview with Lamond.
  Discography; index; musical transcriptions; photographs.

Love, Preston (saxophone, U.S.)

1-111 Love, Preston. *A Thousand Honey Creeks Later: My Life in Music from Basie to Motown—and Beyond.* Introduction by George Lipsitz. Middletown, CT: Wesleyan University Press, 1997. 270 pp.
  Autobiography.
  Illustrations; index; photographs.

Marsalis, Ellis Louis Jr. (piano/composer/teacher, U.S.)

1-112 Handy, D. Antoinette. *Jazz Man's Journey: A Biography of Ellis Louis Marsalis, Jr.* Foreword by David Swanzy. Lanham, MD: Scarecrow Press, 1999. 80 pp.

Biography. Among Marsalis's sons are the jazz musicians Branford, Ellis III, and Wynton. Includes "In His Own Words: An Essay on Jazz."
Discography; index; notes; photographs.

Marsalis, Wynton (trumpet, U.S.)

1-113 Gourse, Leslie. *Wynton Marsalis: Skain's Domain; A Biography.* New York: Schirmer Books, 1999. 311 pp.
Biography. Includes "The History of Jazz at Lincoln Center."
Bibliography; discography; index; notes; photographs; videography.

1-114 Marsalis, Wynton, and Frank Stewart. *Sweet Swing Blues on the Road.* New York: W. W. Norton, 1994. 190 pp.
Account by Marsalis of his band's travels and gigs over the course of a year. Photographs.

Mayerl, Billy (piano/composer, UK)

1-115 Dickinson, Peter. *Marigold: The Music of Billy Mayerl.* Oxford, UK: Oxford University Press, 1999. 302 pp.
Bio-musicological study. Mayerl was the "first prominent British performer to master the implications of the American [jazz] idiom in a virtuoso piano style all his own." Includes a list of works.
Bibliography; chronology; discography; indexes; musical transcriptions; photographs.

McGregor, Chris (piano/bandleader, South Africa)

1-116 McGregor, Maxine. *Chris McGregor and the Brotherhood of Breath: My Life with a South African Jazz Pioneer.* Introduction by Denis-Constant Martin. Flint, MI: Bamberger Books, 1995. 244 pp.
Memoir about McGregor written by his widow. The Brotherhood of Breath, the large jazz orchestra McGregor founded, was "on the verge of international recognition at the time of his death."
Photographs.

McLaughlin, John (guitar/composer, UK)

1-117 Stump, Paul. *Go Ahead, John: The Music of John McLaughlin.* London: SAF Publishing, 1999. 192 pp.
Biography of McLaughlin from the 1960s until the late 1990s.
Bibliography; discography.

McNeely, Big Jay (saxophone, U.S.)

1-118 Dawson, Jim. *Nervous, Man, Nervous: Big Jay McNeely and the Rise of the Honking Tenor Sax.* **Milford, NH: Big Nickel Publications, 1994. 167 pp.**
 Biography.
 Bibliography; discography; index; photographs.

Mezzrow, Mezz (clarinet/saxophone, U.S.)

1-119 Mezzrow, Mezz, and Bernard Wolfe. *Really the Blues.* **Introduction by Barry Gifford. New York: Citadel Underground, 1990. 404 pp.**
 According to this autobiography, Mezzrow attempted to organize the first integrated band in New York in 1930. Originally published by Random House in 1946.
 Index.

Miller, Glenn (trombone/bandleader, U.S.)

1-120 Brown, James. *They Died Too Young: Glenn Miller.* **Avonmouth, UK: Parragon, 1995. 73 pp.**
 Biography.
 Photographs.

1-121 Bruff, Larry. *Glenn Miller: "What Simon Didn't Say."* **Clarinda, IA: Glenn Miller Birthplace Society, 1998. 122 pp.**
 Recollections of Larry Bruff, an adman and later radio and television producer, about his period with the Glenn Miller Chesterfield broadcasts. Excerpted from the author's book *Spoor of a Gofer* (Bloomington, IN: AuthorHouse. 2002.)
 Index; photographs.

1-122 Wright, David G. *Millergate: The Final Solution.* **Southampton, UK: Wright Books, 1998. 187 pp.**
 Investigation into the disappearance of Glenn Miller. Wilbur Wright, the author's late father, wrote two previous books on this subject: *Millergate* and *The Glenn Miller Burial File*.
 Photographs; maps.

Monk, Thelonious (piano/composer, U.S.)

1-123 De Wilde, Laurent. *Monk.* **Translated by Jonathan Dickinson. New York: Marlowe, 1997. 218 pp.**
 Biography.
 Discography.

1-124 Fitterling, Thomas. *Thelonious Monk: His Life and Music.* Revised edition. Translated by Robert Dobbin. Foreword by Steve Lacy. Berkeley, CA: Berkeley Hills Books, 1997. 238 pp.
   Bio-musicological study. Includes "Monk's Life"; "Monk's Music"; and "Monk's Catalog."
   Bibliography; discography; illustrations; index; videography.

1-125 Gourse, Leslie. *Straight, No Chaser: The Life and Genius of Thelonious Monk.* New York: Schirmer Books, 1997. 340 pp.
   Biography. Contains discussion of Monk's music by music critics and interviews with Monk's associates. Includes list of compositions.
   Bibliography; illustrations; index; notes; photographs; sessionography; videography.

Morton, Jelly Roll (piano/composer, U.S.)

1-126 Russell, William. *"Oh, Mister Jelly": A Jelly Roll Morton Scrapbook.* Copenhagen: JazzMedia, 1999. 720 pp.
   Biographical portrait told through Morton's own writing and correspondence. Includes an extensive series of interviews with Morton's friends, family, and associates. Also contains excerpts from two articles by Roy Carew (one previously unpublished).
   Illustrations; indexes; musical transcriptions; photographs.

Nichols, Red (cornet/trumpet/bandleader, U.S.)

1-127 Stroff, Stephen M. *Red Head: A Chronological Survey of "Red" Nichols and His Five Pennies.* Studies in Jazz, no. 21. Lanham, MD: Scarecrow Press, 1996. 187 pp.
   Bio-musicological study. Focuses on the "jazz-oriented recordings made between 1925 and 1932."
   Bibliography; discography; index.

Oxtot, Dick (banjo/bandleader/writer, U.S.)

1-128 Oxtot, Dick, and Jim Goggin. *Jazz Scrapbook: Dick Oxtot—Me and Other Stuff.* Berkeley, CA: Creative Arts Book Co., 1999. 94 pp.
   Autobiography. Includes brief portraits of Oxtot's musical colleagues, including Muggsy Spanier, Paul Lingle, Bob Scobey, and Hots O'Casey.
   Photographs.

Parker, Charlie (saxophone, U.S.)

1-129 Parker, Chan. *Chan Parker.* Interviewed by Will Thornbury. Conversations in Jazz, no. 1. Los Angeles: [Aetheria, 1994]. 32 pp.

Charlie Parker's last wife, Chan, lived with Parker from 1950 until his death in 1955.

Photographs.

1-130 Woideck, Carl. *Charlie Parker: His Music and Life.* Michigan American Music Series. Ann Arbor: The University of Michigan Press, 1996. 277 pp.

Bio-musicological study. Most of the focus is on Parker's music, "tracing his artistic evolution and major achievements as a jazz improviser."

Bibliography; index; musical transcriptions; notes.

1-131 ———, ed. *The Charlie Parker Companion: Six Decades of Commentary.* New York: Schirmer Books, 1998. 294 pp.

Anthology of previously published articles, surveys, interviews, and reviews about Parker and his music. Contributors include Leonard Feather, Nat Hentoff, Ira Gitler, Francis Davis, Barry Ulanov, George T. Simon, Phil Schaap, Bill Coss, and Stanley Crouch.

Bibliography; chronology; discography; index.

Pastorius, Jaco (bass guitar, U.S.)

1-132 Milkowski. Bill. *Jaco: The Extraordinary and Tragic Life of Jaco Pastorius.* San Francisco: Miller Freeman Books, 1995. 264 pp.

Biography. Includes brief recollections from Pastorius's contemporaries.

Discography; index; photographs.

Pearce, Arthur (radio broadcaster, New Zealand)

1-133 Lewis, Laurie. *Arthur and the Nights at the Turntable: The Life and Times of a Jazz Broadcaster.* Wingen, Australia: K'Vrie Press, 1997. 302 pp.

Biography of radio personality Arthur Pearce, known as "Turntable." "Gives an historical account into the development of jazz music and radio broadcasting [in New Zealand]." First published in Great Britain in 1996.

Photographs.

Peterson, Oscar (piano, Canada)

1-134 Lees, Gene. *Oscar Peterson: The Will to Swing.* 2nd ed. Rocklin, CA: Prima Pub., 1990. 293 pp.

Biography first published by Firefly Books in 1988. This edition includes a new chapter covering more recent events in Peterson's life, including his stroke and partial recovery, his appointment as chancellor of York University, and his canceled tour of North America.
Bibliography; index; photographs.

Pizzarelli, Bucky (guitar, U.S.)

1-135   Ripmaster, Terence M. *Mel Bay Presents Bucky Pizzarelli: A Life in Music.* **Pacific, MO: Mel Bay Publications, 1998. 208 pp.**
Biography. Includes "A Short History of Jazz Guitar" and "Influence on Others" (including his son John).
Bibliography; discography; photographs.

Porter, Roy (drums/composer, U.S.)

1-136   Porter, Roy. *There and Back: The Roy Porter Story.* **With David Keller. Baton Rouge: Louisiana State University Press, 1991. 196 pp.**
Autobiography. Discusses Porter's relationships with Charlie Parker, Dizzy Gillespie, and Miles Davis, among others.
Bibliography; discography; index; photographs.

Powell, Bud (piano/composer U.S.)

1-137   Groves, Alan, and Alyn Shipton. *The Glass Enclosure: The Life of Bud Powell.* **Oxford, UK: Bayou Press, 1993. 144 pp.**
Biography.
Bibliography; discography; index; photographs.

1-138   Paudras, Francis. *Dance of the Infidels: A Portrait of Bud Powell.* **Translated by Rubye Monet. Foreword by Bill Evans. New York: Da Capo Press, 1998. 353 pp.**
Memoir that focuses on the author's friendship with Powell. Originally published as *La Danse des Infidèles* in 1986 by Éditions de l'Instant.
Photographs.

Price, Sammy (piano/bandleader, U.S.)

1-139   Price, Sammy. *What Do They Want? A Jazz Autobiography.* **Edited by Caroline Richmond. Discography by Bob Weir. Urbana: University of Illinois Press, 1990. 157 pp.**
Autobiography.
Discography; index; photographs.

Puente, Tito (timbales/vibraphone/bandleader/arranger, U.S.)

1-140 Loza, Steven. *Tito Puente and the Making of Latin Music*. Urbana: University of Illinois Press, 1999. 260 pp.

Biography. Includes "A Conversation with the King"; "The Salazar Perspective"; "Joe Conzo: Reevaluations"; "Reflections on the King: Ray Santos, Chico Sesma, Jerry González, Poncho Sanchez, and Hilton Ruíz"; "Musical Style and Innovation"; and "Identity, Nationalism, and the Aesthetics of Latin Music."

Bibliography; discography; index; musical transcriptions; photographs.

Razaf, Andy (lyricist, U.S.)

1-141 Singer, Barry. *Black and Blue: The Life and Lyrics of Andy Razaf*. New York: Schirmer Books, 1992. 444 pp.

Biography. Razaf's collaborators included Fats Waller, Eubie Blake, J. C. Johnson, and James P. Johnson.

Discography; index; notes; photographs.

Reig, Teddy (record producer, U.S.)

1-142 Reig, Teddy. *Reminiscing in Tempo: The Life and Times of a Jazz Hustler*. Studies in Jazz, no. 10. With Edward Berger. Foreword by Dan Morgenstern. Metuchen, NJ: Scarecrow Press, 1990. 444 pp.

Autobiography. Reig's work included the Charlie Parker sessions for Savoy Records; the first recordings of Miles Davis and Stan Getz as bandleaders; recordings by Count Basie's orchestra; and Latin music sessions by Willie Bobo, Machito, and Candido. Includes recollections by Reig's contemporaries, including Leonard Gaskin and Bob Porter.

Bibliography; discography; index; notes; photographs.

Reinhardt, Django (guitar, Belgium)

1-143 Cherrett, Ted. *The Genius That Was Django: A Fascinating Collection of Press Cuttings, Magazine Articles, Reviews, Photographs and Eyewitness Accounts on the Life and Times of Django Reinhardt*. Woodham, UK: T. Cherrett, 1997. 124 pp.

Biography.

Illustrations; photographs.

Rich, Buddy (drums, U.S.)

1-144 Tormé, Mel. *Traps, the Drum Wonder: The Life of Buddy Rich*. New York: Oxford University Press, 1991. 233 pp.

Biography.
Index; photographs.

Ruff, Willie (French horn/bass, U.S.)

1-145 Ruff, Willie. *A Call to Assembly: The Autobiography of a Musical Storyteller.* New York: Viking, 1991. 432 pp.
  Autobiography.
  Index; photographs.

Russell, Bill (writer/historian, U.S.)

1-146 Kukla, Jon, Mark Cave, Carol O. Bartels, M. Theresa LeFevre, Nancy Ruck, Dan B. Ross, John Magill, Richard Jackson, and Alfred E. Lemmon. *Jazz Scrapbook: Bill Russell and Some Highly Musical Friends.* New Orleans: The Historic New Orleans Collection, 1998. 142 pp.
  Biography. Focuses on Russell as jazz collector and friend of jazz musicians, including Louis Armstrong, Bunk Johnson, Baby Dodds, Natty Dominique, and Fess Manetta.
  Photographs.

Russell, Pee Wee (clarinet, U.S.)

1-147 Hilbert, Robert. *Pee Wee Russell: The Life of a Jazzman.* New York: Oxford University Press, 1993. 300 pp.
  Biography.
  Discography; photographs.

Scott, Ronnie (saxophone/jazz club entrepreneur, UK)

1-148 Fordham, John. *Jazz Man: The Amazing Story of Ronnie Scott and His Club.* Revised and updated edition. London: Kyle Cathie, 1995. 198 pp.
  Biography. Originally published in 1986 as *Let's Join Hands and Contact the Living: Ronnie Scott and His Club.*
  Index; photographs.

Sharrock, Sonny (guitar, U.S.)

1-149 Blass, Charles, and Margaret Davis. *Sweet Butterfingers: Sonny Sharrock, 1940-1994.* Flashback Word Processing, 1994. 45 pp.
  Includes excerpts from interviews with Sharrock and press obituaries.
  Discography; photographs.

Shaw, Artie (clarinet/bandleader, U.S.)

1-150 White, John. *Artie Shaw: Non-Stop Flight.* Hull, UK: University of Hull Press, 1998. 182 pp.
  Biography.
  Photographs.

Short, Bobby (piano/singer, U.S.)

1-151 Short, Bobby. *Bobby Short: The Life and Times of a Saloon Singer.* With Robert Mackintosh. New York: Clarkson Potter, 1995. 265 pp.
  Biography.
  Photographs.

Sinatra, Frank (singer, U.S.)

1-152 Britt, Stan. *Frank Sinatra: A Celebration.* New York: Schirmer Books, 1995. 160 pp.
  Photobiography.
  Discography; filmography; index; photographs; videography.

1-153 Clarke, Donald. *All or Nothing at All: A Life of Frank Sinatra.* New York: Fromm International, 1997. 290 pp.
  Biography.
  Index; photographs.

1-154 Coleman, Ray. *Sinatra: A Portrait of the Artist.* Atlanta: Turner Pub., 1995. 192 pp.
  Photobiography.
  Discography; filmography; index; photographs.

1-155 Friedwald, Will. *Sinatra! The Song Is You: A Singer's Art.* New York: Scribner, 1995. 557 pp.
  Bio-musicological study of Sinatra's style and how it developed over the years. "Examines and evaluates all the classic and less familiar songs."
  Discography; index; notes; photographs.

1-156 Granata, Charles L. *Sessions with Sinatra: Frank Sinatra and the Art of Recording.* Chicago: A Cappella, 1999. 238 pp.
  Musicological study of Sinatra's recording sessions.
  Bibliography; discographies; index; photographs.

1-157 Irwin, Lew. *Sinatra: The Pictorial Biography.* Philadelphia: Courage Books, 1995. 120 pp.

Photobiography.
Bibliography; filmography; index; sessionography.

1-158   Mustazza, Leonard. *Ol' Blue Eyes: A Frank Sinatra Encyclopedia.* **Westport, CT: Greenwood Press, 1998. 436 pp.**
Reference work that concentrates on Sinatra's artistic accomplishments, activities, and recognition. Includes "The Songs"; "The Films"; "Small Screens: Radio, Television, Video and the Internet"; "Major Concerts and Benefit Performances"; and "Awards and Honors."
Bibliography; discography; index; photographs.

1-159   Petkov, Steven, and Leonard Mustazza, eds. *The Frank Sinatra Reader.* **New York: Oxford University Press, 1995. 297 pp.**
Anthology of essays, reviews, and excerpts from memoirs. Writers include Arnold Shaw, Stephen Holden, Gene Lees, Leonard Feather, Whitney Balliett, Ralph J. Gleason, Jonathan Schwartz, and Will Friedwald.
Bibliography; chronology; discography; filmography; index; photographs.

1-160   Sayers, Scott P. Jr., and Ed O'Brien. *Sinatra: The Man and His Music: The Recording Artistry of Francis Albert Sinatra, 1939–1992.* **Austin, TX: Whitley Press, 1992. 303 pp.**
Guide to Sinatra's recording sessions. "Covers his early career with the Dorsey band, and his years with the Columbia, Capitol, and Reprise labels." Includes an alphabetical list of songs he recorded; an alphabetical list of unissued songs; "Sinatra Films"; and "Sinatra Conducts."
Illustrations; photographs.

1-161   Sinatra, Nancy. *Frank Sinatra: An American Legend.* **Los Angeles: General Pub. Group, 1995. 368 pp.**
Biography of Sinatra written by his daughter.
Filmography; index; photographs.

1-162   Vare, Ethlie Ann, ed. *Legend: Frank Sinatra and the American Dream.* **New York: Boulevard Books, 1995. 222 pp.**
Collection of magazine and newspaper articles, excerpts from books, press releases, interviews, and fan letters.
Photographs.

Smith, Stuff (violin, U.S.)

1-163   Smith, Stuff. *Pure at Heart.* **Edited by Anthony Barnett and Eva Løgager. Lewes, UK: Allardyce, Barnett, 1991. 61 pp.**

Autobiography. Includes "An interview" (with the participation of Timme Rosenkrantz); "The Human Side of Jazz" (from Smith's uncompleted autobiography); and "Reflections," by Timme Rosenkrantz (previously published).
Photographs.

Smith, W. O. (bass, U.S.)

1-164 Smith, W. O. *Sideman: The Long Gig of W. O. Smith; A Memoir.* Nashville, TN: Rutledge Hill Press, 1991. 319 pp.
Autobiography.
Index; photographs.

Stewart, Rex (cornet, U.S.)

1-165 Stewart, Rex. *Boy Meets Horn.* Edited by Claire P. Gordon. Michigan American Music Series. Ann Arbor: The University of Michigan Press, 1991. 236 pp.
Autobiography.
Photographs.

Strayhorn, Billy (composer/arranger/pianist, U.S.)

1-166 Hajdu, David. *Lush Life: A Biography of Billy Strayhorn.* New York: Farrar, Straus, Giroux, 1996. 305 pp.
Billy Strayhorn (1915–1967), one of the most accomplished composers in American music, was overshadowed by his friend and collaborator Duke Ellington. Source material includes Strayhorn's private papers and over 500 interviews.
Bibliography; discography; index; photographs.

Sun Ra (keyboards/composer/bandleader, U.S.)

1-167 Szwed, John F. *Space is the Place: The Lives and Times of Sun Ra.* Discography by Robert L. Campbell. New York: Pantheon Books, 1997. 476 pp.
Biography.
Bibliography; discography; index; notes; photographs.

Tanner, Paul O. (trombone, U.S.)

1-168 Tanner, Paul O., and Bill Cox. *Every Night Was New Year's Eve: On the Road with Glenn Miller.* Tokyo: Cosmo Space, 1992. 124 pp.

Autobiography. Tanner was a trombonist with Glenn Miller's civilian orchestra. Includes geographical list of the orchestra's appearances.
Photographs.

Tatum, Art (piano, U.S.)

1-169 Lester, James. *Too Marvelous for Words: The Life and Genius of Art Tatum.* **New York: Oxford University Press, 1994. 240 pp.**
Biography.
Bibliography; index; notes; photographs.

Tipton, Billy (piano/bandleader, U.S.)

1-170 Middlebrook, Diane Wood. *Suits Me: The Double Life of Billy Tipton.* **Boston: Houghton Mifflin, 1998. 326 pp.**
Biography. Tipton was born Dorothy Tipton, but lived as a man from age 19 until her death.
Bibliography; illustrations; index; notes; photographs.

Vaughan, Sarah (singer, U.S.)

1-171 Gourse, Leslie. *Sassy: The Life of Sarah Vaughan.* **New York: C. Scribner's Sons, 1993. 302 pp.**
Biography.
Bibliography; discography; index; notes; photographs.

Wellstood, Dick (piano, U.S.)

1-172 Meyer, Edward N. *Giant Strides: The Legacy of Dick Wellstood.* **Studies in Jazz, no. 32. Lanham, MD: Scarecrow Press, 1999. 269 pp.**
Biography. Wellstood was also a "world-class chess player, a formidable Latinist, and a great writer." Includes "Dick on Music and Musicians"; "Dick on Music Labels"; and "Selected Writings by Dick Wellstood."
Bibliography; discography; index; notes; photographs.

Williams, Mary Lou (piano/composer, U.S.)

1-173 Dahl, Linda. *Morning Glory: A Biography of Mary Lou Williams.* **New York: Pantheon Books, 1999. 463 pp.**
Biography. Includes "Compositions and Arrangements by Mary Lou Williams."
Discography; index; notes; photographs.

Wilson, Teddy (piano, U.S.)

1-174 Wilson, Teddy. *Teddy Wilson Talks Jazz.* With Arie Ligthart and Humphrey van Loo. London: Cassell, 1996. 179 pp.
 Collection of reminiscences.
 Discography; index.

Young, Al (singer, U.S.)

1-175 Young, Al. *Drowning in the Sea of Love: Musical Memoirs.* Hopewell, NJ: Ecco Press, 1995. 273 pp.
 Autobiography.

Young, Lester (saxophone, U.S.)

1-176 Büchmann-Møller, Frank. *You Just Fight for Your Life: The Story of Lester Young.* Foreword by Lewis Porter. New York: Praeger, 1990. 282 pp.
 Biography. Appendixes: "Lists of Jobs and Engagements" and "Members of Lester Young's Permanent Groups, 1941–1955."
 Index; notes; photographs.

1-177 Delannoy, Luc. *Pres: The Story of Lester Young.* Translated by Elena B. Odio. Fayetteville: The University of Arkansas Press, 1993. 252 pp.
 Biography. Translation of *Lester Young: Profesion Président,* first published in 1987.
 Bibliography; discography; index; notes; photographs.

1-178 Porter, Lewis, ed. *A Lester Young Reader.* Washington, DC: Smithsonian Institution Press, 1991. 323 pp.
 Collection of previously published "biographical articles, interviews, and discussions of the music." Contributors include Phil Schaap, John Hammond, Nat Hentoff, Whitney Balliett, Dan Morgenstern, Ralph J. Gleason, Frank Büchmann-Møller, and Loren Schoenberg. Appendixes: "Miscellaneous Short Recordings of Young's Voice" and "Where to Find Unusual Published Photographs of Lester Young."
 Index; musical transcriptions; photographs.

COLLECTIVE BIOGRAPHIES

1-179 Arnaud, Gérald, and Jacques Chesnel. *Masters of Jazz.* Chambers Encyclopedic Guides. Translated by Louis Marcellin-Rice. Edinburgh: Chambers, 1991. 248 pp.

Brief one-to-two-page articles about jazz musicians, organized by instrument. Also includes "Vocal Jazz"; "Jazz Goes Electric"; "Swing Machines"; "Into the Melting Pot"; and "Jazz and Other Forms." Contains portraits of Billie Holiday, Scott Joplin, Django Reinhardt, Benny Goodman, King Oliver, Sidney Bechet, Stephane Grappelli, Tommy Smith, Kenny Clarke, Lionel Hampton, Charles Mingus, J. J. Johnson, Eric Dolphy, Toots Thielemans, Weather Report, and the Duke Ellington Orchestra.

Photographs; index.

1-180 Balliett, Whitney. *American Musicians II: Seventy-Two Portraits in Jazz.* **New York: Oxford University Press, 1996. 520 pp.**

Collection of essays written by Balliett for the *New Yorker* magazine between 1962 and 1991. Originally published in 1986 as *American Musicians*, this expanded edition includes 15 new chapters dealing with Benny Goodman, Mel Powell, Dorothy Donegan, Louie Bellson, Charlie Parker, Dizzy Gillespie, Buddy DeFranco, Jimmy Rowles, George Shearing, Ruby Braff, Paul Desmond, Jimmy Knepper, Walter Norris, and Claude Thornhill.

1-181 Carver, Reginald. *Jazz Profiles: The Spirit of the Nineties.* **New York: Billboard Books, 1998. 304 pp.**

Profiles of 40 musicians. Each profile includes a biographical sketch, interview, and discography. Organized by musical instrument.

Discography; index.

1-182 Crowther, Bruce, and Mike Pinfold. *Singing Jazz: The Singers and Their Styles.* **San Francisco: Miller Freeman, 1997. 256 pp.**

Exploration of the "lives, words, and music" of jazz singers "past and present." Includes profiles of Billie Holiday, Ella Fitzgerald, Sarah Vaughan, Louis Armstrong, and Carmen McRae. Also features "A–Z Reference Section" with "capsule biographies and essential recordings for over 200 singers."

Bibliography; index.

1-183 Crumpacker, Chick, and Bunny Crumpacker. *Jazz Legends.* **Layton, UT: G. Smith, 1995. 93 pp.**

Brief biographical sketches of prominent jazz musicians, including Louis Armstrong, Billie Holiday, Duke Ellington, Dizzy Gillespie, Charlie Parker, Benny Goodman, Oscar Peterson, Ella Fitzgerald, Fats Waller, Earl Hines, Miles Davis, Art Tatum, Sarah Vaughan, Count Basie, Sonny Rollins, Dave Brubeck, Lena Horne, John Coltrane, Thelonious Monk, Lester Young, Coleman Hawkins, Gerry Mulligan, Stan Getz, and the Modern Jazz Quartet.

Photographs.

1-184 Davis, Francis. *Outcats: Jazz Composers, Instrumentalists, and Singers.* **New York: Oxford University Press, 1990. 261 pp.**

Profiles and critical essays about 37 musicians and composers, written for various newspapers and periodicals between 1986 and 1989. Includes "Composers" (Duke and Mercer Ellington, Sun Ra); "Instrumentalists" (Miles Davis, Doc Cheatham); "Eight Singers and a Comic" (Ella Fitzgerald); and "Combos, Movements, Issues, and Isolated Events."

Index.

1-185 Deffaa, Chip. *In the Mainstream: 18 Portraits in Jazz.* **Studies in Jazz, no. 11. Metuchen, NJ: Scarecrow Press, 1992. 390 pp.**

Profiles of 18 musicians, including Mahlon Clark, Bill Dillard, George Kelly, Ray McKinley, Sonny Igoe, Ken Peplowski, Joe Wilder, Jake Hanna, Oliver Jackson, Bill Challis, Bob Haggart, Doc Cheatham, Bucky and John Pizzarelli, Erskine Hawkins, Johnny Mince, Buddy Morrow, and Dick Hyman. Shorter versions of most of these pieces were previously published in *The Mississippi Rag*.

Bibliography; index; photographs.

1-186 ———. *Jazz Veterans: A Portrait Gallery.* **Photographs by Nancy Miller Elliott and John and Andreas Johnsen. Fort Bragg, CA: Cypress House, 1996. 259 pp.**

Photo-biographical essays of over 100 "older" jazz artists, including Jabbo Smith, Benny Carter, Jonah Jones, Lester Young, Freddie Green, Vic Dickenson, Nat Pierce, Illinois Jacquet, Harold Ashby, Charlie Parker, Sarah Vaughan, Ellis Larkins, Toshiko Akiyoshi, and Sonny Rollins.

Bibliography; index; photographs.

1-187 ———. *Traditionalists and Revivalists in Jazz.* **Studies in Jazz, no. 16. Metuchen, NJ: Scarecrow Press, 1993. 391 pp.**

Portraits of 14 musicians who play within the traditional jazz framework, including Vince Giordano, Terry Waldo, Eddy Davis, Peter Ecklund, Marty Grosz, Joe Muranyi, Richard Sudhalter, Dan Barrett, Ed Polcer, Stan Rubin, Carrie Smith, Sandra Reeves-Phillips, Orange Kellin, and Vernel Bagneris. Appendix: "Revivalists of Another Sort: Restorers of Vintage Recordings."

Bibliography; index; photographs.

1-188 ———. *Voices of the Jazz Age: Profiles of Eight Vintage Jazzmen.* **Urbana: University of Illinois Press, 1990. 255 pp.**

Profiles of eight jazzmen who came up during the 1920s, including Sam Wooding, Benny Waters, Bix Beiderbecke, Joe Tarto, Bud Freeman, Jimmy McPartland, Freddie Moore, and Jabbo Smith. Told largely in their own words.

Bibliography; discography; index; photographs.

1-189   Dietrich, Kurt. *Duke's 'Bones: Ellington's Great Trombonists.* **Rottenburg N., Germany: Advance Music, 1995. 229 pp.**

Biographical and musicological study of Duke Ellington's trombonists, including "Tricky Sam" Nanton, Juan Tizol, and Lawrence Brown. Also covers "Ellington's Scoring for Trombones" and "Register of Ellington's Trombonists."

Bibliography; index; musical transcriptions; photographs.

1-190   Enstice, Wayne, and Paul Rubin. *Jazz Spoken Here: Conversations with Twenty-Two Musicians.* **Rottenburg N., Germany: Advance Music, 1995. 316 pp.**

Interviews with 22 jazz musicians, including Mose Allison, Art Blakey, Ruby Braff, Anthony Braxton, Bob Brookmeyer, Dave Brubeck, Ray Bryant, Larry Coryell, Mercer Ellington, Bill Evans, Gil Evans, Tommy Flanagan, Dizzy Gillespie, Chico Hamilton, Lee Konitz, Charles Mingus, Joe Pass, Sonny Stitt, Gábor Szabó, Clark Terry, Henry Threadgill, and Bill Watrous.

Discography, index, photographs.

1-191   Fernett, Gene. *Swing Out: Great Negro Dance Bands.* **New York: Da Capo Press, 1993. 174 pp.**

Reprint of 1970 edition, with new introduction by Dan Morgenstern. Includes profiles of Fate Marable, James Reese Europe and the Hellfighters, McKinney's Cotton Pickers, Alphonso Trent, Noble Sissle, Lawrence "Speed" Webb and His Hollywood Blue Devils, Andy Kirk and His Clouds of Joy, Erskine Hawkins, The Jeter-Pillars Band, and Harlan Leonard and His Rockets.

Index, photographs.

1-192   Fordham, John. *Jazz Heroes.* **London: Collins & Brown, published in association with Channel Four Television Corp., 1998.**

"Life stories" of six "key heroes" of the postwar world of jazz: Dizzy Gillespie, Thelonious Monk, Gerry Mulligan, Ella Fitzgerald, Wes Montgomery, and John Coltrane.

Discography, index, photographs.

1-193   Fox, Jo Brooks, and Jules Fox. *The Melody Lingers On: Scenes from the Golden Years of West Coast Jazz.* **Santa Barbara, CA: Fithian Press, 1996. 125 pp.**

Autobiography of press agents Jo Brooks Fox and Jules Fox. Their clients included Sarah Vaughan, Woody Herman, Ella Fitzgerald, and the Red Feather nightclub.

Photographs.

1-194   Friedwald, Will. *Jazz Singing: America's Great Voices from Bessie Smith to Bebop and Beyond.* **New York: C. Scribner's Sons, 1990. 477 pp.**

History of jazz singing through portraits of jazz vocalists, including Bing Crosby, Billie Holiday, Ella Fitzgerald, Mildred Bailey, Connee Boswell, Lee Wiley, Jack Teagarden, Chet Baker, Mel Tormé, and Anita O'Day.

Discography; index; photographs.

1-195   Giddins, Gary. *Visions of Jazz: The First Century.* **New York: Oxford University Press, 1998. 690 pp.**

Bio-musicological essays covering more than 70 American jazz musicians, including Louis Armstrong, Duke Ellington, Fats Waller, Roy Eldridge, Billy Strayhorn, Chico O'Farrill, Charlie Parker, Miles Davis, Nat "King" Cole, Art Tatum, and John Coltrane.

Index; musical transcriptions.

1-196   Griffiths, David. *Hot Jazz: From Harlem to Storyville.* **Studies in Jazz, no. 28. Lanham, MD: Scarecrow Press, 1998. 257 pp.**

Interviews with over 30 jazz performers, including Lester Boone, Cliff Olson, Lizzie Miles, George Guesnon, Emanuel Sayles, Emanuel Paul, Kid Thomas, Kid Sheik Cola, Barclay Draper, Sal Dentici, Nappy Howard, and Kat Cowens. Some material was previously published in the magazines *Storyville*, *Doctor Jazz*, *Mississippi Rag*, and *Jazz Journal*.

Discography; index; photographs.

1-197   Grudens, Richard. *The Best Damn Trumpet Player: Memories of the Big Band Era and Beyond.* **Stony Brook, NY: Celebrity Profiles Pub., 1997. 186 pp.**

Previously published interviews (conducted from 1980 to 1995) of "Big Band personalities," including Harry James, Arvell Shaw, The Andrews Sisters, Ray Anthony, Frankie Laine, Count Basie, Tony Bennett, Fran Warren, Teddy Wilson, Larry Elgart, and Budd Johnson.

Index; photographs.

1-198   ———. *Jukebox Saturday Night: More Memories of the Big Band Era and Beyond.* **Stony Brook, NY: Celebrity Profiles Pub., 1999. 235 pp.**

Profiles of the "dance bands, ballrooms, Big Bands, songwriters, vocalists, arrangers broadcasters, and European counterparts, all contributing to the legacy of the Big Bands." Includes profiles of Artie Shaw, Les Brown, Stan Kenton, Duke Ellington, Red Norvo, Harry James, Tommy and Jimmy Dorsey, and Glenn Miller.

Bibliography; index; photographs.

1-199   ———. *The Music Men: The Guys Who Sang with the Bands and Beyond.* **Stony Brook, NY: Celebrity Profiles Pub., 1998. 234 pp.**

Exploration of the world of male vocalists, with tributes to such late artists as Bing Crosby, Fats Waller, and Nat "King" Cole, and interviews with Frank Sinatra, Mel Tormé, and Joe Williams.
Bibliography; index; photographs.

1-200   Hager, Andrew G. *Jazz Duets.* **Life, Times & Music Series. New York: Friedman/Fairfax, 1996. 64 pp.**
Mini-biographies of Bing Crosby and the Andrews Sisters, the Boswell Sisters, Billy Eckstine and Sarah Vaughan, Ivie Anderson with the Duke Ellington Orchestra, Ella Fitzgerald and Louis Armstrong, and Annie Ross.
Bibliography; discography; index; photographs.

1-201   Hall, Fred. *More Dialogues in Swing: Intimate Conversations with the Stars of the Big Band Era.* **Ventura, CA: Pathfinder Pub., 1991. 231 pp.**
Collection of interviews (originally conducted for Hall's radio show *Swing Thing*) with bandleaders, solo performers, singers and composers of the swing era, including Kay Starr, Count Basie, Teddy Wilson, Alvino Rey, the King Sisters, Herb Jeffries, Johnny Green, Les Brown, Helen Forrest, Helen O'Connell, Harry James, and Tony Bennett.
Bibliography; discography; index; photographs.

1-202   Hargrove, Rich. *Satchmo, Duke, Rabbit, and Me: Anecdotal Jazz.* **With M. Eleanor Fisher. Elizabeth City, NC: Saxy Jazz Musique, 1998. 163 pp.**
Short biographical essays about Louis Armstrong, Duke Ellington, and Johnny Hodges, plus an autobiographical essay by the author, a saxophonist.
Bibliography; discography; musical transcriptions; photographs.

1-203   Heath, Moira. *I Haven't Said Thanks: The Story of Ted and Moira Heath.* **[UK]: M. Heath, 1998. 172 pp.**
Memoir about her husband, trombonist Ted Heath, and his band. Includes list of band personnel.
Index; photographs.

1-204   Kennedy, Don. *Big Band Jump Personality Interviews: A Dozen Interviews of Big Band Era Bandleaders and Vocalists.* **Atlanta: Crawford Houston Group, [1993]. 70 pp.**
Collection of interviews previously published in the *Big Band Jump* newsletter. Includes Count Basie, Yank Lawson, Bob Haggart, Artie Shaw, Frankie Carle, Helen O'Connell, Ray Anthony, Erskine Hawkins, Charlie Barnet, Stan Kenton, Ray McKinley, and Mel Tormé.
Photographs.

1-205 Lees, Gene. *Cats of Any Color.* New York: Oxford University Press, 1994. 246 pp.

Essays, unified through the central topic of racism, about jazz artists such as Dave Brubeck, Ernie Andrews, Horace Silver, Red Rodney, and Benny Golson.

1-206 Liebman, David. *Miles Davis and David Liebman: Jazz Connections.* Lewiston, NY: Edwin Mellen Press, 1996. 206 pp.

Oral history of saxophonist David Liebman, based on three extended interviews. The first half of the book deals with Liebman's life, work as a musician, and influences. The second half focuses on Liebman's experiences as a member of Miles Davis's band and Liebman's reflections on Davis after his death.

Index.

1-207 Lock, Graham. *Blutopia: Visions of the Future and Revisions of the Past in the Work of Sun Ra, Duke Ellington, and Anthony Braxton.* Durham, NC: Duke University Press, 1999. 314 pp.

Study of the work of Sun Ra, Duke Ellington, and Anthony Braxton, based on Lock's doctoral dissertation. "Blutopia," a short Ellington instrumental composition, signals to the author "a utopia tinged with the blues."

Bibliography; discography; indexes; notes.

1-208 ———. *Chasing the Vibration: Meetings with Creative Musicians.* Exeter, Devon, UK: Stride Publications, 1994. 192 pp.

Profiles of musicians that originally appeared in the *Wire* and *NME* (*New Musical Express*). Musicians covered include Mal Waldron, Abdullah Ibrahim, Billie Holiday, Max Roach, Betty Carter, Horace Tapscott, and Sun Ra. Also includes a previously unpublished piece on Sunny Murray.

Discography; index.

1-209 Mathieson, Kenny. *Giant Steps: Bebop and the Creators of Modern Jazz 1945–65.* Edinburgh: Payback, 1999. 339 pp.

Study of bebop with a focus on the music of Dizzy Gillespie, Charlie Parker, Fats Navarro, Bud Powell, and Thelonious Monk. The book then moves through subsequent developments in jazz composition, modal jazz, and free jazz as reflected in the work of Charles Mingus, Max Roach, Sonny Rollins, Miles Davis, Herbie Nichols, and John Coltrane.

Bibliography; discography; photographs.

1-210 McLeod, Jim. *Jim McLeod's JazzTrack.* Sydney: ABC Books, 1994. 240 pp.

Interviews by Australian jazz deejay McLeod, conducted from 1992 to 1994. Parts of these interviews have appeared in *24 Hours* magazine. Interviewees include Don Burrows, Artie Shaw, Bryce Rohde, Jack Brokensha, Betty Carter, Bob Bertles, Bob Mintzer, Judy Bailey, McCoy Tyner, Mike Nock, Delfeayo Marsalis, Dale Barlow, Paul Grabowsky, Kate Dunbar, George Wein, Howard Alden, and Warren Vaché Jr.

1-211 Milkowski, Bill. *Rockers, Jazzbos and Visionaries.* **New York: Billboard Books, 1998. 286 pp.**

Interviews with 30 musicians, including Keith Jarrett, David Sanborn, Wynton Marsalis, Jimmy Smith, Joe Henderson, Tony Williams, Steve Coleman, Branford Marsalis, Larry Coryell, John McLaughlin, and David Murray.

Index; photographs.

1-212 ———. *Swing It: An Annotated History of Jive.* **New York: Billboard Books, 2001. 288 pp.**

Bio-historical study of jive music through its key musicians, including Louis Jordan, T-Bone Walker, Huey "Piano" Smith, Ella Fitzgerald and "retro jivester" Brian Setzer.

Bibliography; index; photographs.

1-213 Moody, Bill. *The Jazz Exiles: American Musicians Abroad.* **Reno: University of Nevada Press, 1993. 193 pp.**

Study of the "phenomenon of American jazz musicians touring, working, and most important, living" in Europe, Japan, Puerto Rico, and Morocco. Includes Garvin Bushell, Bud Freeman, Jay Cameron, Bob Dorough, Art Farmer, Mark Murphy, Eddie "Lockjaw" Davis, Phil Woods, Jon Hendricks, Nathan Davis, Red Mitchell, and Donald "Duck" Bailey.

Bibliography; index; notes; photographs.

1-214 Perry, David. *Jazz Greats.* **London: Phaidon, 1996. 240 pp.**

Biographical portraits of twelve jazz musicians: Buddy Bolden, Louis Armstrong, Sidney Bechet, Duke Ellington, Lester Young, Charlie Parker, Charles Mingus, John Coltrane, Miles Davis, Ornette Coleman, Wynton Marsalis, and Keith Jarrett.

Bibliography; discography; index; photographs.

1-215 Roland, Paul, ed. *Jazz Singers.* **London: Hamlyn, 1999. 160 pp.**

Interviews from *Melody Maker* magazine of jazz singers: Louis Armstrong, Chet Baker, Tony Bennett, Ray Charles, June Christy, Nat "King" Cole, Billy Eckstine, Ella Fitzgerald, Billie Holiday, Peggy Lee, Anita O'Day, Annie Ross, Nina Simone, Frank Sinatra, Mel Tormé, Sarah Vaughan, Dinah Washington, Joe Williams, and Jimmy Witherspoon.

Photographs.

1-216 Rowland, Mark, and Tony Scherman, eds. *The Jazz Musician.* New York: St. Martin's Press, 1994. 261 pp.

Essays selected from *Musician* magazine on jazz musicians, including Wayne Shorter, Lester Bowie, Charlie Haden, Miles Davis, John Coltrane, Jaco Pastorius, Tony Williams, and Dizzy Gillespie. Also includes a tribute to John Coltrane by various musicians, and interviews of Chet Baker, Wynton Marsalis, Herbie Hancock, and Sonny Rollins.

Photographs.

1-217 Schiedt, Duncan. *Twelve Lives in Jazz.* Parma, Italy: Delta Pub., 1996. 176 pp.

Brief portraits of twelve jazz musicians, including Louis Armstrong, Bix Beiderbecke, Bessie Smith, Jelly Roll Morton, Fletcher Henderson, Duke Ellington, Fats Waller, Benny Goodman, Count Basie, Billie Holiday, Coleman Hawkins, and Charlie Parker.

Index; photographs.

1-218 Shadwick, Keith. *Jazz: Legends of Style.* Edison, NJ: Chartwell Books, 1998. 352 pp.

Profiles of some 300 jazz musicians, with "special features" on such artists as Albert Ayler, Sidney Bechet, Dave Brubeck, Benny Carter, Ornette Coleman, John Coltrane, Bill Evans, Stan Getz, Fletcher Henderson, Keith Jarrett, Louis Jordan, Stan Kenton, Gene Krupa, Wynton Marsalis, Charles Mingus, Jelly Roll Morton, Gerry Mulligan, Bud Powell, Max Roach, Sonny Rollins, George Russell, Archie Shepp, Nina Simone, Sun Ra, Cecil Taylor, Sarah Vaughan, Fats Waller, Mary Lou Williams, and Lester Young.

Discography; index; photographs.

1-219 Sidran, Ben. *Talking Jazz: An Illustrated Oral History.* San Francisco: Pomegranate Artbooks, 1992. 210 pp.

Interviews ("directed conversations") with jazz artists, which took place from 1984 to 1990. Includes Gil Evans, Jay McShann, Red Rodney, Frank Morgan, Jon Hendricks, Max Roach, Willie Ruff, Art Blakey, Betty Carter, Horace Silver, Abdullah Ibrahim, Pepper Adams, McCoy Tyner, Max Gordon, Archie Shepp, Herbie Hancock, Tony Williams, Keith Jarrett, Rudy Van Gelder, Charles Brown, Joe Sample, Denny Zeitlin, Don Cherry, and Donald Fagen.

Index; photographs.

1-220 Such, David G. *Avant-Garde Jazz Musicians: Performing "Out There."* Iowa City: University of Iowa Press, 1993. 206 pp.

Focuses not only on "avant-garde" musicians and their respective approaches to performing "out" or "free" jazz, but also on the cultural and personal factors that have influenced their music. Musicians covered include Charles Mingus,

Ornette Coleman, Cecil Taylor, John Coltrane, Albert Ayler, Jemeel Moondoc, and Billy Bang.

Bibliography; discography; illustrations; index; musical transcriptions; notes; photographs; tables.

1-221 Sudhalter, Richard M. *Lost Chords: White Musicians and Their Contributions to Jazz, 1915–1945.* **New York: Oxford University Press, 1999. 890 pp.**

Collective biography of white musicians, featuring analysis of their musical styles and achievements. Includes Miff Mole, Red Nichols, Bud Freeman, Jean Goldkette, Ben Pollack, Jimmy and Tommy Dorsey, the Boswell sisters, Bix Beiderbecke, Frank Trumbauer, Jack Purvis, Bunny Berigan, Benny Goodman, Artie Shaw, Bobby Hackett, Red Norvo, Pee Wee Russell, and Jack Teagarden.

Bibliography; notes; illustrations; indexes; notes.

1-222 Taylor, Arthur. *Notes and Tones: Musician-to-Musician Interviews.* **New York: Da Capo Press, 1993. 300 pp.**

Interviews of jazz musicians taped from 1968 to 1972, including Miles Davis, Randy Weston, Ornette Coleman, Philly Joe Jones, Don Byas, Ron Carter, Johnny Griffin, Charles Tolliver, Eddie "Lockjaw" Davis, Erroll Garner, Leon Thomas, Max Roach, Dizzy Gillespie, Carmen McRae, Nina Simone, Tony Williams, and Don Cherry. This expanded edition includes a new introduction by the author, new photographs, and previously unpublished interviews with Dexter Gordon and Thelonious Monk. First published in 1977.

Index; photographs.

1-223 Tormé, Mel. *My Singing Teachers.* **New York: Oxford University Press, 1994. 338 pp.**

Mel Tormé's "role models" include Louis Armstrong, Billie Holiday, Bing Crosby, Ella Fitzgerald, Mabel Mercer, and Lee Wiley. Also covers intrumentalists and arrangers who have influenced him.

Index; photographs.

BANDS/ORCHESTRAS

General

1-224 Raymond, Al. *Swinging Big Bands into the 90s.* **Broomall, PA: Harmony Press, 1992. 245 pp.**

Discussion of big bands from the 1940s to 1992. Includes recollections of Raymond, a bandleader himself.

Index; photographs.

1-225 Tracy, Sheila. *Talking Swing: The British Big Bands.* Edinburgh: Mainstream, 1997. 256 pp.

Interviews with members of British big bands led by Ambrose, Ivy Benson, John Dankworth, Eric Delaney, Teddy Foster, Roy Fox, Geraldo, Nat Gonella, Ted Heath, Jack Hylton, Syd Lawrence, Vic Lewis, Joe Loss, Ken Mackintosh, Oscar Rabin, Harry Davis, Harry Roy, and Lew Stone.

Photographs.

1-226 Wood, Ean. *Born to Swing: The Story of the Big Bands.* London: Sanctuary, 1996. 264 pp.

History of the big bands from the 1920s through the 1940s. Bandleaders covered include Fletcher Henderson, Duke Ellington, Benny Goodman, the Dorsey Brothers, Count Basie, Artie Shaw, Glenn Miller, Charlie Barnet, and Woody Herman. Also focuses on lesser-known black and white bands of the twenties and thirties.

Bibliography; index; photographs.

Bama State Collegians (U.S.)

1-227 Stewart, Thomas W. *Great College Jazz Orchestras, Part One: The Bama State Collegians.* Birmingham, AL: Thomasina Pub., 1990. [unpaged]

Story of the Bama State Collegians of Alabama State Teachers College in Birmingham, Alabama, from their origin as a college band to their rise to international renown in 1939 with the hit record "Tuxedo Junction."

Photographs.

George Gruntz Concert Jazz Band (Switzerland)

1-228 Rentsch, Christian, ed. *25 Years: George Gruntz Concert Jazz Band; "Breaking Walls."* Therwil, Switzerland: Euromusic Association, 1996. [unpaged]

Collection of essays in German, French, and English about the George Gruntz Concert Jazz Band. Topics include the origins of the band, the Swiss-German tour of 1978, and recollections by past and present band members. Contributors include Flavio Ambrosetti, Mike Zwerin, Peter Erskine, Randi Hultin, Lance Tschannen, and Art Lange.

Photographs.

Italian Instabile Orchestra (Italy)

1-229 Lorrai, Marcello, and Roberto Masotti. *Italian Instabile Orchestra.* Translated by Melinda Male and Paul Smith. Milan: Auditorium, 1997. 123 pp.

Essays cover the history of the group, concert and festival performances, profiles of band members; and the group's influence on other jazz groups.

Index; photographs.

WOMEN IN JAZZ

General

1-230 Davis, Angela Y. *Blues Legacies and Black Feminism: Gertrude "Ma" Rainey, Bessie Smith, and Billie Holiday.* **New York: Pantheon Books, 1998. 427 pp.**

Examines three women artists who shaped the history of popular music in the United States, and "the ways their recorded performances divulge unacknowledged traditions of feminist consciousness in working-class communities." Includes "'When a Man Loves a Woman': Social Implications of Billie Holiday's Love Songs" and "'Strange Fruit': Music and Social Consciousness."

Bibliography; index; notes; photographs.

1-231 Gourse, Leslie. *Madame Jazz: Contemporary Women Instrumentalists.* **New York: Oxford University Press, 1995. 273 pp.**

Interviews with female jazz musicians, including saxophonist Virginia Mayhew, bassist Tracy Wormworth, vocalist Shirley Horn, and pianists Dorothy Donegan and Marian McPartland. Also presents interviews with Cobi Narita, organizer of the "Salute to Women in Jazz" festival, and talent agents Helen Keane and Linda Goldstein.

Bibliography; index; photographs.

1-232 Grudens, Richard. *The Song Stars: The Ladies Who Sang with the Bands and Beyond.* **Stony Brook, NY: Celebrity Profiles Pub., 1997. 224 pp.**

Portraits of famous and lesser-known female vocalists, including Bessie Smith, Ella Fitzgerald, Josephine Baker, Helen Forrest, Kitty Kallen, Connie Haines, Doris Day, Helen O'Connell, Peggy Lee, Rosemary Clooney, Teresa Brewer, Lena Horne, Frances Langford, Jo Stafford, Anita O'Day, Dolly Dawn, Patti Page, the Lennon Sisters, Lynn Roberts, and Diana Krall.

Bibliography; illustrations; index; photographs.

1-233 Handy, D. Antoinette. *Black Women in American Bands and Orchestras.* **2nd ed. Lanham, MD: Scarecrow Press, 1998. 359 pp.**

Profiles of female jazz and classical American band and orchestra members. Includes: "Orchestras and Orchestra Leaders"; "String Players"; "Wind and Percussion Players"; "Keyboard Players"; and "Non-Playing Orchestra/Band Affiliates." Profiles from first edition have been updated and new profiles have been added.

Bibliography; index; photographs.

2
History

The 1990s brought forth a broad gamut of works about jazz history—ranging from *Jazz for Dummies* by Dick Sutro to Lewis Porter's *Jazz: From Its Origins to the Present*. Swing music was a very popular subject. There were also multiple titles on bebop, free jazz, fusion, and contemporary jazz.

The historical section is organized into the following areas: General History; Pre-jazz and Early Jazz; Swing; Bebop & Cool Jazz; 1960s through 1990s; Latin Jazz; Institutions; Media; and Recordings.

GENERAL HISTORY

2-1 Adams, Simon. *Jazz: A Crash Course.* New York: Watson-Guptill, 1999. 143 pp.

Illustrated history of jazz from its origins to the present—and the future. Includes short bios of musicians (King Oliver, Louis Armstrong, Paul Whiteman, Sidney Bechet, Bix Beiderbecke, Duke Ellington, Coleman Hawkins, Lester Young, Billie Holiday, Miles Davis, John Coltrane, Sun Ra); jazz terminology; key movements; and jazz record labels.

Bibliography; chronology; discography; illustrations; index; photographs.

2-2 Axelrod, Alan. *The Complete Idiot's Guide to Jazz.* New York: Alpha Books, 1999. 347 pp.

Beginner's guide intended for the layperson, with brief biographical annotations and introductions to jazz history and jazz styles. Topics include "What jazz is—and why you should listen to it"; "Jazz in clubs, concert halls, festivals, on the air, and on disk"; "Strategies for listening to, understanding, and enjoying jazz"; "The essential heritage and basic elements of jazz"; "Instruments of jazz"; and "The jazz singer."

Bibliography; chronology; discography; glossary; illustrations; index; photographs.

2-3   Berendt, Joachim E. *The Jazz Book: From Ragtime to Fusion and Beyond*. 6th ed. Revised by Günther Huesmann. Translated by H. and B. Bredigkeit with Dan Morgenstern and Tim Nevill. Brooklyn, NY: Lawrence Hill Books, 1992. 541 pp.

History of the "whole range of jazz" from "ragtime and New Orleans to the present." New sections in this sixth revised edition include "David Murray and Wynton Marsalis"; "From the Eighties to the Nineties"; "Saxophone Groups"; and "Organs, Synthesizer, Keyboards." In addition, "the sections on Ornette Coleman and Miles Davis have been much expanded, taking into account their development into the eighties." Organized into the following sections: "The Styles of Jazz"; "The Musicians of Jazz"; "The Elements of Jazz"; "The Instruments of Jazz"; "The Vocalists of Jazz"; "The Big Bands of Jazz"; "The Jazz Combos"; "Towards a Definition of Jazz."

Chronology; discography; index; musical transcripts; notes; photographs.

2-4   Boggs, Vernon W. *Salsiology: Afro-Cuban Music and the Evolution of Salsa in New York City*. Contributions to the Study of Music and Dance. New York: Greenwood Press, 1992. 386 pp.

Collection of essays that explore the "origin, contours, and present state" of the Afro-Hispanic music called salsa. Includes "The Roots," by John Storm Roberts; "Popular Music in Puerto Rico: Toward an Anthropology of Salsa," by Jorge Duany; "Founding Fathers and Changes in Cuban Music Called Salsa," by Vernon W. Boggs; and "Afro-American Latinized Rhythm," by Max Salazar.

Bibliography; musical transcriptions; photographs.

2-5   Carlin, Richard. *Jazz*. New York: Facts on File, 1991. 142 pp.

Brief overview of jazz, covering its history, styles, and musicians.

Bibliography; discography; glossary; index; photographs.

2-6   Carr, Roy. *A Century of Jazz*. London: Hamlyn, 1997. 256 pp.

Pictorial history of jazz. Topics include "Jazz at the Philharmonic"; "West Coast Jazz"; "East Coast Hard Bop"; "Free Jazz"; "Jazz-Rock Fusion"; "Jazz Festivals"; and "African Jazz."

Photographs.

2-7   Chiswick, Linton. *Milestones of Jazz: A Chronological History of Jazz Music in Photographs*. Godalming, UK: CLB International, 136 pp.

Photo-historical overview of jazz from 1902 to today. Photographers represented include William Gottlieb, Chuck Stewart, Duncan Schiedt, and Danny Gignoux.

Bibliography; discography; index; photographs.

2-8   Cooke, Mervyn. *Jazz.* New York: Thames and Hudson, 1998. 200 pp.

History of jazz "from its early balancing of African and European influences" to the present.

Bibliography; glossary; illustrations; index.

2-9   Craker, Chris. *Get into Jazz: A Comprehensive Beginner's Guide.* New York: Bantam Books, 1994. 273 pp.

Includes "Jazz: An Outline History—The First Eighty Years"; "The Giants of Jazz"; "Where to Go to Hear Jazz"; and "Building a Jazz Record Collection."

Bibliography; discography; index.

2-10   Dewe, Michael. *The Skiffle Craze.* Discography by Paul Redmond Drew. Aberystwyth, Wales, UK: Planet Books, 1998. 268 pp.

History of "skiffle" music, which has elements of jazz and blues. Focuses primarily on the revival of skiffle music in Britain in the 1950s.

Bibliography; discography; index; photographs.

2-11   Gioia, Ted. *The History of Jazz.* New York: Oxford University Press, 1997. 471 pp.

Chronicle of jazz from its prehistory in 19th-century slave dances in New Orleans to the present.

Bibliography; discography; index; notes.

2-12   King, Jonny. *What Jazz Is: An Insider's Guide to Understanding and Listening to Jazz.* Foreword by Christian McBride. New York: Walker and Co., 1997. 162 pp.

Exploration of "how jazz works in simple terms and from the perspective of a working professional musician." Organized into three major areas: "Jazz Basics"; "The Key Players and Their Repertoire"; and "A Guide to Recordings at the Heart of Modern Jazz."

Discography; index; photographs.

2-13   Porter, Lewis, and Michael Ullman. *Jazz: From Its Origins to the Present.* With Edward Hazell. Englewood Cliffs, NJ: Prentice Hall, 1993. 496 pp.

"One-volume history of jazz and its major figures," including in-depth studies of musicians Sidney Bechet, Louis Armstrong, Duke Ellington, Count

Basie, Charlie Parker, Miles Davis, John Coltrane, Ornette Coleman, and Bill Evans.
Bibliography; discography; glossary; index; musical transcriptions; photographs.

2-14   Shadwick, Keith. *The Illustrated Story of Jazz.* **New York: Crescent Books, 1991. 181 pp.**
History of jazz from its "first flowering" in New Orleans to the present.
Bibliography; discography; illustrations; index; photographs.

2-15   Sutro, Dirk. *Jazz for Dummies.* **Foster City, CA: IDG Books Worldwide, 1998. 358 pp.**
Overview of jazz history and instruments, with short bios of instrumentalists and vocalists. Also includes "Ten Trustworthy Jazz Labels"; "Catching Real Live Jazz"; and "Resources for Further Jazz Enlightment."
Bibliography; discography; index; photographs; videography; webliography.

2-16   Vail, Ken. *Jazz Milestones: A Pictorial Chronicle of Jazz 1900–1990.* **Cambridge, UK: Vail, 1993. 176 pp.**
"Chronological look" at the history of jazz. Entries include important events, births, deaths, books, records, and films.
Bibliography; discography; index; musical transcripts.

ERAS & STYLES

Pre-Jazz and Early Jazz

2-17   Cliffe, Peter. *Fascinating Rhythm: Dance Tunes from between the Wars and the Stars Who Made Them Magical.* **Baldock, UK: Egon, 1990. 282 pp.**
History of popular dance music in the United States and the United Kingdom from 1920 to 1939, with details on composers, singers, musicians, bandleaders, and recordings.
Bibliography; index; photographs.

2-18   Hennessey, Thomas J. *From Jazz to Swing: African-American Jazz Musicians and Their Music, 1890–1935.* **Detroit: Wayne State University Press, 1994. 217 pp.**
Describes the process by which jazz was created from within the life experiences of the artists. Includes "Raising the Curtain on Jazz"; "Jazz Goes on Record 1914–1923"; "Territory Bands 1914–1923"; "Chicago Sounds 1923–1929"; "New York Scores 1923–1929"; "Territory Scuffles 1923–1929"; "The Rise of the National Bands 1929–1935"; and "The Impact of the National Bands."
Bibliography; index; notes.

2-19 Pasternak, Judith. *Dixieland: The Birth of Jazz.* **New York: Friedman/Fairfax Publishers, 1995. 64 pp.**

Brief history of Dixieland jazz, dealing mostly with the historically contributing styles of blues and ragtime.

Bibliography; discography; index.

Swing

2-20 Batchelor, Christian. *This Thing Called Swing: A Study of Swing Music and the Lindy Hop.* **London: The Original Lindy Hop Collection, 1997. 347 pp.**

Study of swing music and the dances that arose around it, including the Lindy Hop.

Illustrations; index; maps; photographs; timelines.

2-21 Erenberg, Lewis A. *Swingin' the Dream: Big Band Jazz and the Rebirth of American Culture.* **Chicago: The University of Chicago Press, 1998. 320 pp.**

Socio-cultural history of big band jazz. Topics include "Just One More Chance: The Fall of the Jazz Age and the Rise of Swing, 1929–1935"; "The Crowd Goes Wild: The Youth Culture of Swing"; "Swing Is Here: Benny Goodman and the Triumph of American Music"; "News from the Great Wide World: Count Basie, Duke Ellington, and Black Swing Bands"; "Swing Left: The Politics of Race and Culture in the Swing Era"; "The City of Swing: New York and the Dance Band Business in Black and White"; "Swing Goes to War: Glenn Miller and the Popular Music of World War II"; and "Coda and Conclusion: Red Scares and Head Scares" (the Cold War and jazz).

Index; notes; photographs.

2-22 Scanlan, Tom. *The Joy of Jazz: Swing Era, 1935–1947.* **Golden, CO.: Fulcrum Pub., 1996. 148 pp.**

Historical study of swing music. Includes "Racial Problems and Racial Equity" and brief portraits of musicians, including Louis Armstrong, Benny Goodman, Lester Young, Charlie Christian, Art Tatum, and Erroll Garner.

Bibliography; discography; index; notes; photographs.

2-23 Shaw, Arnold. *Let's Dance: Popular Music in the 1930s.* **Edited by Bill Willard. New York: Oxford University Press, 1998. 241 pp.**

Year-by-year history of popular music in the 1930s, including biographies and interviews with musicians and composers. Sequel to Shaw's *The Jazz Age: Popular Music in the 1920s*.

Indexes.

2-24   Stowe, David W. *Swing Changes: Big-Band Jazz in New Deal America.* **Cambridge, MA: Harvard University Press, 1994. 299 pp.**

Exploration of "New Deal America through its music." "Shows us how the contradictions and tensions within swing—over race, politics, its own cultural status, the role of women—mirrored those played out in the larger society." Draws on "memoirs, oral histories, newspapers, magazines, recordings, photographs, literature, and films."

Index; notes; photographs.

2-25   Way, Chris. *The Big Bands Go to War.* **Edinburgh: Mainstream Pub., 1991. 288 pp.**

Story of the service bands and orchestras from Britain, Canada, and the United States, from 1939 to 1945. Chronological narratives of each band are followed by a "listing of the many radio broadcasts of these service bands, plus known details of recording sessions."

Discography; index; photographs.

2-26   Wood, Ean. *Born to Swing: The Story of the Big Bands.* **London: Sanctuary, 1996. 264 pp.**

Account of major U.S. swing bands, including those led by Fletcher Henderson, Benny Goodman, Duke Ellington, Glenn Miller, Charlie Barnet, and Woody Herman.

Index; photographs.

2-27   Woods, Bernie. *When the Music Stopped: The Big Band Era Remembered.* **New York: Barricade Books, 1994. 304 pp.**

Essays by Woods, the music editor of *Variety*, on swing music and the memorable people involved in the "big band era." Discusses agents, press agents, and disk jockeys as well as musicians, including Benny Goodman, Tommy Dorsey, Jimmy Dorsey, Artie Shaw, Woody Herman, Sammy Kaye, Duke Ellington, Glenn Miller, Count Basie, and Lionel Hampton.

Index; photographs.

Bebop & Cool Jazz

2-28   Bergerot, Frank, and Arnaud Merlin. *The Story of Jazz: Bop and Beyond.* **Translated from the French by Marjolijn de Jager. New York: Harry N. Abrams, 1993. 160 pp.**

History of "bop" music (including "free" jazz, "West Coast," "cool," "hard bop," modal, and fusion) and its influence on today's jazz scene. Contains documents, interviews, and essays on bebop musicians.

Discography; illustrations; photographs.

2-29 DeVeaux, Scott. *The Birth of Bebop: A Social and Musical History.* **Berkeley: University of California Press, 1997. 572 pp.**
Analytical study of the "various social and musical factors that culminated" in the emergence of bebop. Topics include "College of Music: Coleman Hawkins and the Swing Era"; "Professionals After Hours: Young Black Musicians in the 1940s"; and "Taking Advantage of the Disadvantages: Bop Meets the Market."
Bibliography; discography; index; musical transcriptions; photographs.

2-30 Owens, Thomas. *Bebop: The Music and Its Players.* **New York: Oxford University Press, 1995. 323 pp.**
Historical overview and musical analysis of bebop and its key players. Organized by instrument. Includes material on Charlie Parker, Dizzy Gillespie, Thelonious Monk, and Wynton Marsalis.
Bibliography; glossary; illustrations; index; musical transcriptions; notes.

2-31 Rosenthal, David H. *Hard Bop: Jazz and Black Music, 1955–1965.* **New York: Oxford University Press, 1992. 208 pp.**
Study of "hard bop" jazz (which incorporated bebop and R&B) focusing on the recordings and styles of its practitioners, including Lee Morgan, Miles Davis, Clifford Brown, Sonny Rollins, Horace Silver, Art Blakey, Wynton Kelly, Elmo Hope, Charlie Mingus, Thelonious Monk, John Coltrane, and Sonny Clark. Contains previously published material.
Discography; index.

1960s through 1990s

2-32 Budds, Michael J. *Jazz in the Sixties: The Expansion of Musical Resources and Techniques.* **Expanded edition. Iowa City: University of Iowa Press, 1990. 185 pp.**
Musical study of jazz innovations in the 1960s. This expanded edition explores the "purpose assigned to jazz by its creators" and the "significance of its development from a vantage point of more than ten years later." Topics include "color and instrumentation"; "texture and volume"; "melody and harmony"; "meter and rhythm"; and "structural design." First published in 1978.
Bibliography; discography; index.

2-33 Jost, Ekkehard. *Free Jazz.* **New York: Da Capo Press, 1994. 214 pp.**
Jost defines "free jazz" as a "musical form with some degree of syncopation or swing inflection, which also includes some combination of four basic characteristics: nonreliance on traditional musical norms and priorities, emphasis on tone color, open ensemble roles, and collective improvisation." Includes portraits and style analyses of John Coltrane, Charles Mingus, Ornette Coleman, Cecil Taylor,

Archie Shepp, Albert Ayler, Don Cherry, the Chicago-based AACM (which included Muhal Richard Abrams, Joseph Jarman, Roscoe Mitchell, Lester Bowie, Anthony Braxton, and the Art Ensemble of Chicago), and Sun Ra.

Bibliography; discography; index; photographs.

2-34 Mandel, Howard. *Future Jazz.* **New York: Oxford University Press, 1999. 235 pp.**

Covers jazz from the 1970s to the 1990s. Includes interviews with Wynton Marsalis, David Murray, George Benson, and John Scofield.

Index.

2-35 Nicholson, Stuart. *Jazz: The 1980s Resurgence.* **New York: Da Capo Press, 1995. 402 pp.**

Told through "snapshot critiques" of representative musicians. Includes "Past Masters and Keepers of the Faith: Mainstream and Cool"; "Big Bands: Ancient to Modern"; "The Hard Bop Mainstream"; "Miles and the Fusion Junta"; "Post-Bop and Beyond: The Expansion of the Mainstream"; "Neo Faces: The Hard-Bop Renaissance"; "Village Voices and Downtown Sounds: Freebop and Beyond"; "Voice: Gospel and Vocal Group"; "European Dreams and the Global Democracy." Originally published as: *Jazz: the Modern Resurgence* (London: Simon & Schuster, 1990).

Bibliography; discography; index; notes; photographs.

2-36 ———. *Jazz-Rock***:** *A History.* **New York: Schirmer Books, 1998. 454 pp.**

Traces the main developments of jazz-rock and attempts to show "why jazz-rock was a logical step for jazz to have taken in the context of its time." Includes such musicians as Miles Davis, Ornette Coleman, Tony Williams, Wayne Shorter, Alexis Korner, Kenny G, David Sanborn, George Benson, and Grover Washington Jr.

Discography; indexes; photographs.

Latin Jazz

2-37 Roberts, John Storm. *Latin Jazz: The First of the Fusions, 1880s to Today.* **New York: Schirmer Books, 1999. 306 pp.**

Historical survey of Latin jazz. Includes discussion of tango, rumba, swing, mambo, bossa nova, funk, fusion, and Brazilian and Caribbean music.

Bibliography; discography; glossary; illustrations; index; photographs.

INSTITUTIONS

2-38 Hazell, Ed. *Berklee: The First Fifty Years*. **Boston: Berklee Press, 1995. 296 pp.**
Pictorial history of the Berklee College of Music in Boston, Massachusetts.
Illustrations; photographs.

MEDIA

2-39 Gabbard, Krin. *Jammin' at the Margins: Jazz and the American Cinema*. **Chicago: University of Chicago Press, 1996. 350 pp.**
Account of "the representation of jazz in American movies." Includes "The Ethnic Oedipus: *The Jazz Singer* and Its Remakes"; "*Black and Tan Fantasies*: The Jazz Biopic"; "Jazz Becomes Art"; "Signifying the Phallus: Representations of the Jazz Trumpet"; "Duke's Place: Visualizing a Jazz Composer"; "Actor and Musician: Louis Armstrong and His Films"; "Nat King Cole, Hoagy Carmichael and the Fate of the Jazz Actor"; and "New York, New York and Short Cuts."
Bibliography; index; notes; photographs.

RECORDINGS

2-40 Piazza, Tom, ed. *Setting the Tempo: Fifty Years of Great Jazz Liner Notes*. **New York: Anchor Books, 1996. 369 pp.**
Collection of "forty-nine of the best liner notes ever written" by "most of the best writers in the field" as well as some musicians. According to the editor, the best jazz liner notes "tell a listener, in many subtle ways, what it means to be a jazz fan." Writers include George Avakian, Charles Edward Smith, George Frazier, David Stuart, Gunther Schuller, David Himmelstein, Tom Piazza, Dan Morgenstern, Ira Gitler, Nat Hentoff, Martin Williams, Leonard Feather, Whitney Balliett, Benny Green, Stanley Dance, Orrin Keepnews, Frank Kofsky, Amiri Baraka (LeRoi Jones), J. B. Figi, Robert Palmer, Stanley Crouch, Loren Schoenberg, and Felicity Howlett. Also includes contributions by the musicians themselves, including Art Hodes, Duke Ellington, Danny Barker, Charles Mingus, Bill Evans, Dick Wellstood, Andrew White, and Ornette Coleman.
Photographs.

3
Individual Instruments

Only a dozen books dealing with specific musical instruments in jazz were published during the 1990s. The largest number dealt with drums and drumming (five), followed by guitar (three). The general books on saxophone and trombone were included because they contained significant amounts of information relating to jazz and jazz musicians. Also included were a book on the bass guitar and a book dealing exclusively with the "stride" piano style.

BASS GUITAR

3-1 Bacon, Tony, and Barry Moorhouse. *The Bass Book.* San Francisco: GPI Books, 1995. 108 pp.

History of the electric bass guitar, including a section on "jazz bass guitar." Jazz musicians mentioned include Jaco Pastorius, John Patitucci, John Entwistle, and Marcus Miller. Contains a reference guide to "the specifications and production histories of most of the instruments [the reader] will come across on a regular basis," including bass guitars produced by 46 companies.

Photographs.

DRUMS

3-2 Cangany, Harry. *The Great American Drums and the Companies That Made Them, 1920–1969.* Edited by Rick Van Horn. Cedar Grove, NJ: Modern Drummer Publications, 1996. 72 pp.

Survey of the biggest American drum manufacturers. Contains information on jazz and rock drummers who used (and sometimes endorsed) particular brands.

Drum manufacturers include Camco, Fibes, Fred Gretsch, Leedy, L&S (Leedy & Strupe), Ludwig, Rogers, Slingerland, WFL, George Way, and Walberg & Auge.

Glossary; photographs.

3-3 Koenig, Dr. Karl. *Sonic Boom: Drums, Drummers and Drumming in Early Jazz.* **Edited by Mike Stagg. Covington, LA: Basin Street Press, 1990. 38 pp.**

Discussion of the role of drums and drummers in early New Orleans jazz. "This work notates what the early drummers have to say about their art and how the various drumming techniques helped evolve a new style of dance music—jazz."

Photographs.

3-4 Korall, Burt. *Drummin' Men: The Heartbeat of Jazz; The Swing Years.* **Foreword by Mel Tormé. New York: Schirmer Books, 1990. 381 pp.**

History of the drummers who came to the forefront during the swing years. Includes recollections by Chick Webb, Gene Krupa, Buddy Rich, Ray McKinley, Jo Jones, Sid Catlett, and Dave Tough.

Discography; index; notes; photographs.

3-5 Riley, Herlin, and Johnny Vidacovich. *New Orleans Jazz and Second Line Drumming.* **Interviews by Dan Thress and Val Wilmer. Miami: Manhattan Music, 1995. 119 pp.**

"This book traces the evolution of New Orleans jazz and second line drumming from the early styles of ragtime and traditional jazz to their modern applications in contemporary jazz." Includes biographical profiles of Baby Dodds and James Black, and interviews with David Lee, Smokey Robinson, James Black, and Freddie Kohlman.

Charts; discography; index; musical transcriptions; photographs.

3-6 Spagnardi, Ronald. *Great Jazz Drummers.* **Edited by William F. Miller. Cedar Grove, NJ: Modern Drummer Publications, 1992. 128 pp.**

One-page biographical portraits of 62 drummers. Each portrait attempts to "pinpoint the artist's style, his contribution to drumming, and the overall extent of his influence on other players." Drummers profiled include Zutty Singleton, Baby Dodds, Jo Jones, Chick Webb, Max Roach, Buddy Rich, Louie Bellson, Art Blakey, Ed Thigpen, Joe Morello, Paul Motian, and Kenny Washington.

Photographs.

GUITAR

3-7 Alexander, Charles, ed. *Masters of Jazz Guitar: The Story of the Players and Their Music.* **London: Balafon, 1999. 192 pp.**

Collection of essays, including "Soloists of the Swing Era," by Brian Priestley; "Django Reinhardt," by Max Harrison; "Charlie Christian," by Dave Gelly; "Wes Montgomery," by Kenny Mathieson; "Joe Pass," by John Fordham; "Pat Metheny," by Kenny Mathieson; "Brazilian Guitar," by John Zaradin; and "The Acoustic Guitar in Jazz," by Charles Alexander.

Bibliography; discography; index; photographs.

3-8 Sallis, James, ed. *The Guitar in Jazz: An Anthology.* **Lincoln: University of Nebraska Press, 1996. 210 pp.**

Collection of previously published articles and book excerpts focusing on jazz guitar history, styles, and performers. Includes "The Guitar in Jazz," by Leonard Feather; "Nick Lucas," by Nick Lucas and Jas Obrecht; "Eddie Lang," by James Sallis; "Charlie Christian," by Bill Simon; "Django's Blues," by Dan Lambert; "Oscar Moore," by Michael H. Price; "Joe Pass," by Wayne Enstice and Paul Rubin; and "The Guitar," by Joachim E. Berendt.

Illustrations; musical transcriptions; photographs.

3-9 Summerfield, Maurice J. *The Jazz Guitar: Its Evolution, Players and Personalities since 1900.* **4th ed. Gateshead, UK: Ashley Mark, 1998. 238 pp.**

Examination of "the guitar's role in jazz," including "Its Evolution"; "Its Players and Personalities"; "Its Instrument Makers"; and "Sources of Information and Supply." The first edition was published in 1978.

Bibliography; discography; index.

PIANO

3-10 Fell, John L., and Terkild Vinding. *Stride! Fats, Jimmy, Lion, Lamb, and All the Other Ticklers.* **Studies in Jazz, no. 31. Lanham, MD: Scarecrow Press, 1999. 237 pp.**

Study of "stride" piano style, including its prehistory, history, and technique. Stride pianists portrayed include James P. Johnson, Willie "The Lion" Smith, Fats Waller, Joe Turner, Luckey Roberts, Johnny Guarnieri, Ralph Sutton, Dick Hyman, and Dick Wellstood. Appendixes include "Clubs, Theaters, and Ballrooms"; "The Compositions of Luckey Roberts"; "The Compositions of Willie 'The Lion' Smith"; and "The Compositions of Fats Waller."

Bibliography; discography; index; musical transcriptions; photographs.

SAXOPHONE

3-11 Lindemeyer, Paul. *Celebrating the Saxophone.* **New York: Hearst Books, 1996. 96 pp.**

Pictorial history of the saxophone. Includes brief biographical sketches of Sidney Bechet, Coleman Hawkins, Lester Young, Charlie Parker, Sonny Rollins, John Coltrane, and the "Four Brothers" sax section of the Woody Herman Orchestra.

Bibliography; illustrations; photographs.

TROMBONE

3-12   Lane, G. B. *The Trombone: An Annotated Bibliography.* **Lanham, MD: Scarecrow Press, 1998. 425 pp.**

"The trombone has frequently been relegated to the status of footnotes and afterthoughts in much of the research on brass instruments. This book is designed to feature the trombone, its history, music, performers, performance practices (including jazz performance), instruments and equipment, and pedagogical topics that are of concern to those who teach the instrument." Each chapter or section is organized alphabetically by author.

Bibliographies; discographies; index.

4
Essays and Criticism

In the 1990s, books of jazz essays and criticism included historical studies, biographical portraits, and works on jazz in literature, dance, film, and photography. Several covered African Americans in jazz, or as Tom Piazza put it, "race, the individual, and the group in a democracy." One author, Francis Davis, dealt with his "growing disenchantment with contemporary jazz," while another, Eric Nisenson, expressed his belief that "jazz is stagnating." Collections of writings appeared by Whitney Balliett, Dan Bied, James Lincoln Collier, Francis Davis, John Fordham, Warren Vaché Sr., and Tex Wyndham. New editions of essays by Hayden Carruth, Francis Davis, Ralph J. Gleason, Benny Green, and Burnett James introduced these writers to a new generation of jazz enthusiasts. Older writings also resurfaced in anthologies such as Ralph de Toledano's *Frontiers of Jazz* (3rd revised edition) and Lewis Porter's *Jazz: A Century of Change.*

4-1 Alkyer, Frank, ed. *Down Beat: 60 Years of Jazz.* **Milwaukee, WI: Hal Leonard, 1995. 270 pp.**

"More than 100 classic articles and photographs from *Down Beat* Magazine," from 1935 to 1994. Arranged chronologically by decade. Includes articles by John Hammond, Jelly Roll Morton, W. C. Handy, Count Basie, Dave Dexter Jr., Bill Gottlieb, John S. Wilson, Leonard Feather, Ralph J. Gleason, Oscar Peterson, Nat Hentoff, Charles Mingus, Quincy Jones, Ira Gitler, John Tynan, Don Nelson, John Coltrane, Stanley Dance, Marian McPartland, Dan Morgenstern, Mel Tormé, Art Lange, and Bill Milkowski.

Index; photographs.

4-2 Balliett, Whitney. *Goodbyes and Other Messages: A Journal of Jazz, 1981–1990.* **New York: Oxford University Press, 1991. 295 pp.**

Short essays on jazz written by Balliett for the *New Yorker* magazine, including pieces on jazz bands and festivals, reviews of recordings and books, and over a dozen obituaries. Also includes two previously unpublished pieces: "The Sound of Jazz" (on the 1957 television show of that name) and "Romantic Agony" (on Bill Evans). Subjects include "The New Red Norvo Trio"; "Sonny Greer"; "Otis Ferguson"; "Earl Hines and Peck Kelley"; "Vic" (on Vic Dickenson); and "The Mulligan Sextet and Paul Gonsalves."

Index.

4-3 Bied, Dan. *Dan Bied's Jazz Reader.* **Burlington, IA: Craftsman Press, 1997. 254 pp.**

"Interviews, reviews, commentaries and nostalgic reminiscences." Musicians discussed include Benny Goodman, Duke Ellington, Stan Kenton, Count Basie, Maynard Ferguson, Ella Fitzgerald, Bob Haggart, Ray McKinley, Artie Shaw, Doc Cheatham, Ralph Sutton, and Art Hodes.

4-4 ———. *Jazz Memories.* **Burlington, IA: Craftsman Press, 1994. 244 pp.**

Collection of essays. Subjects include Duke Ellington, Benny Goodman, Count Basie, Roy McKinley, Si Zentner, Ellis Larkins, Dorothy Donegan, Pearl Bailey, Peggy Lee, Kay Starr, and the jazz clubs Eddie Condon's, Sweet Basil, and the Metropole.

Photographs.

4-5 Buckner, Reginald T., and Steven Weiland, eds. *Jazz in Mind: Essays on the History and Meanings of Jazz.* **Detroit: Wayne State University Press, 1991. 185 pp.**

Essays concerning the important role of writing in jazz. Most of the essays were initially presented at a scholarly conference at the University of Minnesota in fall 1987. Includes "James Reese Europe and the Prehistory of Jazz," by R. Reid Badger; "Negotiating the Color Line: Louis Armstrong's Autobiographies," by William H. Kenney III; "Soviet Jazz: Transforming American Music," by Greg Gaut; "The Problem of Local Jazz History: The Example of South Carolina," by Benjamin Franklin V; "The Quoter and His Culture," by Krin Gabbard; "'Jazz Isn't Just Me': Jazz Autobiographies as Performance Personas," by Kathy Ogren; "Jazz and Modernism: Changing Conceptions of Innovation and Tradition," by Mark S. Harvey; and "Jazz as Social Structure, Process, and Outcome," by David T. Bastien and Todd J. Hostager.

Discographies ("James Reese Europe"; "Soviet Jazz"; "Jazz and Modernism"); index.

4-6 Campbell, James. *The Picador Book of Blues and Jazz.* **London: Picador, 1995. 406 pp.**

Anthology of essays, poems, songs, fiction, and biography, with an eye toward the social context from which the music emerged. Includes "Early Ideas on the Origin of the Word Jazz," by David Boulton; "Jazz Comes to Revolutionary Russia," by S. Frederick Starr; "Remembering Jimmy Rushing," by Ralph Ellison; "The International Sweethearts of Rhythm," by Marian McPartland; "Jazz in a Nazi Concentration Camp," by Eric Vogel; "The Court Martial of Lester Young," by John McDonough; "Mingus and His Psychiatrist," by Charles Mingus; "In the Studio with Miles and Louis," by Nat Hentoff; "Bendin' the Horn," by Dizzy Gillespie; "Black Consciousness and the White Jazz Fan," by James Lincoln Collier; and "Ornette Coleman Learns to Play the Saxophone," by John Litweiler.

Bibliography; index.

4-7 Carruth, Hayden. *Sitting In: Selected Writings on Jazz, Blues, and Related Topics.* **Expanded edition. Iowa City: University of Iowa Press, 1993. 223 pp.**

Collection of previously published essays, reviews, and poems. Includes "Influences: The Formal Idea of Jazz"; "The Main Thing about Improvisation"; and "Eleven Memoranda on the Culture of Jazz." First published in 1986.

4-8 Collier, James Lincoln. *Jazz: The American Theme Song.* **New York: Oxford University Press, 1993. 326 pp.**

Collection of essays that "examine jazz from a variety of positions." Includes "The Inevitability of Jazz in America"; "Art and the Academy"; "The Rise of Individualism and the Jazz Solo"; "Jazz and Pop"; "The Critics"; and "Local Jazz."

Index; notes.

4-9 Coolidge, Clark. *Now It's Jazz: Writings on Kerouac and the Sounds.* **Albuquerque, NM: Living Batch Press, 1999. 136 pp.**

Essays on author Jack Kerouac and jazz. Includes "A Note on Bop"; "The Miles Problem"; and "Sonny's Well" (on Sonny Rollins).

4-10 Crow, Bill. *From Birdland to Broadway: Scenes from a Jazz Life.* **New York: Oxford University Press, 1992. 273 pp.**

Collection of the author's "personal stories." Most of the material is previously unpublished, but some appeared in slightly different form in Gene Lees's *Jazzletter* or in Crow's column "The Band Room" in *Allegro*, the monthly newspaper of Local 802, the New York chapter of the American Federation of Musicians. Includes "Dave Lambert"; "Slim Gaillard"; "Stan Getz"; "Pee Wee Marquette"; "Claude Thornhill"; "Gene Quill"; "Terry Gibbs"; "The Marian McPartland Trio"; "Popsie Randolph"; "Vic Dickenson"; "Bird"; "Gerry Mulligan"; "Duke Ellington"; "Garner & Monk"; "Pee Wee Russell"; "The Sherwood Inn"; "The Half Note"; and "Condon's, the Playboy Club."

Index.

4-11 ———. *Jazz Anecdotes.* **New York: Oxford University Press, 1990. 350 pp.**

Contains stories culled from interviews, biographies, autobiographies, oral histories compiled by the Institute of Jazz Studies at Rutgers University, and Crow's columns. "Organized around general topics—teaching and learning, stage fright, life on the road, prejudice and discrimination, and the importance of a good nickname." Contains extended sections on musicians such as Bessie Smith, Louis Armstrong, Fats Waller, Duke Ellington, Tommy Dorsey, Dizzy Gillespie, Charlie Parker, Zoot Sims, Art Tatum, and Eddie Condon.

4-12 Davis, Francis. *Bebop and Nothingness: Jazz and Pop at the End of the Century.* **New York: Schirmer Books, 1996. 304 pp.**

Collection of previously published articles from 1989 to 1995. The author writes that his unifying theme "might be [his] growing disenchantment with contemporary jazz." Pieces include "Better with Age" (Benny Carter); "Pres and his Discontents" (Lester Young); "Bebop and Nothingness" (Charlie Parker/Art Pepper); "Anthony Braxton, All American"; "This Is Not Just Jazz" (Sonny Sharrock); "Sun Ra, Himself"; and "Bagels and Dreadlocks" (Don Byron).

Index.

4-13 ———. *In the Moment: Jazz in the 1980s.* **New York: Da Capo Press, 1996. 258 pp.**

Collection of essays on jazz, originally published in 1986 by Oxford University Press. This edition includes a new introduction by the author. Includes "The Right Stuff" (Wynton and Branford Marsalis); "Swing Redux" (Scott Hamilton and Warren Vaché Jr.); "An Improviser Prepares" (Sonny Rollins); "There's No Success Like Failure and Failure's No Success at All: Ornette Coleman's Permanent Revolution"; "Don Cherry Sees the World"; "Henry Threadgill Leads the Parade"; and "The Unsure Egoist is Not Good for Himself" (Miles Davis).

Index.

4-14 Folley-Cooper, Marquette, Deborah Macanic, and Janice McNeil, compilers. *Seeing Jazz: Artists and Writers on Jazz.* **Edited by Elizabeth Goldson. San Francisco: Chronicle Books in association with the Smithsonian Institution Traveling Exhibition Service, 1997. 144 pp.**

Includes artwork by such artists as Henri Matisse, Man Ray, and Jean-Michel Basquiat; photographs by William Gottlieb and Gordon Parks; and brief excerpts from jazz fiction, poetry, and nonfiction, including "Treat It Gentle," by Sidney Bechet; "Earl and the Duke," by Stanley Crouch; "Baquet on Bolden," by George Baquet; and "The Last Generation," by Billy Taylor.

4-15 Fordham, John. *Shooting from the Hip: Changing Tunes in Jazz.* **London: Kyle Cathie, 1996. 352 pp.**

Collection of brief essays written by Fordham for various publications from 1970 to 1995. Organized by decade, with a background narrative prefacing each section.

Index.

4-16 Gabbard, Krin, ed. *Jazz among the Discourses.* **Durham, NC: Duke University Press, 1995. 288 pp.**

Anthology of essays "concerned primarily with jazz history and aesthetics or with specific jazz artists." Includes "'Moldy Figs' and Modernists: Jazz at War (1942–1946)," by Bernard Gendron; "Jazz in Crisis, 1948–1958," by Steven B. Elworth; "Historical Context and the Definition of Jazz: Putting More of the History in 'Jazz History'," by William Howland Kenney; "The Media of Memory: The Seductive Menace of Records in Jazz History," by Jed Rasula; "Ephemera Underscored: Writing around Free Improvisation," by John Corbett; and "Double V, Double Time: Bebop's Politics of Style," by Eric Lott.

Bibliography; index; musical transcriptions; notes.

4-17 ———, ed. *Representing Jazz.* **Durham, NC: Duke University Press, 1995. 320 pp.**

Collection of essays that deal with jazz in literature, dance, film, and photography. Includes "Jammin' the Blues, or the Sight of Jazz, 1944," by Arthur Knight; "Improvising and Mythmaking in Eudora Welty's 'Powerhouse'," by Leland H. Chambers; "Fabulating Jazz," by Frederick Garber; "Signifyin(g) the Phallus: *Mo' Better Blues* and Representations of the Jazz Trumpet," by Krin Gabbard; "Jazz Autobiography: Theory, Practice, Politics," by Christopher Harlos ; and "Jazz and the New York School," by Mona Hadler.

Bibliography; illustrations; index; photographs.

4-18 Giddins, Gary. *Faces in the Crowd: Players and Writers.* **New York: Oxford University Press, 1992. 278 pp.**

Collection of essays, reviews, and profiles about musicians, actors, and filmmakers. Includes "Lady Gets Her Day" (Billie Holiday); "Divine" (Sarah Vaughan); "The Wizard of Bop" (Frank Morgan); and "Of Thad and Mel" (Thad Jones and Mel Lewis).

Index; musical transcriptions.

4-19 Gleason, Ralph J. *Celebrating the Duke: And Louis, Bessie, Billie, Bird, Carmen, Miles, Dizzy and Other Heroes.* **New York: Da Capo Press 1995. 280 pp.**

Collection of essays originally published in 1975, with a new introduction by Ira Gitler. Includes "Jazz Black Art/American Art"; "Bessie Smith"; "Louis Armstrong"; " Jimmie Lunceford"; "Billie Holiday—Lady Day"; "Pres: Lester Young"; "Charlie 'Bird' Parker"; "John Birks 'Dizzy' Gillespie"; "John Lewis and the Modern Jazz Quartet"; "Carmen McRae"; "John Coltrane"; "Miles Davis"; "The Death of Albert Ayler"; and "Farewell to the Duke."

Discography; index; photographs.

4-20   Gottlieb, Robert, ed. *Reading Jazz: A Gathering of Autobiography, Reportage, and Criticism from 1919 to Now.* **New York: Vintage Books, 1996. 1068 pp.**

Includes autobiographical excerpts by Jelly Roll Morton, Sidney Bechet, Louis Armstrong, Willie "The Lion" Smith, Duke Ellington, Sonny Greer, Leora Henderson, Art Hodes, Buck Clayton, Eddie Condon, Mary Lou Williams, Cab Calloway, Lionel Hampton, John Hammond, Hampton Hawes, Paul Desmond, Cecil Taylor, and Anthony Braxton. The "Reportage" section includes "King Oliver: A Very Personal Memoir," by Edmond Souchon; "Thomas 'Fats' Waller," by John S. Wilson; "The Spirit of Jazz," by Otis Ferguson; "The Mirror of Swing" (Benny Goodman), by Gary Giddins; "Jimmie Lunceford," by Ralph J. Gleason; "Two Rounds of the Battling Dorseys," by Tommy and Jimmy Dorsey; "Minton's," by Ralph Ellison; "Minton's Playhouse," by Dizzy Gillespie; "At the Hi-De-Ho," by Hampton Hawes; "Bird," by Miles Davis; "An Evening with Monk," by Dan Morgenstern; "Thelonious and Me," by Orrin Keepnews; "John Coltrane," by Nat Hentoff; "Bessie Smith: Poet," by Murray Kempton; "Lady Day Has Her Say," by Billie Holiday; "The Untold Story of the International Sweethearts of Rhythm," by Marian McPartland; "Moonbeam Moscowitz: Sylvia Syms," by Whitney Balliett; "A Night at the Five Spot," by Martin Williams; and "Jazz in America," by Jean-Paul Sartre. The "Criticism" section includes "Bechet and Jazz Visit Europe, 1919," by Ernst-Alexandre Ansermet; "Harpsichords and Jazz Trumpets," by Roger Pryor Dodge; "Has Jazz Influenced the Symphony?" by Gene Krupa and Leonard Bernstein; "Bix Beiderbecke," by Benny Green; "James P. Johnson," by Max Harrison; "Coleman Hawkins," by Dan Morgenstern; "Bop," by LeRoi Jones; "On Bird, Bird-Watching, and Jazz," by Ralph Ellison; "Why Did Ellington 'Remake' His Masterpiece?" by André Hodeir; "On the Corner: The Sellout of Miles Davis," by Stanley Crouch; "Space Is the Place," by Gene Santoro; "The Divine Sarah" (Sarah Vaughan), by Gunther Schuller; and "Fifty Years of 'Body and Soul'," by Gary Giddins.

4-21   Green, Benny. *The Reluctant Art: Five Studies in the Growth of Jazz.* **Expanded edition. New York: Da Capo Press, 1991. 210 pp.**

Collection of essays originally published in 1962, with the addition of a new preface and a chapter on Art Tatum originally published as "liner notes to a boxed set of his recordings in 1976." Includes essays on Bix Beiderbecke, Benny Goodman, Lester Young, Billie Holiday, and Charlie Parker.

4-22   Hentoff, Nat. *Listen to the Stories: Nat Hentoff on Jazz and Country Music.* **New York: Harper Collins, 1995. 220 pp.**

Collection of essays, some previously published in the "Leisure and Arts" page of the *Wall Street Journal*. Includes "Duke Ellington, 1899–1974"; "The Duke, in Private"; "Kansas City, Walking in Time"; "What Makes a Jazz Singer?"; "The Last Days of Lady Day"; "Carmen McRae Meets Thelonious Monk"; "Is There a Charlie Parker among the New Generation of Jazz Players?"; "Danny Barker: A Very Long Life in Jazz"; "The Limitless Mingus"; "The Impresario Who Brought Civil Rights to Jazz" (Norman Granz).

Bibliography; index.

4-23 Hobsbawm, Eric J. *The Jazz Scene*. Revised edition. New York: Pantheon Books, 1993. 392 pp.

History of jazz. This revised edition includes "twenty-three pieces that have never appeared in book form—concert reviews, record reviews, and essays from the *New Statesman* and the *New York Review of Books*." Musicians covered include Thelonious Monk, Duke Ellington, Sidney Bechet, and Count Basie. Originally published in 1959 under the pseudonym Francis Newton.

Bibliography; notes.

4-24 James, Burnett. *Essays on Jazz*. New York: Da Capo Press, 1990. 211 pp.

Collection of essays, originally published in 1961, with a new introduction and index by the author. Includes "Billie Holiday and the Art of Communication"; "Lester Young"; "King Oliver as Father Figure"; "Bix Beiderbecke and a White Style in Jazz"; "Oscar Peterson"; "Johnny Hodges"; "The Impressionism of Duke Ellington"; and "Such Sweet Thunder."

Index.

4-25 Kington, Miles, ed. *The Jazz Anthology*. London: HarperCollins, 1992. 317 pp.

Collection of excerpts from books and other archival sources. Includes "Musicians on Music"; "Places"; "Race"; "Jazz Is"; and "Sleeve Notes."

Index.

4-26 Lancaster, Byard. *Horn Works: Music Discipline*. Philadelphia: Jazzversity Press, 1992. 95 pp.

Essays on elementary business techniques, and lists of radio stations and publications. Also includes "Electro/Acoustical Concepts in 20th Century Composition," by Youseff Yancy.

Bibliography; photographs.

4-27 Larkin, Philip. *Reference Back: Philip Larkin's Uncollected Jazz Writings 1940–1984*. Edited by Richard Palmer and John White. Hull, UK: University of Hull Press, 1999. 170 pp.

Collection of Larkin's writings, including "Reviews in Newspapers & Periodicals"; "Miscellany of Essays, Book Reports, and Letters"; "*Daily Telegraph* Records of the Year, 1961–70"; and "Larkin's First Essay on Jazz (1940)."
Bibliography; index; notes.

4-28 Meltzer, David, ed. *Reading Jazz.* San Francisco: Mercury House, 1993. 317 pp.
Collection that explores the literary and critical use of jazz during four historical moments of cultural transition. According to the author, the readings represent the ways jazz was mythologized, colonialized, demonized, defended, and ultimately neutralized by white Americans and Europeans. Writers include Hoagy Carmichael, Philip Larkin, Artie Shaw, Norman Mailer, Art Pepper, Simone de Beauvoir, Julio Cortázar, William Carlos Williams, and Robert Creeley.
Bibliography; index.

4-29 ———, ed. *Writing Jazz.* San Francisco: Mercury House, 1999. 315 pp.
Anthology of writings representing African-American perceptions of jazz as a subject and practice. Includes selections from Louis Armstrong, Amiri Baraka, Sidney Bechet, Miles Davis, Ralph Ellison, Dizzy Gillespie, Nikki Giovanni, Billie Holiday, Son House, Langston Hughes, Furry Lewis, Albert Murray, Ishmael Reed, Sonia Sanchez, Willie "The Lion" Smith, Wole Soyinka, Ethel Waters, Booker White, Richard Wright, Eileen Southern, and Samuel Floyd.
Bibliography; index.

4-30 Nisenson, Eric. *Blue: The Murder of Jazz.* New York: St. Martin's Press, 1997. 262 pp.
Exploration of the viewpoint held by some jazz musicians and musicologists that jazz is stagnating. Reviews historical and sociological causes and possible "progressive and visionary" rescuers.
Bibliography; discography; index; notes.

4-31 O'Meally, Robert G., ed. *The Jazz Cadence of American Culture.* New York: Columbia University Press, 1998.
Includes "Forward Motion: An Interview with Benny Golson," by Benny Golson and Jim Merod; "Improvisation and the Creative Process," by Albert Murray; "Jazz and the White Critic," by Amiri Baraka; "Improvisation in Jazz," by Bill Evans; "Characteristics of Negro Expression," by Zora Neale Hurston; and "Double V, Double Time: Bebop's Politics of Style," by Eric Lott.
Bibliography; illustrations; index; photographs.

4-32 Piazza, Tom. *Blues Up and Down: Jazz in Our Time.* New York: St. Martin's Press, 1997. 194 pp.

Collection of essays, articles, and reviews written between 1979 and 1997, addressing issues such as "race, the individual and the group in a democracy, the role of the arts in a commercial culture, the relationship of so-called 'high art' to so-called 'popular art,' and the question of whether there is such a thing as progress in the arts." Includes "McCoy Tyner's Present Tense"; "Mary Lou Williams Keeps the Faith"; "Portrait of Wynton Marsalis"; "How Two Pianists Remade a Tradition" (Thelonious Monk and Bud Powell); "Jazz Piano's Heavyweight Champ" (Art Tatum); and "Lincoln Center and Its Critics Swing Away."

4-33   Porter, Lewis. *Jazz: A Century of Change.* **New York: Schirmer Books, 1997. 298 pp.**

Collection of essays by Porter that frame a selection of excerpts from writings ranging from 1856 to 1997. Among the writers included are Scoop Gleeson, Henry F. Gilbert, James Reese Europe, Richard Rodney Bennett, Winthrop Sargeant, and Billy Taylor. Includes "Where Did the Word *Jazz* Come From?"; "Analyzing Jazz"; "Where Did the Music Come From?"; "Responses to Early Jazz, 1919 to 1934"; "African Americans and the Swing Era"; "Reactions to Bebop"; "The Drug Problem"; "Race Politics and Jazz in the 1950s and 1960s"; "Avant-garde and Fusion: Two Opposites? 1960 to the Present"; "Traditionalism, Revivalism, and the 'Young Lions,' 1980 to the Present"; and "Crossing Boundaries, 1980 to the Present."

Bibliography; illustrations; index; musical transcriptions; table.

4-34   Rust, Brian. *My Kind of Jazz.* **London: Elm Tree Books, 1990. 200 pp.**

Essays on "some of the outstanding events in the evolution of jazz." Topics include early New Orleans jazz, the Chicago style of jazz, the New York jazz scene, and the influence of jazz overseas.

Discography; index.

4-35   Santoro, Gene. *Dancing in Your Head: Jazz, Blues, Rock, and Beyond.* **New York: Oxford University Press, 1994. 308 pp.**

Collection of previously published essays on jazz, blues, rock, and rap. Includes the following jazz musicians: Ornette Coleman, John Coltrane, Miles Davis, Duke Ellington, Bill Frisell, Charles Mingus, Thelonious Monk, Charlie Parker, Django Reinhardt, and Sun Ra.

Bibliography; index.

4-36   ———. *Stir It Up: Musical Mixes from Roots to Jazz.* **New York: Oxford University Press, 1997. 193 pp.**

Collection of previously published essays on jazz, R&B, reggae, rock, and world music. Includes material on Thelonious Monk, John Coltrane, Ornette Coleman, Abbey Lincoln, Charles Mingus, Ray Drummond, Tom Harrell, Don Pullen, Joe Lovano, Marty Ehrlich, and Manu Dibango.

Index.

4-37 Swanson, Bill. *Little Red Book of Jazz Definitions*. Grand Rapids, MI: Moonlight Graphics, 1994. 125 pp.

Collection of short essays and quotations about jazz.

4-38 Toledano, Ralph de, ed. *Frontiers of Jazz*. 3rd revised edition. Gretna, LA: Pelican Publishing, 1994. 178 pp.

Historical compilation of previously published critical and biographical articles on jazz. Includes "Harpsichords and Jazz Trumpets," by Roger Pryor Dodge; "Notes on Boogie Woogie," by William Russell; "Jazz Pre-History, and Bunk Johnson," by Morroe Berger; "I Discovered Jazz in 1902," by Jelly Roll Morton; and "Grandfather of Hot Piano" (James P. Johnson), by Ross Russell. First published in 1947.

Index; musical transcriptions.

4-39 Vaché, Warren W. Sr. *Jazz Gentry: Aristocrats of the Music World*. Studies in Jazz, no. 33. Lanham, MD: Scarecrow Press, 1999. 379 pp.

Collection of previously published essays that "represent a cross section of [Vaché's] writings on jazz and jazz musicians over the past fifteen years." Includes material on Bobby Hackett, Pee Wee Russell, Joe Venuti, Chris Griffin, Jack Pettis, Jane Jarvis, George Masso, Fred Norman, Wild Bill Davison, Dolly Dawn, Johnny Varro, Tony Spargo, Al Duffy, Bill Challis, Dick Wellstood, Chauncey Morehouse, Doc Cheatham, Ray Noble, and Johnny Mince.

Index; photographs.

4-40 Walser, Robert, ed. *Keeping Time: Readings in Jazz History*. New York: Oxford University Press, 1999. 450 pp.

Anthology of writings by jazz critics and musicians, arranged in chronological order. Includes "Sidney Bechet's Musical Philosophy," by Sidney Bechet; "A Negro Explains Jazz," by James Reese Europe; "The 'Inventor of Jazz'," by Jelly Roll Morton; "Jazz and African Music," by Nicholas G. J. Ballanta-Taylor; "A Black Journalist Criticizes Jazz," by Dave Peyton; "What is Swing?" by Louis Armstrong; "On the Road with Count Basie," by Billie Holiday; "The Cult of Bebop," by Dizzy Gillespie; "Jazz in the Classroom," by Marshall W. Stearns; "Sonny Rollins and the Challenge of Thematic Improvisation," by Gunther Schuller; "Jazz and the White Critic," by LeRoi Jones; "Jazz as a Progressive Social Force," by Leonard Feather; and "Ring Shout, Signifyin(g), and Jazz Analysis," by Samuel A. Floyd Jr.

Bibliography; index.

4-41 Wiener Musik Galerie. *Incident in Jazz*. Vienna: Wiener Musik Galerie, 1992. 178 pp.

Program book, with extensive essays in German and English, for the concerts celebrating the tenth anniversary of the Wiener Musik Galerie (October 2–4,

1992). Some essays previously published. English essays include "Pete Rugolo's Mirage," by Gunther Schuller; "Blake on Russo," by Will Friedwald; "The Murderous Music of Edward Vesala," by Steve Lake; "Precision in Melancholy: The Vienna Flugelhorn Player and (Jazz) Composer Franz Koglmann," by Peter Niklas Wilson; "The Music of Magic Realism: A Portrait of the Composer Denys Bouliane," by Peter Niklas Wilson; and "The NDR Bigband," by Wolfgang Kunert.

4-42 Williams, Martin T. *Jazz Changes*. New York: Oxford University Press, 1992. 317 pp.

Compilation of previously published pieces, including "brief appreciation profiles" of musicians; pieces on "musicians observed in recording studios, at rehearsals, and in clubs"; interviews and "give and take conversations" with musicians; and record and concert reviews, "some of which go back to [Williams's] earliest days as a record and concert reviewer." Includes material on Earl Hines, Bob Wilber, Billie Holiday, Ross Russell, John Lewis, Steve Kuhn, Ornette Coleman, Scott LaFaro, Steve Swallow, Gary Peacock, Jelly Roll Morton (at the Library of Congress), Dinah Washington, Thelonious Monk, Art Blakey, John Coltrane, Art Pepper, Eric Dolphy, Herbie Nichols, Cannonball Adderley, Oscar Peterson, Martial Solal, George Shearing, and Ahmad Jamal.

Index.

4-43 Wyndham, Tex. *Texas Shout: How Dixieland Jazz Works*. Seattle, WA: Light, Words & Music, 1997 346 pp.

Collection from Wyndham's column "Texas Shout" in *West Coast Rag/The American Rag* from 1989 to 1996. According to Wyndham, "Texas Shout" is based on two of his "most deeply held beliefs: (1) The more you know about something, the more likely you are to enjoy it and stick with it. (2) Dixieland Jazz and ragtime, like all other valid art forms, are not in any way dated." Includes "Women in Dixieland"; "Dixieland vs. Ragtime"; "Economics of Dixieland"; "Fats Waller, Etc."; Contemporary Ragtimers"; "West Coast Revival"; and "Melodic Improvisation."

Photographs.

5
Musicology

Books about musicology published in the 1990s ranged from general beginner's guides to intricate theoretical studies. Six books went under the heading of jazz and race.

MUSICAL THEORY/IMPROVISATION

5-1   Berliner, Paul F. *Thinking in Jazz: The Infinite Art of Improvisation.* **Chicago: University of Chicago Press, 1994. 883 pp.**
   Study of the art of improvisation focusing on "the remarkableness of the training and rigorous musical thinking that underlie this art." Contains "Initial Preparation for Jazz"; "Cultivating the Soloist's Skills"; and "Collective Aspects of Improvisation." Incorporates interviews with over fifty jazz musicians.
   Bibliography; discography; index; musical transcriptions; notes; videography.

5-2   Dean, Roger T. *New Structures in Jazz and Improvised Music since 1960.* **Philadelphia: Open University Press, 1992. 230 pp.**
   Analysis of "changes in the nature and structure of improvised music between 1960 and around 1985." Topics include "improvised music as object and evolution," "improvised music as process," "the evolution of improvisation in the work of the individual," and "improvised work and the artistic context." Artists covered include Paul Bley, Andrew Hill, Wolfgang Dauner, and Joachim Kuhn.
   Bibliography; diagrams; discography; index; musical transcriptions; videography.

5-3   Kernfeld, Barry. *What to Listen for in Jazz.* **New Haven, CT: Yale University Press, 1995. 247 pp.**

Exploration of the "process of making jazz," organized around seven topics: rhythm, forms, arrangement, composition, improvisation, sound, and style.

Bibliography; discography; index; musical transcriptions; notes.

5-4   Martin, Henry. *Charlie Parker and Thematic Improvisation.* **Studies in Jazz, no. 24. Lanham, MD: Scarecrow Press, 1996. 155 pp.**

Overall assessment of the importance of Charlie Parker through an analysis of his improvisations in a variety of genres. Includes "Improvisation and Linear Theory"; "Rhythm Changes"; "Popular Song"; "The Blues"; and "Master Soloist."

Bibliography; discography; index.

5-5   Monson, Ingrid. *Saying Something: Jazz Improvisation and Interaction.* **Chicago: University of Chicago Press, 1996. 253 pp.**

Study of improvisation, focusing primarily on the interaction among rhythm section players. Includes "Talking to Musicians"; "Music, Language, and Cultural Styles: Improvisation as Conversation"; "Intermusicality"; "Interaction, Feeling, and Musical Analysis"; and "Ethnomusicology, Interaction, and Poststructuralism."

Bibliography; discography; index; musical transcriptions; notes.

5-6   Sturm, Fred. *Changes over Time: The Evolution of Jazz Arranging.* **Rottenburg, Germany: Advance Music, 1995. 222 pp.**

"Comparative case studies" illustrate "the dramatic development of rhythmic, melodic, harmonic, orchestrational, and structural variation in jazz arranging from the 1920s to the present." The case studies are 35 different arrangements of three classic jazz compositions and one standard: Jelly Roll Morton's "King Porter Stomp," Don Redman's "Chant of the Weed," Gerald Marks and Seymour Simon's "All of Me," and Billy Strayhorn's "Take the 'A' Train." Examines arrangements by Don Redman, Fletcher Henderson, Benny Carter, Duke Ellington, Billy Strayhorn, Gil Evans, Thad Jones, Bill Holman, Bob Brookmeyer, and Clare Fischer, among others.

Bibliography; discography; musical notations.

JAZZ AND RACE

5-7   Gerard, Charley. *Jazz in Black and White: Race, Culture and Identity in the Jazz Community.* **Westport, CT: Praeger, 1998. 202 pp.**

Study of racial attitudes in the jazz community and the "formulation of identity in the face of racial difference." Includes "Black Music, Black Identity"; "African Music, African Identity"; "Race and Religious Identity"; "Race and Jazz Communities"; "Black Music, White Identity"; "Colorless Swing"; and "Racial Identity Embedded in Performance."

Bibliography; index; musical transcriptions; notes; photographs.

Musicology

5-8 Hennessey, Thomas J. *From Jazz to Swing: African-American Jazz Musicians and Their Music, 1890–1935.* **Detroit: Wayne State University Press, c1994. 217 pp.**

Explores how "black jazz musicians transformed their art—a series of regional musics—into America's most popular music." Also "examines the historical context of jazz within the changing situation of the African-American community and notes the tensions created by the structures of segregation, stereotypes, and prejudice." Sources include African-American newspapers, such as the *Chicago Defender*, as well as published and archival oral history interviews. Includes material on Louis Armstrong, Coleman Hawkins, Duke Ellington, James Reese Europe, King Oliver, Don Redman, and Fletcher Henderson.
Bibliography; index.

5-9 Kofsky, Frank. *Black Music, White Business: Illuminating the History and Political Economy of Jazz.* **New York: Pathfinder, 1998. 165 pp.**

Investigation of the "conflicts between the artistry of Black musicians and the control by largely white-owned businesses of jazz distribution—the recording companies, booking agencies, festivals, clubs, and magazines." Expanded from parts of Kofsky's earlier book *Black Nationalism and the Revolution in Music*.
Bibliography; illustrations; index; photographs.

5-10 Panish, Jon. *The Color of Jazz: Race and Representation in Postwar American Culture.* **Jackson: University Press of Mississippi, 1997. 166 pp.**

"Study of America's attitudes toward jazz from the end of World War II to the beginning of the Black Power Movement." Explores the "diverse representations of jazz and jazz musicians in literature and popular culture."
Bibliography; index.

5-11 Peretti, Burton H. *The Creation of Jazz: Music, Race, and Culture in Urban America.* **Urbana: University of Illinois Press, 1992. 277 pp.**

Examines the creation of jazz within the contexts of American "urbanization, race relations, individual development, professionalism, and capitalism."
Bibliography; index; photographs.

5-12 Yoshida, George. *Reminiscing in Swingtime: Japanese Americans in American Popular Music, 1925–1960.* **San Francisco: National Japanese American Historical Society, 1997. 300 pp.**

Contents include "The Original Jazz Syncopators: Pre-World War II Jazz Bands"; "Bata-Kusai Jazz Singers: Nisei Music Makers in Prewar Japan"; "Of Jive Bombers and Stardusters: Dance Bands in Assembly Centers & Detention

Camps"; "Goin' to Chicago Blues: From War to Peacetime"; and "Establishing New Roots: Postwar Music." Musicians covered include Mikados of Swing; Oakland Sons and Daughters Orchestra; Richard's Original Syncopators Orchestra; Japanese Sandmen; Tekisei Ongaku; Helen Honda; George Igawa Orchestra; Jive Bombers; Hideo Kawano; Eager Beavers; Paul Togawa; and Pat Suzuki. Appendix: "Nisei Dance Bands and Band Personnel."

Glossary; index; photographs.

6
Regional Studies

The English-language books about jazz that were published abroad during the 1990s came from such diverse places as Finland, Slovakia, Australia, and South Africa. Readers can trace unique developments of jazz in different parts of the world—from "township jazz" in South Africa to "bodgie" followers in Australia to "underground jazz" and "propaganda swing" in Germany—while finding universality in the challenges that jazz musicians worldwide confront. Some books are devoted to specific areas of the United States, including Ohio; Rhode Island; Nashville, Tennessee; and Seattle, Washington. Canadian jazz was represented by titles on Canadian jazz history, jazz in Toronto, and the Festival International de Jazz de Montréal.

AFRICA—SOUTH AFRICA

6-1   Ballantine, Christopher. *Marabi Nights: Early South African Jazz and Vaudeville.* **Johannesburg: Ravan Press, 1993. 116 pp.**
History of jazz in South Africa. (Marabi is a "rhythmically propulsive dance music.") Discusses "The Foundations of Black jazz in South Africa"; "The Social Role of Black Jazz and Vaudeville in South Africa"; and "Race, Class, and Gender in Black South African Jazz Culture."
Bibliography; index; photographs.

6-2   Breakey, Basil. *Beyond the Blues: Township Jazz in the '60s and '70s.* **Commentary by Steve Gordon. Cape Town: David Philip, 1997. 82 pp.**
Photographs and commentary about "township jazz" (a blend of American jazz and indigenous African music) and some of its musicians, including Kippie Moeketsi, Abdullah Ibrahim (Dollar Brand), Chris McGregor, Basil Coetzee,

Barney Rachabane, Louis Moholo, Dudu Pukwana, Mongezi Feza, and Johnny Dyani. Contains the previously published piece "Louis Moholo on the Blue Notes."
Discography; photographs.

AUSTRALIA

6-3   Clare, John. *Bodgie Dada and the Cult of Cool.* Sydney: University of New South Wales, 1995. 218 pp.
Study of postwar Australian jazz, particularly the followers of West Coast cool jazz, known as "bodgies." Includes material on Don Burrows, the Australian Jazz Quartet, Johnny Bamford, Ron Falson, and the jazz clubs Jazz Centre 44 and El Rocco.
Index; photographs.

6-4   Myers, Eric, ed. *Australian Jazz Directory 1998.* Millers Point, NSW, Australia: Jazz Co-ordination Association of New South Wales, 1998. 333 pp.
Not reviewed. Includes jazz festivals.
Index.

EUROPE

6-5   Fanø, Mette, and Arnvid Meyer, eds. *Directory of Jazz Festivals and Related Major Jazz Events, Part One: Europe.* 3rd ed. Rønnede, Denmark: Danish Jazz Center in collaboration with the International Jazz Federation, 1990. 120 pp.
Listing of jazz festivals held in Europe. Organized by country. *Note*: Fourth edition not examined.

Finland

6-6   Vuorela, Jari-Pekka, and Jari Muikku. *What about Jazz in Finland?* 4th ed. Translated by Susan Sinisalo. Helsinki: Finnish Music Information Centre, 1992. 112 pp.
Collection of portraits of prominent Finnish jazz musicians, including Otto Donner, Markku Johansson, Markku Kanerva, Antti Sarpila, Eero Koivistoinen, Pentti Lahti, Reino Laine, Jukka Linkola, and Esko Linnavalli. First published in 1974 under the title *Finnish Jazz*.
Photographs.

Germany

6-7 Bergmeier, Horst J. P. and Rainer E. Lotz. *Hitler's Airwaves: The Inside Story of Nazi Radio Broadcasting and Propaganda Swing.* **New Haven: Yale University Press, 1997. 368 pp.**

Chronicles the "Reich Ministry for Public Enlightenment and Propaganda" and the "propaganda swing orchestra" fronted by Charlie Schwedler.
Bibliography; discography; index; notes; photographs.

6-8 Kater, Michael H. *Different Drummers: Jazz in the Culture of Nazi Germany.* **New York: Oxford University Press, 1992. 291 pp.**

History of underground jazz in Germany during the Third Reich. Jazz groups include the Weintraub Syncopators, the Hamburg Swingers, and the Harlem Group of Frankfurt.
Bibliography; index; notes; photographs.

Hungary

6-9 Simon, Géza Gábor. *The Book of Hungarian Jazz.* **Translated by Borbála Molnaár, et al. Budapest: Hotelinfo, 1992. 199 pp.**

Not reviewed.
Bibliography; discography; index; photographs.

Netherlands

6-10 Whitehead, Kevin. *New Dutch Swing.* **New York: Billboard Books, 1998. 338 pp.**

Musicological study of the development of jazz (particularly experimental jazz) in Amsterdam. Includes profiles of Louis Andriessen, Eric Boeren, Han Bennink, and Guus Janssen.
Bibliography; discography; index.

Slovakia

6-11 Lábska,Yvetta, ed. *Slovak Popular Music and Jazz.* **Bratislava, Slovakia: Music Information Centre of the Slovak Music Fund, 1990. 35 pp.**

Examination of Slovak jazz and popular music. Includes short biographies of Peter Lipa, Ladislav Gerhardt, Laco Déczi, Gabriel Jonáš, Jozef Šošoka, and Dušan Húščava.
Bibliography; photographs.

Former Soviet Republics

6-12 Minor, William. *Unzipped Souls: A Jazz Journey through the Soviet Union.* Philadelphia: Temple University Press, 1995. 226 pp.

The author travels through six republics of the former Soviet Union, tracing the development of contemporary Russian jazz in response to cultural changes.

Index; photographs.

Spain

6-13 Festival de Jazz de San Sebastián. *Donostiako Jazzaldia: lehenengo 30 urteak; los primeros 30 años.* Translated by Jesús Lasa. [Irun, Spain]: Litografía Valverde, 1996. 159 pp.

History of the San Sebastián jazz festival. Most material is in Spanish or Basque, with one essay in English.

Illustrations; index; photographs.

United Kingdom

6-14 Ingless, Steve. *The Day Before Yesterday: Rock, Rhythm and Jazz in the Bishop's Stortford Area from 1957 to 1969.* Bishop's Stortford, UK: Scila, 1999. 229 pp.

History of jazz, rock, and other forms of popular music in Bishop's Stortford, Hertfordshire, England, from 1957 to 1969. Includes concert listings.

Bibliography; discography; photographs.

6-15 Hoctor, Michelle, ed. *Directory of Musicians in Ireland: Featuring 1,600 Classical, Traditional and Jazz Musicians and Performing Groups, in and from Ireland, North and South.* Dublin: Music Network, 1998. 321 pp.

Not reviewed.

Map.

NORTH AMERICA

Canada

6-16 Miller, Mark. *Such Melodious Racket: The Lost History of Jazz in Canada, 1914–1949.* Toronto: Mercury Press, 1997. 288 pp.

Development of jazz in Canada from the 1914 debut of the Creole Band to Oscar Peterson's first U.S. appearance in 1949. Other musicians covered include Slap Rags White, Shirley Oliver, Melody Kings, Ollie Wagner, and the Knights of Harlem.

Bibliography; index; photographs.

Ontario

6-17   Litchfield, Jack. *Toronto Jazz: A Survey of Live Appearances and Radio Broadcasts of Dixieland Jazz Experienced in Toronto during the Period 1948–1950.* **Toronto: J. Litchfield, 1992. 103 pp.**
   Chronicle of live appearances and radio broadcasts in Toronto from 1948 to 1950. Includes magazine and newspaper reviews and posters.
   Chronology; illustrations; index; photographs.

Quebec

6-18   Rosenthall, Ron. *Festival International de Jazz de Montréal: Portrait d'un Festival (Portrait of a Festival).* **Montréal: Le Festival, 1999. 161 pp.**
   Collection of brief essays in French and English about the festival. Includes "Strings"; "Keyboards"; "The Sax"; "Voice"; "Percussion"; "The Oscar Peterson Award"; "The Miles Davis Award"; and "General Motors Grand Prix de Jazz."
   Photographs.

United States

6-19   Bird, Christiane. *The Jazz and Blues Lover's Guide to the U.S.: With More than 900 Hot Clubs, Cool Joints, Landmarks, and Legends, from Boogie-woogie to Bop and Beyond.* **Updated edition. Reading, MA: Addison Wesley, 1994. 434 pp.**
   Directory of clubs, museums, and other venues and institutions that focus on jazz or the blues in 26 cities or regions. Each chapter contains a brief historical introduction; "Sources" (local publications and information); "Notes on the Neighborhood"; "Landmarks and Legends"; "Clubs, Etc."; "Other Venues and Special Events"; "Radio"; "Record Stores"; "Other Nearby Locations"; and sometimes the author's "Personal Choices." Also includes "A Brief History of Jazz and Blues" and "Major Festivals."
   Bibliography; index; notes; photographs.

6-20   Jenkins, Willard, ed. *Lost Jazz Shrines.* **Brooklyn, NY: 651, An Arts Center, 1998. 65 pp.**
   Concentrates on "unique and historic [jazz] venues—ranging from corner bars to small nightclubs to 'music rooms' with particular focus on the African American shrines and their founding contributions." Includes "Brooklyn, New York," by K. Leander Williams; "Cleveland, Ohio," by Gregory Reese; "Harlem, New York," by Clarence Atkins; "Indianapolis, Indiana," by David N. Baker; "Kansas City, Missouri," by Bob Blumenthal; "Lower Manhattan, New York," by Willard

Jenkins; "Newark, New Jersey," by Amiri Baraka; "Philadelphia, Pennsylvania," by James G. Spady; "San Antonio, Texas," by Berneice Williams; and "Washington, D.C.," by W. A. Brower. The Lost Jazz Shrines project "is designed to establish a national program where each presenter has artistic control over the development of a performance event honoring the historic jazz venues or artists of their own community."

Photographs.

Southwest

6-21 Boyd, Jean A. *The Jazz of the Southwest: An Oral History of Western Swing.* **Austin: University of Texas Press, 1998. 269 pp.**

Exploration of the origins and development of western swing. Includes "Western Swing Fiddlers"; "Western Swing Guitarists"; "The Steel Guitar in Western Swing"; "The Western Swing Rhythm Section: Banjo and Bass"; "The Western Swing Rhythm Section: Piano and Drums"; and "The Rest of the Western Swing Band: Horn Players and Vocalists."

Bibliography; index; notes; photographs.

California

6-22 Bryant, Clora, Buddy Collette, William Green, Steven Isoardi, Jack Kelson, Horace Tapscott, Gerald Wilson, and Marl Young, eds. *Central Avenue Sounds: Jazz in Los Angeles.* **Berkeley: University of California Press, 1998. 442 pp.**

Oral histories of musicians from the Central Avenue area in Los Angeles. Includes the recollections of Marshal Royal, Lee Young, Fletcher Smith, Coney Woodman, William "Brother" Woodman Jr., Britt Woodman, Buddy Collette, David Bryant, Big Jay McNeely, Jack Kelson (Jackie Kelso), Bill Douglass, Melba Liston, Art Farmer, Horace Tapscott, Gerald Wiggins, Gerald Wilson, Clora Bryant, Bill Green, and Marl Young.

Bibliography; index; notes; photographs.

6-23 Cox, Bette Yarbrough. *Central Avenue: Its Rise and Fall (1890–c. 1955); Including the Musical Renaissance of Black Los Angeles.* **Los Angeles: BEEM Publications, 1996. 336 pp.**

Collective oral history of the African-American community in Los Angeles and its major contributions to the world of music. Oral histories include Bessie Williams Dones, Samuel Rodney Browne, Tiny Bradshaw, Lorenza Jordan-Cole, Freita Shaw Johnson, Jester Hairston, Marion Downs Smith, Ivan Harold Browning, Walter Robert Rousseau, Verna Arvey Still and William Grant Still, Leroy

Hurte, Deedie McGehee, Albert McNeil, Esvan Mosby, Marshal Royal, Teddy Buckner, Eddie Beal, Buddy Collette, Ginger Smock, and Marl Young.
Bibliography; chronology; illustrations; index; maps; photographs.

6-24   Gioia, Ted. *West Coast Jazz: Modern Jazz in California, 1945–1960.* **Berkeley: University of California Press, 1998. 418 pp.**
Study of this jazz substyle from its origins in postwar Los Angeles to its decline in the 1960s. Musicians covered include Dexter Gordon, Dave Brubeck, and Chet Baker. Also explores "California jazz nightspots." Originally published by Oxford University Press in 1992. This edition has a new preface and also includes photographs by William Claxton. Appendix: "Fifty Representative West Coast Jazz Recordings 1945–1960."
Discography; index; notes; photographs.

6-25   Goggin, Jim, and Peter Clute. *The Great Jazz Revival: A Pictorial Celebration of Traditional Jazz.* **San Rafael, CA: Donna Ewald, 1994. 159 pp.**
Photo-history of the traditional jazz scene in San Francisco from the 1930s through 1994.
Bibliography; discography; photographs.

6-26   Minor, William. *Monterey Jazz Festival: Forty Legendary Years.* **Santa Monica, CA: Angel City Press, 1997. 176 pp.**
Pictorial history of the Monterey Jazz Festival from 1958 to 1997. Contains biographical sketches of founders Jimmy Lyons and Ralph Gleason, and a list of festival performances.
Bibliography; index; photographs.

Georgia

6-27   Elmore, Charles J. *All That Savannah Jazz: From Brass Bands, Vaudeville, to Rhythm and Blues.* **Savannah, GA: Savannah State University, 1998. 268 pp.**
History of jazz in Savannah from 1918 to the 1960s. Includes biographies of Arthur Dilworth, Bobby Dilworth, George Doerner, King Oliver, and Estella Jackson.
Bibliography; index; notes; photographs.

6-28   Hornstein, Julius. *Sites and Sounds of Savannah Jazz.* **Savannah, GA: Gaston Street Press, 1994. 144 pp.**
Essays on nightclubs and Savannah Jazz Festival. Includes biographical sketches of Johnny Mercer, George Doerner, Emma Kelly, Ben Tucker, and Jess Mooney.
Bibliography; index; photographs.

Illinois

6-29 Kenney, William Howland. *Chicago Jazz: A Cultural History, 1904–1930.* **New York: Oxford University Press, 1993. 233 pp.**

Cultural history of Chicago jazz from its origins to the Depression. Includes "South Side Jazz: Cultural Context"; "The Evolution of South Side Jazz"; "White Jazz and Dance Halls"; "White Chicago Jazz: Cultural Context"; "Chicago's Jazz Records"; and "'Syncopated Threnody': The End of Chicago's Jazz Age."

Bibliography; index; notes.

Indiana

6-30 Kennedy, Rick. *Jelly Roll, Bix, and Hoagy: Gennett Studios and the Birth of Recorded Jazz.* **Bloomington: Indiana University Press, 1994. 233 pp.**

Account of the small record company that released the debut recordings of jazz artists Louis Armstrong, King Oliver, Bix Beiderbecke, Jelly Roll Morton, Earl Hines, Muggsy Spanier, Johnny Dodds, Leon Roppolo, and Hoagy Carmichael, among others. Includes "Gennett on Reissue Anthologies."

Bibliography; indexes; notes; photographs.

Louisiana

6-31 Bissonnette, Big Bill. *The Jazz Crusade: The Inside Story of the Great New Orleans Jazz Revival of the 1960s.* **Bridgeport, CT: Special Request Books & Recordings Division, 1992. 338 pp.**

Account of the endeavor by the author and a "handful of New Orleans jazz enthusiasts to help preserve" jazz by promoting tours and recordings of the "elderly jazz musicians still playing" in the city.

Discography; index; photographs.

6-32 Carter, William. *Preservation Hall: Music from the Heart.* **New York: W. W. Norton, 1991. 315 pp.**

Story of the institution where the "pioneers of traditional jazz have played" since the early 1960s. Also includes "Sunburst of the Soul: An Interview with Alan Lomax."

Index; notes; photographs.

6-33 Collins, R. *New Orleans Jazz: A Revised History; The Development of American Music from the Origin to the Big Bands.* **New York: Vantage Press, 1996. 296 pp.**

Study of the origin of jazz that disputes opposing theories (including the African origin theory) and credits the evolution of Creole musical culture in New Orleans. Also discusses the development of New Orleans jazz and its musical principles.
Bibliography; illustrations; indexes; photographs.

6-34 Koenig, Karl. *Jazz Map of New Orleans.* **Covington, LA: Basin Street Press, 1991. 22 pp.**
Compilation of more than 600 marked locations of performance venues (halls, clubs, cabarets, etc.) and musician residences (Buddy Bolden, Kid Ory, etc.). Included are supplemental maps of West End, Bucktown, Spanish Fort, and Milneburg.
Maps, photographs.

6-35 Martyn, Barry. *New Orleans Jazz: The End of the Beginning.* **New Orleans: Jazzology, 1998. 200 pp.**
"Stories of many of the pioneers of jazz in their own words," based on interviews conducted by the author. Includes Joe Watkins, "Kid Sheik" Cola, Emanuel Sayles, Alfred Williams, Cié Frazier, Alex Bigard, Eddie Dawson, Peter Bocage, Emile Barnes, Harold Dejan, Eddie Summers, Jack Kelly, DeDe Pierce, Billie Pierce, John Handy, George Guesnon, Lionel Ferbos, Andrew Morgan, Paul Barnes, Jeanette Kimball, Kid Valentine, Rose Winn-Tio, Louis Gallaud, Alton Purnell, Percy Humphrey, Leonard Bechet, Mike Delay, Leo Dejan, Alvin Alcorn, Reginald Koeller, Walter Lewis, Harold Christophe, Sylvester Handy, Charlie Hamilton, Emile Maurice, and Leroy Thompson.
Index; photographs.

6-36 Russell, Bill. *New Orleans Style.* **Edited by Barry Martyn and Mike Hazeldine. New Orleans: Jazzology Press, 1994. 224 pp.**
Interviews with musicians conducted by Russell in the 1950s and 1960s, trying to define the "New Orleans Style." Musicians interviewed include Baby Dodds, Chinee Foster, Paul Barbarin, Johnny St. Cyr, George Guesnon, Lawrence Marrero, Louis Keppard, Edward Garland, Pops Foster, Wellman Braud, Slow Drag Pavageau, Manuel Manetta, Sweet Emma Barrett, Bunk Johnson, Louis Armstrong, Natty Dominique, Johnny Wiggs, Kid Ory, Roy Palmer, George Brunis, Omer Simeon, Edmond Hall, Raymond Burke, and Lawrence Duhé.
Photographs; index.

6-37 Smith, Michael P. *A Joyful Noise: A Celebration of New Orleans Music.* **Introduction and interviews by Alan Govenar. Dallas, TX: Taylor Pub. Co., 1990. 210 pp.**

Collection of Smith's photographs of "several customary traditions of the city," interspersed with Govenar's interviews. Musicians interviewed include Harold Dejan and Kool Stephenson.
Bibliography; photographs.

6-38 ———. *New Orleans Jazz Fest: A Pictorial History.* **Foreword by Ben Sandmel. Gretna, LA: Pelican Publishing, 1991. 207 pp.**
Pictorial history of the New Orleans Jazz and Heritage Festival from 1970 through 1990. Jazz musicians covered include Duke Ellington and Dizzy Gillespie.
Index; photographs.

6-39 Touchet, Leo. *Rejoice When You Die: The New Orleans Jazz Funerals.* **Text by Vernel Bagneris. Introduction by Ellis L. Marsalis Jr. Baton Rouge: Louisiana State University Press, 1998. 152 pp.**
Compilation of black-and-white photographs of New Orleans jazz funerals, mostly taken from 1968 to 1970.
Photographs.

Missouri

6-40 Kansas City Jazz Museum. *Kansas City . . . and All That's Jazz.* **Kansas City, MO: Andrews McMeel, 1999. 120 pp.**
Study of Kansas City jazz from the 1920s through the 1960s. Includes profiles of Jay McShann, Mary Lou Williams, and Lester Young. Published in conjunction with the new museum's first exhibition.
Bibliography; discography; illustrations; photographs; videography.

New Jersey

6-41 Kukla, Barbara J. *Swing City: Newark Nightlife, 1925–50.* **Philadelphia: Temple University Press, 1991. 269 pp.**
History of jazz and other forms of entertainment in Newark, concentrating on performers' lives and personalities. Describes the house rent parties of the 1930s, the "colored only" clubs, and the entertainment at Newark's 1,000 saloons during Prohibition. Appendixes: "Who's Who of Newark Nightlife, 1925–50"; "Newark Bands, 1925–50"; "Big Band Appearances in Newark"; and "Clubs, Theaters, Halls, and Hangouts."
Bibliography; index; photographs.

6-42 Ripmaster, Terence M. *A History of Jazz in Paterson.* **Hackettstown, NJ: T. M. Ripmaster, 1996. 50 pp.**

Chronicle of the jazz scene and musicians in Paterson. Includes oral histories of Gil Benson, Joe Dailey, Fred Dittamo, Andy Fitzgerald, Amos Kaune, Dr. Martin Krivin, John Napodano, and Joseph Sellitti.
Bibliography; discography.

New York

6-43   Albert, Margaret, et al., eds. *100 Years of Jazz & Blues: Festival.* **Brooklyn, NY: 651/Kings Majestic Corp., 1992. 84 pp.**
Program for a two-month-long jazz and blues festival held in Brooklyn and put together with the assistance of the Brooklyn Academy of Music. Essays include "Jazz, America's Classical Music," by Dr. Billy Taylor; "Jazz Improvisation," by Dr. David N. Baker; "Sweet and Hot: Black Women in Blues and Jazz," by Dr. Daphne Duval-Harrison; "African Roots and Contemporary Manifestations of Blues and Jazz in African Popular Music," by Dr. J. H. Kwabena Nketia; and "Jazz Styles from Bebop to Fusion," by Dan Morgenstern. Also includes biographies of the musicians and panelists.
Bibliography; photographs.

6-44   Chevigny, Paul. *Gigs: Jazz and the Cabaret Laws in New York City.* **New York: Routledge, 1991. 215 pp.**
Study of the social, political, cultural, and legal ramifications of cabaret laws governing live entertainment in New York. The author, a lawyer, represented jazz musicians and the musicians union in their fight against the system.
Bibliography; charts; index; notes.

6-45   Stokes, W. Royal. *Swing Era New York: The Jazz Photographs of Charles Peterson.* **Foreword by Stanley Dance. Philadelphia: Temple University Press, 1994. 220 pp.**
Categories include "Harlem"; "52nd Street"; "Nick's, The Village Vanguard, Café Society, and Other Venues"; "Jam Sessions"; and "The Big Bands."
Bibliography; index; photographs.

Ohio

6-46   Arts Foundation of Olde Towne. *Listen for the Jazz: Key Notes in Columbus History.* **Columbus, OH: Arts Foundation of Olde Towne, 1990. 149 pp.**
Study of the jazz scene in and around the Near East Side of Columbus, Ohio, from the 1890s to 1960. Includes "The Jazz Cradle of Columbus," by William T. McDaniel, and material on local jazz clubs and jam sessions. Also contains portraits

of native Columbus musicians, including Thomas Howard, Sammy Stewart, Rusty Bryant, Roland Kirk, and Nancy Wilson.

Maps; photographs.

6-47 Berger, Harris M. *Metal, Rock, and Jazz: Perception and the Phenomenology of Musical Experience.* **Hanover, NH: University Press of New England, 1999. 334 pp.**

"Ethnography of heavy metal, rock and jazz musicians in Cleveland and Akron, Ohio."

Bibliography; glossary; index; maps; notes.

6-48 Mosbrook, Joe. *Cleveland Jazz History.* **Cleveland Heights, OH: Northeast Ohio Jazz Society, 1993. 122 pp.**

Includes: "Cleveland's Links to Jazz History"; "The Early Years"; "The Jazz Age in Cleveland"; "Count Basie's Cleveland Connections"; "Central High"; and "Jazz Clubs of the 1950s." Musicians covered include Will Marion Cook, Noble Sissle, Jimmie Lunceford, Art Tatum, Mary Lou Williams, Benny Goodman, Buddy DeFranco, Tadd Dameron, Freddie Webster, Benny Bailey, Django Reinhardt, Dave Brubeck, and Joe Lovano.

Discography; index; photographs.

Rhode Island

6-49 Kaplan, Lloyd S., and Robert E. Petteruti. *Who's Who in Rhode Island Jazz c. 1925–1988.* **West Greenwich, RI: Consortium Pub., 1991. 107 pp.**

Tribute to jazz performers who have contributed to jazz in Rhode Island. Contains a historical overview of jazz in Rhode Island; information on jazz clubs; biographical sketches; essays by Lloyd Kaplan on Art Pelosi, Bobby Hackett, and Roomful of Blues; and an essay by Ken Franklin on Dave McKenna.

Photographs.

Tennessee

6-50 Broome, P. J., and Clay Tucker. *The Other Music City: The Dance Bands and Jazz Musicians of Nashville 1920 to 1970.* **Nashville, TN: American Press Print. Co., 1990. 80 pp.**

Story of Nashville dance bands and jazz musicans from 1920 to 1970. Topics covered: African-American musicians, sidemen and bands; "Club Bands, Jabbers, and Small Groups"; and "Beasley Smith and Francis Craig."

Bibliography; photographs.

Texas

6-51　Oliphant, Dave. *Texan Jazz.* **Austin: University of Texas Press, 1996. 481 pp.**

"Lives, careers, and recordings" of Texan musicians, including Scott Joplin, Hersal Thomas, Blind Lemon Jefferson, Sippie Wallace, Jack Teagarden, Buster Smith, Hot Lips Page, Eddie Durham, Herschel Evans, Charlie Christian, Red Garland, Kenny Dorham, Jimmy Giuffre, Ornette Coleman, and John Carter.

Bibliography; index; notes; photographs.

Washington

6-52　de Barros, Paul. *Jackson Street after Hours: The Roots of Jazz in Seattle.* **Seattle: Sasquatch Books, 1993. 238 pp.**

History of the "authentic black jazz scene" that developed in nightclubs around the hub of Jackson Street and Twelfth Avenue. Explores such musicians as Ernestine Anderson, Quincy Jones, and Ray Charles. Photographs by Eduardo Calderón.

Bibliography; illustrations; index; notes; photographs.

7
Discographies

A plethora of jazz discographies was published in the 1990s. In addition to works on individual musicians and bands, there were discographies focusing on record labels and specific geographic areas. Several discographies were also solographies, with listings of musicians' solos.

I have indicated whether discographies list unissued material, reissues, and recording formats other than LPs, EPs, and CDs, when this information is provided.

The discographies below are listed under five categories: Artists/Groups, Comprehensive, Geographical, Recording Companies, and Miscellaneous.

ARTISTS/GROUPS

Alexander, Van (arranger/composer/bandleader, U.S.)

7-1 Garrod, Charles, and Bill Korst. "Van Alexander and His Orchestra." In *Al Donahue and His Orchestra: Plus Van Alexander and His Orchestra*. Zephyrhills, FL: Joyce Record Club Publication, 1991. 33 pp.
  Not reviewed.
  Index.

Allen, Pete (saxophone/clarinet/singer, UK)

7-2 Bielderman, Gerard. *Pete Allen Discography*. Eurojazz Discos, no. 74. Zwolle, Netherlands: Gerard Bielderman, 1998. 28 pp.
  Covers 1976 to 1997, with a brief biography. Includes unissued material.
  Bibliography; illustrations; indexes (releases, musicians, song titles); photographs.

Andrews Sisters (vocal group, U.S.)

7-3 Garrod, Charles. *The Andrews Sisters.* Zephyrhills, FL: Joyce Record Club Publication, 1992. 49 pp.
Not reviewed.
Index.

Antolini, Charly (drums, Switzerland)

7-4 Bielderman, Gerard. *Charly Antolini Discography.* Eurojazz Discos, no. 49. Zwolle, Netherlands: Gerard Bielderman, 1996. 48 pp.
Covers 1957 to 1996, with a biography. Includes unissued material.
Bibliography; illustrations; indexes (musicians, releases, song titles); photographs.

Armstrong, Louis (trumpet/singer, U.S.)

7-5 Dürr, Klaus-Uwe. *Louis Armstrong 1923–1932.* Revised edition. Hamburg: Klaus-Uwe Dürr, 1996. 39 pp.
Covers 1923 to 1932, with a brief biography. Includes unissued material. No reissue information.
Chronology; photographs.

Ashman, Mickey (bass, UK)

7-6 Bielderman, Gerard. *Mickey Ashman Discography.* 4th ed. Eurojazz Discos, no. 4. Zwolle, Netherlands: Gerard Bielderman, 1995. 48 pp.
Covers 1949 to 1995, with a brief biography. Includes unissued material. First published in 1984.
Bibliography; indexes (musicians, releases, song titles); photographs.

Auld, Georgie (saxophone/bandleader, Canada)

7-7 Garrod, Charles, and Bill Korst. *Georgie Auld and His Orchestra.* Revised edition. Portland, OR: Joyce Record Club Publication, 1999. 30 pp.
Not reviewed. First published in 1992.
Index.

Avon Cities Skiffle Group & Jazz Band (band, UK)

7-8 Bielderman, Gerard. "Discography of the Avon Cities Skiffle Group & Jazz Band." In *Discography of British Traditional Jazz Bands/Musicians, vol. 1: Avon Cities Skiffle Group 1956–1958; Avon Cities [Jazz Band] 1956–1997; Dick Charlesworth 1957–1994; Clyde Valley Stompers 1956–1983; Saints Jazz*

Band 1956–1983. **Eurojazz Discos, no.72. Zwolle, Netherlands: Gerard Bielderman, 1999. pp. 3–11.**
Covers 1955 to 1997. Formats include audio cassettes. Contains unissued material. First published in 1997.
Bibliography; illustrations; indexes (album titles, song titles).

Ayres, Mitchell (violin/bandleader, U.S.)

7-9   Garrod, Charles. *Mitchell Ayres and His Orchestra.* **Zephyrhills, FL: Joyce Record Club Publication, 1991. 57 pp.**
Not reviewed.
Index.

Ball, Kenny (trumpet/bandleader/singer, UK)

7-10   Bielderman, Gerard. *Kenny Ball Discography.* **4th ed. Eurojazz Discos, no. 17. Zwolle, Netherlands: Gerard Bielderman, 1996. 60 pp.**
Covers 1954 to 1995, with a biography. Includes unissued material; "Musicians of Kenny Ball's Jazzmen"; and list of Sid Phillips LP titles. First published in 1989.
Bibliography; illustrations; indexes (musicians, releases, song titles); photographs.

Barber, Chris (trombone/bandleader, UK)

7-11   Bielderman, Gerard, and Julian Purser. *Chris Barber Discography: Chris Barber, 40 Years in Music.* **2nd ed. Eurojazz Discos, no. 100. Zwolle, Netherlands: Gerard Bielderman, 1996. 100 pp.**
Covers 1949 to 1992, with an addendum for 1992 to 1995. Includes interviews with Chris Barber and Pat Halcox, by Julian Purser. Contains unissued material. First published in 1976. Appendix: "Related Recording Sessions."
Illustrations; indexes (releases, musicians, song titles); photographs.

Barda, Daniel (trombone, France)

7-12   Bielderman, Gerard. *Daniel Barda Discography.* **Eurojazz Discos, no. 108. Zwolle, Netherlands: Gerard Bielderman, 1996. 36 pp.**
Covers 1964 to 1999, with a biography. Includes unissued material.
Bibliography; indexes (musicians, releases, song titles); photographs.

Barnes, John (reeds/singer, UK)

7-13   Simpson, Norman, and Gerard Bielderman. *John Barnes Discography.* **Eurojazz Discos, no. 43. Zwolle, Netherlands: Gerard Bielderman, 1995. 64 pp.**

Covers 1955 to 1995, with a biography. Formats include audio cassettes and videotapes.

Bibliography; illustrations; indexes (musicians, releases, song titles); photographs.

Barnet, Charlie (saxophone/bandleader, U.S.)

7-14 Garrod, Charles. *Charlie Barnet and His Orchestra 1933–1973.* 4th ed. Portland, OR: Joyce Record Publication, 1999. 103 pp.

Not reviewed. First published in 1973.

Index.

Barrelhouse Jazzband (band, Germany)

7-15 Elvers, Erwin, and Gerard Bielderman. *Barrelhouse Jazzband Discography.* 3rd ed. Eurojazz Discos, no. 35. Zwolle, Netherlands: Gerard Bielderman, 1996. 36 pp.

Covers 1956 to 1994, with a band profile by Reimer von Essen in German and English. Includes unissued material and list of "Other Recordings by Members of Barrelhouse Jazzband 1958–1994."

Illustrations; indexes (musicians, releases, song titles); photographs.

Beecham, John (trombone, UK)

7-16 Bielderman, Gerard. *John Beecham Discography.* Eurojazz Discos, no. 98. Zwolle, Netherlands: Gerard Bielderman, 1999. 36 pp.

Covers 1961 to 1998, with a biography. Formats include audio cassettes. Contains unissued material.

Bibliography; indexes (musicians, releases, song titles).

Beiderbecke, Bix (cornet, U.S.)

7-17 Evans, Philip R., and Linda K. Evans. *Bix: The Leon Bix Beiderbecke Story.* Bakersfield, CA: Prelike Press, 1998. 602 pp.

Annotated bio-discography, covering 1924 to 1930, with information on soloists. Includes unissued material.

Illustrations; indexes (names, song titles); photographs.

Beneke, Tex (saxophone/singer/bandleader, U.S.)

7-18 Garrod, Charles. *Tex Beneke and His Orchestra.* Revised edition. Zephyrhills, FL: Charles Garrod, 1997. 74 pp.

Not reviewed. First published in 1986.

Index.

Benkó Dixieland Band (band, Hungary)

7-19 Simon, Géza Gábor. *Benkó Dixieland Band.* 2nd ed. Eurojazz Discos, no. 25. Zwolle, Netherlands: Gerard Bielderman, 1997. 24 pp.
 Covers 1967 to 1993. Includes a band profile. Formats include videotapes. First published in 1991.
 Bibliography; illustrations; indexes (band compositions, musicians, releases, song titles).

Bernie, Ben (violin/bandleader, U.S.)

7-20 Garrod, Charles. *Ben Bernie and His Orchestra.* Zephyrhills, FL: Joyce Record Club Publication, 1991. 24 pp.
 Not reviewed.
 Index.

Bilk, Acker (clarinet/bandleader/singer, UK)

7-21 Bielderman, Gerard. *Acker Bilk Discography.* 4th ed. Eurojazz Discos, no. 98. Zwolle, Netherlands: Gerard Bielderman, 1996. 56 pp.
 Covers 1954 to 1996, with a biography. Includes unissued material. First published in 1988.
 Bibliography; illustrations; indexes (musicians, releases, song titles); photographs.

Billett, Cuff (trumpet/bandleader/singer, UK)

7-22 Lee, Raymond. *Cuff Billett Discography.* 2nd ed. Eurojazz Discos, no. 39. Zwolle, Netherlands: Gerard Bielderman, 1999. 40 pp.
 Covers 1962 to 1998, with a brief biography. Includes unissued material. First published in 1994.
 Bibliography; indexes (musicians, releases, song titles); photographs.

Black Bottom Stompers (band, UK)

7-23 Bielderman, Gerard. "Black Bottom Stompers Discography." In *Discography of British Traditional Jazz Bands/Musicians, vol. 2: Black Bottom Stompers 1971–1982; Bill Brunskill's Jazzmen 1972–1986; Brian Green 1965–1968, 1994–1996; Colin Kingwell's Jazz Bandits 1964–1995.* Eurojazz Discos, no. 76. Zwolle, Netherlands: Gerard Bielderman, 1997. pp. 12–21.
 Covers 1971 to 1982. No reissues or unissued material.
 Bibliography; indexes (album titles, song titles); photographs.

Bley, Paul (piano, Canada)

7-24 Kluck, Henk. *Bley Play: The Paul Bley Recordings.* Emmen, Netherlands: H. Kluck, 1996. 212 pp.

Covers 1952 to 1994. Includes unissued material.

Bibliography; indexes (groups, musicians, record labels, song titles); photographs.

Blount, Chris (clarinet/bandleader, UK)

7-25 Lee, Raymond. *Chris Blount Discography.* 6th ed. Eurojazz Discos, no. 29. Zwolle, Netherlands: Gerard Bielderman, 1999. 52 pp.

Covers 1956 to 1998, with a biography by Brian Wood. Includes unissued material. First published in 1992.

Bibliography; illustrations; indexes (musicians, releases, song titles); photographs.

Bothwell, Johnny (bandleader/saxophone, U.S.)

7-26 Garrod, Charles, and Bill Korst. "Johnny Bothwell." In *Boyd Raeburn and His Orchestra; Plus: Johnny Bothwell and George Handy.* Revised edition. Zephyrhills, FL: Joyce Record Club Publication, 1997. 39 pp.

Not reviewed. First published in 1985.

Index.

Bourbon Street Jazzband (band, Denmark)

7-27 Bielderman, Gerard, and Erwin Elvers. "Discography of the Bourbon Street Jazz Band." In *Discography of Danish Traditional Jazz Bands, vol. 1: Bourbon Street Jazzband 1975–1998; Gentlemen of Jazz 1989–1998; Pee Dee Jazzband 1988–1999; Vestre Jazzværk 1979–1997.* Eurojazz Discos, no. 103. Zwolle, Netherlands: Gerard Bielderman, 1999. pp. 3–11.

Covers 1975 to 1998. No reissues.

Indexes (album titles, song titles); photographs.

Bowden, Colin (drums, UK)

7-28 Lee, Raymond. *Colin Bowden Discography.* 3rd ed. Eurojazz Discos, no. 32. Zwolle, Netherlands: Gerard Bielderman, 1999. 60 pp.

Covers 1952 to 1999, with a biography. Includes unissued material. First published in 1993.

Bibliography; illustrations; indexes (album titles, musicians); photographs.

Bradley, Will (trombone/bandleader, U.S.)

7-29 Garrod, Charles. "Will Bradley and His Orchestra." In *Will Bradley and His Orchestra; Plus: Freddie Slack and His Orchestra.* Revised edition. Zephyrhills, FL: Joyce Record Club Publication, 1997. 32 pp.
 Not reviewed. First published in 1986.
 Index.

Bradshaw, Tiny (drums/singer/bandleader, U.S.)

7-30 Garrod, Charles, and Bill Korst. "Tiny Bradshaw and His Orchestra." In *Tiny Bradshaw and His Orchestra; Plus: Lucky Millinder and His Orchestra.* Zephyrhills, FL: Joyce Record Club Publication, 1994. 31 pp.
 Not reviewed.
 Index.

Brennan, Dave (banjo/bandleader, UK)

7-31 Bielderman, Gerard. *Dave Brennan Discography.* Eurojazz Discos, no. 83. Zwolle, Netherlands: Gerard Bielderman, 1998. 28 pp.
 Covers 1971 to 1998, with a biography. Includes unissued material.
 Bibliography; indexes (musicians, releases, song titles); photographs.

Brooks, Randy (trumpet/bandleader, U.S.)

7-32 Garrod, Charles, and Bill Korst. "Randy Brooks." In *Bobby Sherwood and His Orchestra; Plus: Randy Brooks and His Orchestra.* Revised edition. Portland, OR: Joyce Record Club Publication, 1999. 43 pp.
 Not reviewed. First published in 1999.
 Index.

Brown, Sandy (clarinet/bandleader, UK)

7-33 Bielderman, Gerard, and John Latham. *Sandy Brown Discography.* Eurojazz Discos, no. 5. Zwolle, Netherlands: Gerard Bielderman, 1997. 64 pp.
 Covers 1949 to 1974, with a biography. Contains unissued material. First published in 1985.
 Illustrations; indexes (musicians, records, song titles); photographs.

Bill Brunskill's Jazzmen (band, UK)

7-34 Bielderman, Gerard. "Discography of Bill Brunskill's Jazzmen." In *Discography of British Traditional Jazz Bands/Musicians, vol. 2: Black Bottom*

Stompers 1971–1982; Bill Brunskill's Jazzmen 1972–1986; Brian Green 1965–1968, 1994–1996; Colin Kingwell's Jazz Bandits 1964–1995. Eurojazz Discos, no. 76. Zwolle, Netherlands: Gerard Bielderman, 1997. pp. 12–21.

Covers 1972 to 1986. Contains unissued material but no reissues. Formats include audio cassettes.

Bibliography; indexes (album titles, song titles).

Bryden, Beryl (singer, UK)

7-35 Bielderman, Gerard. *Beryl Bryden Discography.* Eurojazz Discos, no. 1. 7th ed. Zwolle, Netherlands: Gerard Bielderman, 1998. 32 pp.

Covers 1948 to 1997, with a brief biography. Includes unissued material. Originally published in 1972.

Bibliography; illustrations; indexes (musicians, recording units, releases, song titles); photographs.

Bue, Papa (trombone/bandleader, Denmark)

7-36 Elvers, Erwin, et al. *Papa Bue Discography 1954–1998.* 4th ed. Eurojazz Discos, no. 19. Zwolle, Netherlands: Gerard Bielderman, 1999. 56 pp.

Covers 1954 to 1998. Includes unissued material. First published in 1989.

Bibliography; indexes (musicians, records, song titles); photographs.

Burbank, Albert (clarinet/singer, U.S.)

7-37 Lee, Raymond, and Guus Smits. *Clarinet Wizard: A Discography of Albert Burbank.* Sounds of New Orleans, no. 3. Zwolle, Netherlands: Gerard Bielderman, 1997. 40 pp.

Covers 1945 to 1976, with a biography by Brian Wood. Includes unissued material.

Bibliography; indexes (musicians, releases, song titles); photographs.

Burke, Sonny (violin/piano/bandleader, U.S.)

7-38 Garrod, Charles. "Sonny Burke and His Orchestra." In *Sonny Burke and His Orchestra; Plus: Skinnay Ennis and His Orchestra.* Zephyrhills, FL: Joyce Record Club Publication, 1994. 42 pp.

Not reviewed.

Index.

Busse, Henry (trumpet/bandleader, Germany)

7-39 Garrod, Charles. "Henry Busse and His Orchestra." In *Henry Busse and His Orchestra; Plus: Clyde McCoy and His Orchestra.* Zephyrhills, FL: Joyce Record Club Publication, 1990.

Covers 1925 to 1954.
Index (song titles).

Byrne, Bobby (trombone/bandleader, U.S.)

7-40 Garrod, Charles, and Bill Korst. "Bobby Byrne and His Orchestra." In *Bobby Byrne and His Orchestra; Plus: Dean Hudson and His Orchestra*. Zephyrhills, FL: Joyce Record Club Publication, 1992.
Not reviewed.
Index.

Chaix, Henri (piano/bandleader, Switzerland)

7-41 Bielderman, Gerard, and Arild Widerøe. *Henri Chaix Discography*. Eurojazz Discos, no. 65. Zwolle, Netherlands: Gerard Bielderman, 1997. 56 pp.
Covers 1945 to 1996, with a biography. Includes unissued material.
Bibliography; indexes (musicians, releases, song titles); photographs.

Chaloff, Serge (saxophone, U.S.)

7-42 Simosko, Vladimir. *Serge Chaloff: A Musical Biography and Discography*. Studies in Jazz, no. 27. Lanham, MD: Scarecrow Press, 1998. 186 pp.
Serge Chaloff "is most widely remembered as the flamboyant baritone saxophone star with Woody Herman's Second Herd whose problems with drugs extended to erratic personal behavior. Nevertheless, there were many brilliant sessions featuring his work before and after his stint with Herman. This work attempts to bring them the recognition they deserve."
Photographs.

Charlestown Jazzband (band, Netherlands)

7-43 Bielderman, Gerard. "Discography of the Charlestown Jazzband." In *Discography of Dutch Traditional Jazz Bands, vol. 2: Circus Square Jazz Band 1968–1995; Storyville Jassband 1968–1995; Freetime Old Dixie Jassband 1975–1995; Charlestown Jazzband 1971–1998*. Eurojazz Discos, no. 93. Zwolle, Netherlands: Gerard Bielderman, 1999. pp. 32–39.
Covers 1971 to 1998. Formats include audio cassettes. Contains unissued material but no reissues.
Bibliography; illustrations; indexes (album titles, song titles); photographs.

Charlesworth, Dick (clarinet/saxophone/singer, UK)

7-44 Bielderman, Gerard. "Dick Charlesworth Discography." In *Discography of British Traditional Jazz Bands/Musicians, vol. 1: Avon Cities Skiffle*

Group 1956–1958; Avon Cities [Jazz Band] 1956–1997; Dick Charlesworth 1957–1994; Clyde Valley Stompers 1956–1983; Saints Jazz Band 1956–1983. **2nd ed. Eurojazz Discos, no. 72. Zwolle, Netherlands: Gerard Bielderman, 1999. pp. 12–21.**

Covers 1957 to 1994. Formats include videocassettes. Contains unissued material. First published in 1997.

Bibliography; indexes (album titles, song titles); photographs.

Charquet & Co.; see Morel, Jean-Pierre

Chescoe, Laurie (drums/bandleader, UK)

7-45 Bielderman, Gerard. *Laurie Chescoe Discography.* **Eurojazz Discos, no. 99. Zwolle, Netherlands: Gerard Bielderman, 1999. 24 pp.**

Covers 1951 to 1999. Includes a biography.

Bibliography; indexes (musicians, releases, song titles); photographs.

Chester, Bob (saxophone/bandleader, U.S.)

7-46 Garrod, Charles, and Bill Korst. *Bob Chester and His Orchestra.* **Revised edition. Zephyrhills, FL: Joyce Record Club Publication, 1997. 32 pp.**

Not reviewed. First published in 1987.

Index.

Chesterman, Chez (cornet/trumpet/singer, UK)

7-47 Bielderman, Gerard. "Chez Chesterman Discography." In *Discography of British Traditional Jazz Bands, vol. 4: Chez Chesterman 1960–1998; Mike Daniels' Delta Jazz Band 1948–1995; Roy Kirby Paragon Jazz Band; John Maddocks 1971–1998.* **Eurojazz Discos, no. 89. Zwolle, Netherlands: Gerard Bielderman, 1998. pp. 3–11.**

Covers 1960 to 1998. Formats include audio cassettes and videocassettes. Contains unissued material.

Bibliography; indexes (album titles, song titles); photographs.

Chisholm, George (trombone, UK)

7-48 Clutten, Michael N., and Syd R. Gallichan. *George Chisholm Discography.* **2nd ed. Revised and updated by Gerard Bielderman. Eurojazz Discos, no. 41. Zwolle, Netherlands: Gerard Bielderman, 1999. 112 pp.**

Covers 1934 to 1990. First published in 1977. Includes a biography.

Bibliography; illustrations; indexes (musicians, releases, song titles); photographs.

Chittison, Herman (piano, U.S.)

7-49 Doran, James M. *Herman Chittison: A Bio-Discography.* IAJRC monograph series, no. 2. Bel Air, MD: International Association of Jazz Record Collectors, 1993. 136 pp.
Bio-discography. Includes oral history.
Bibliography; chonology; illustrations; indexes; photographs.

Christian, Charlie (guitar, U.S.)

7-50 Broadbent, Peter. *Charlie Christian.* Milwaukee, WI: Hal Leonard, 1997. 120 pp.
Bio-discography, covers 1939 to 1941. No reissue information.
Bibliography; illustrations; indexes (essential recordings, non-essential recordings, LPs, CDs); photographs.

Circus Square Jazz Band (band, Netherlands)

7-51 Bielderman, Gerard. "Discography of the Circus Square Jazz Band." In *Discography of Dutch Traditional Jazz Bands, vol. 2: Circus Square Jazz Band 1968–1995; Storyville Jassband 1968–1995; Freetime Old Dixie Jassband 1975–1995; Charlestown Jazzband 1971–1998.* Eurojazz Discos, no. 93. Zwolle, Netherlands: Gerard Bielderman, 1999. pp. 3–13.
Covers 1968 to 1995. No unissued material.
Bibliography; illustrations; indexes (album titles, song titles); photographs.

Clark, Buddy (bass/arranger, U.S.)

7-52 Garrod, Charles, and Bob Gottlieb. *Buddy Clark.* Zephyrhills, FL: Joyce Record Club Publication, 1991. 53 pp.
Not reviewed.
Index.

Clinton, Larry (trumpet/arranger/composer/bandleader, U.S.)

7-53 Garrod, Charles. *Larry Clinton and His Orchestra.* Revised edition. Zephyrhills, FL: Joyce Record Club Publications, 1990. 36 pp.
Not reviewed.
Index.

Cola, Kid Sheik (trumpet/singer, U.S.)

7-54 Lee, Raymond. *Sheik's Blues: A Discography of Kid Sheik Cola.* Sounds of New Orleans, no. 5. Zwolle, Netherlands: Gerard Bielderman, 1998, 120 pp.

Covers 1954 to 1985, with a biography by Brian Wood. Includes unissued material.

Bibliography; illustrations; indexes (musicians, releases, song titles); photographs.

Cole, Geoff (trombone/bandleader, UK)

7-55 Bielderman, Gerard. *Geoff Cole Discography.* Eurojazz Discos, no. 86. Zwolle, Netherlands: Gerard Bielderman, 1998. 36 pp.

Covers 1958 to 1998, with a biography. Contains unissued material. Formats include audio cassettes and videotapes.

Bibliography; indexes (musicians, releases, song titles); photographs.

Cole, Nat King (piano/singer/bandleader, U.S.)

7-56 Teubig, Klaus. *Straighten Up and Fly Right: A Chronology and Discography of Nat King Cole.* Westport, CT: Greenwood Press, 1994. 297 pp.

Covers 1936 to 1952. Includes a brief biography and a listing of Cole's uncredited appearances as piano accompanist. Formats include 16-inch discs. Lists transcriptions.

Chronology; indexes (releases, song titles).

Collie, Max (trombone/bandleader/singer, Australia)

7-57 Bielderman, Gerard. *Max Collie Discography.* 4th ed. Eurojazz Discos, no. 13. Zwolle, Netherlands: Gerard Bielderman, 1999. 28 pp.

Covers 1966 to 1998. Includes a biography and band personnel list. First published in 1987.

Bibliography; illustrations; indexes (releases, song titles); photographs.

Coltrane, John (saxophone, U.S.)

7-58 Fujioka, Yasuhiro. *John Coltrane: A Discography and Musical Biography.* Studies in Jazz, no. 20. With Lewis Porter and Yoh-ichi Hamada. Metuchen, NJ: Scarecrow Press, 1995. 377 pp.

Covers 1946 to 1993. Includes annotations and unissued material. Formats include audio cassettes and videotapes.

Bibliography; illustrations; indexes; photographs.

Colyer, Ken (cornet/guitar/trumpet/bandleader, UK)

7-59 Bielderman, Gerard. *Ken Colyer Discography: Incorporating the Crane River Jazz Band.* 9th ed. Eurojazz Discos, no. 3. Zwolle, Netherlands: Gerard Bielderman, 1999. 76 pp.

Covers 1948 to 1997, with a biography. Contains unissued material. Lists radio and TV broadcasts. First published in 1983.

Bibliography; illustrations; indexes (musicians, releases, song titles); photographs.

Courtney, Del (piano/bandleader, U.S.)

7-60 Garrod, Charles. "Del Courtney and His Orchestra." In *Del Courtney and His Orchestra; Plus: Gray Gordon and His Orchestra*. Zephyrhills, FL: Joyce Record Club Publication, 1992. 34 pp.

Not reviewed.

Index.

Crane River Jazz Band; *see* Colyer, Ken

Crosby, Bob (singer/bandleader, U.S.)

7-61 Garrod, Charles. *Bob Crosby and His Orchestra*. 2 vols. Revised edition. Zephyrhills, FL: Joyce Record Club Publication, 1996. Vol. 1: 60 pp.; vol. 2: 72 pp.

Not reviewed. Volume 1 covers 1935 to 1945, and volume 2 covers 1946 to 1985.

Indexes.

Cugat, Xavier (violin/bandleader, Spain)

7-62 Garrod, Charles. *Xavier Cugat and His Orchestra*. Zephyrhills, FL: Joyce Record Club, 1995. 92 pp.

Not reviewed.

Index.

Daniels, Mike (cornet/trumpet/bandleader, UK)

7-63 Bielderman, Gerard. "Mike Daniels Discography." In *Discography of British Traditional Jazz Bands, vol. 4: Chez Chesterman 1960–1998; Mike Daniels' Delta Jazz Band 1948–1995; Roy Kirby Paragon Jazz Band; John Maddocks 1971–1998*. Eurojazz Discos, no. 89. Zwolle, Netherlands: Gerard Bielderman, 1998. pp. 12–23.

Covers 1948 to 1995. Formats include audio cassettes and videocassettes. Contains unissued material.
Bibliography; indexes (album titles, song titles); photographs.

Davies, John R. T. (saxophone/trombone, UK)

7-64 Bielderman, Gerard. *John R. T. Davies Discography.* **Eurojazz Discos, no. 71. Zwolle, Netherlands: Gerard Bielderman, 1998. 48 pp.**
Covers 1949 to 1995, with a biography. Includes unissued material.
Bibliography; indexes (musicians, releases, song titles); photographs.

Davis, Miles (trumpet, U.S.)

7-65 Lohmann, Jan. *The Sound of Miles Davis: The Discography; A Listing of Records and Tapes 1945–1991.* **Copenhagen: JazzMedia, 1993. 396 pp.**
Includes brief biography, unissued material, and radio and TV broadcasts. Also includes a "List of Equivalents of Issued Records."
Bibliography; indexes (musicians, song titles.)

Day, Doris (singer, U.S.)

7-66 Garrod, Charles. *Doris Day.* **Zephyrhills, FL: Joyce Record Club Publication, 1997. 71 pp.**
Not reviewed.
Index.

DeFranco, Buddy (clarinet, U.S.)

7-67 Kuehn, John, and Arne Astrup. *Buddy DeFranco: A Biographical Portrait and Discography.* **Studies in Jazz, no. 12. Foreword by Leonard Feather. Metuchen, NJ: Scarecrow Press, 1993. 261 pp.**
Bio-discography covering 1943 to 1988, compiled by Astrup and including unissued material. Also contains an interview with DeFranco; lists of AFRS transcriptions and V-Discs; and addenda up to 1992.
Bibliography; indexes (subject, song titles); photographs.

Delange, Eddie (lyricist/bandleader, U.S.)

7-68 Garrod, Charles. "Eddie Delange and His Orchestra." In *Will Hudson and His Orchestra; The Hudson-Delange Orchestra; Eddie Delange and His Orchestra; George Paxton and His Orchestra; Bob Strong and His Orchestra.* **Zephyrhills, FL: Joyce Record Club Publication, 1993. 39 pp.**
Not reviewed.
Index

Dickenson, Vic (trombone, U.S.)

7-69 Selchow, Manfred. *Ding! Ding! A Bio-Discographical Scrapbook on Vic Dickenson.* Westoverledingen, Germany: M. Selchow, 1998. 947 pp.

Bio-discography covering 1930 to 1985. Includes unissued material and lists of solos and radio/TV broadcasts. Also includes "Vic Dickenson on Compositions."

Bibliography; illustrations; indexes (names, song titles); musical transcriptions; photographs.

Dickie, Neville (piano, UK)

7-70 Bielderman, Gerard. *Neville Dickie Discography.* 2nd edition. Eurojazz Discos, no. 40. Zwolle, Netherlands: Gerard Bielderman, 1999. 36 pp.

Covers 1966 to 1999, with a biography. Contains unissued material. Formats include audio cassettes. First published in 1995.

Bibliography; illustrations; indexes (musicians, releases, song titles); photographs.

Dixieland Pipers (band, Netherlands)

7-71 Bielderman, Gerard. "Discography of the Dixieland Pipers." In *Discography of Dutch Traditional Jazz Bands, vol. 1: Eric Krans' Dixieland Pipers 1950–1963; Bert de Kort's Dixieland Pipers 1977–1985; Harbour Jazz Band 1967–1996; Reunion Jazz Band 1966–1998; Revival Jassband 1977–1993.* Eurojazz Discos, no. 82. Zwolle, Netherlands: Gerard Bielderman, 1998. pp. 3–14.

Covers 1950 to 1985. Includes unissued material.

Bibliography; indexes (album titles, song titles); photographs.

Dixon, Bill (trumpet/piano/composer, U.S.)

7-72 Young, Ben. *Dixonia: A Bio-Discography of Bill Dixon.* Westport, CT: Greenwood Press, 1998. 418 pp.

Annotated bio-discography, covering 1951 to 1997. Includes unissued material. Also contains descriptions of Dixon's unrecorded live performances. Formats include videos. Appendixes include "Known Class Recordings."

Bibliography; index.

Donahue, Al (bandleader, U.S.)

7-73 Garrod, Charles, and Bill Korst. "Al Donahue and His Orchestra." In *Al Donahue and His Orchestra: Plus Van Alexander and His Orchestra.* Zephyrhills, FL: Joyce Record Club Publication, 1991. 33 pp.

Not reviewed.

Index.

Donahue, Sam (saxophone/bandleader, U.S.)

7-74   Garrod, Charles, and Bill Korst. *Sam Donahue and His Orchestra.* Zephyrhills, FL: Joyce Record Club Publication, 1992. 29 pp.
   Not reviewed.
   Index.

Dorsey Brothers (band, U.S.)

7-75   Garrod, Charles. *The Dorsey Brothers and Their Orchestra.* Zephyrhills, FL: Joyce Record Club Publication, 1992. 25 pp.
   Not reviewed.
   Index.

Dorsey, Jimmy (saxophone/clarinet/bandleader, U.S.)

7-76   Stockdale, Robert L. *Jimmy Dorsey: A Study in Contrasts.* Studies in Jazz, no. 30. Lanham, MD: Scarecrow Press, 1999. 688 pp.
   Annotated bio-discography, covering 1923 to 1957. Formats include 78s, 45s, EPs, 8-track, and audio cassettes. Lists solos and unissued material as well as AFRS transcriptions and radio/TV broadcasts. Includes "listings of Broadway musicals where Dorsey was a member of the pit band."
   Bibliography; illustrations; indexes (general, musicians, recording groups, song titles, concerts/broadcasts/telecasts); photographs.

Dorsey, Tommy (trombone/bandleader, U.S.)

7-77   Stockdale, Robert L. *Tommy Dorsey: On the Side.* Studies in Jazz, no. 19. Metuchen, NJ: Scarecrow Press, 1995. 448 pp.
   Annotated, covering 1923 to 1956, and lists solos. Author distinguishes between "positive," "probable," and "possible" participation by Dorsey in a given session. Includes unissued material.
   Bibliography; illustrations; indexes (general, composers/lyricists, recording groups, performing artists, song titles).

Down Town Jazz Band (band, Netherlands)

7-78   Bielderman, Gerard. *Discography of the Down Town Jazz Band, Leaders: Eelco van Velzen and Roefie Hueting.* Eurojazz Discos, no. 63. Zwolle, Netherlands: Gerard Bielderman, 1997. 32 pp.
   Covers 1954 to 1995. Includes band history; unissued material; "Band Members, 1949–1997"; and "Roefie Hueting Compositions."
   Bibliography; illustrations; indexes (musicians, releases, song titles); photographs.

Dunham, Sonny (trumpet/trombone/bandleader, U.S.)

7-79 Garrod, Charles, and Bill Korst. "Sonny Dunham and His Orchestra." In *Sonny Dunham and His Orchestra; Plus: Ziggy Elman and His Orchestra.* Zephyrhills, FL: Joyce Record Club Publication, 1990. 30 pp.
Not reviewed.
Index.

Durham, Mike (trumpet/bandleader, UK)

7-80 Bielderman, Gerard. *Discography of Mike Durham and West Jesmond Rhythm Kings.* Eurojazz Discos, no. 70. Zwolle, Netherlands: Gerard Bielderman, 1997. 32 pp.
Covers 1981 to 1997. Includes a biography and band personnel list. Also contains recordings of the West Jesmond Rhythm Kings, led by Durham. Includes unissued material but no reissues.
Indexes (releases, song titles); photographs.

Dutch Swing College Band (band, Netherlands)

7-81 Bielderman, Gerard. *Dutch Swing College Band Discography.* 4th ed. Eurojazz Discos, no. 21. Zwolle, Netherlands: 1999. 98 pp.
First published in 1990.
Indexes (album titles, song titles); photographs.

Eckstine, Billy (singer/bandleader, U.S.)

7-82 Brown, Denis. *Billy Eckstine: A Discography.* Zephyrhills, FL: Joyce Record Club Publication, 1996. 142 pp.
Not reviewed.
Index.

Elgart, Larry (saxophone, U.S.)

7-83 Palmer, Richard F., and Charles Garrod. *Les & Larry Elgart and Their Orchestras.* Zephyrhills, FL: Joyce Record Club Publication, 1992. 64 pp.
Not reviewed.
Index.

Elgart, Les (trumpet, U.S.)

7-84 Palmer, Richard F., and Charles Garrod. *Les & Larry Elgart and Their Orchestras.* Zephyrhills, FL: Joyce Record Club Publication, 1992. 64 pp.
Not reviewed.
Index.

Ellington, Duke (piano/composer/bandleader, U.S.)

7-85 Lambert, Eddie. *Duke Ellington: A Listener's Guide.* **Studies on Jazz, no. 26. Foreword by Dan Morgenstern. Bibliography compiled by Sjef Hoefsmit. Lanham, MD: Scarecrow Press, 1999. 374 pp.**

Critical survey of Duke Ellington's entire recorded output from 1924 to 1984. Lists "outstanding records" and includes brief portraits of Ellington's sidemen. Appendixes include "French RCA Integrale, Volumes 14 to 17: A Guide."

Bibliography; index; photographs.

7-86 Massagli, Luciano. *The New Desor: An Updated Edition of Duke Ellington's Story on Records, 1924–1974.* **2 vols. Milan: Luciano Massagli, Giovanni M. Volonté, 1999. 1515 pp.**

Volume 1 is a complete Ellington discography from 1929 to 1974, including unissued material, rehearsal sessions, film soundtracks, AFRS transcriptions, and radio and TV broadcasts. Volume 2 is a solography of Ellington and his musicians. Does not include 78s. List of alternative song titles.

Indexes (general, musicians, releases, song titles).

7-87 Moulé, François-Xavier. *A Guide to the Duke Ellington Recorded Legacy on LPs and CDs.* **Vol. 1. Le Mans, France: Madly Production, 1992. 684 pp.**

Guide to "concert recordings, radio and TV programs, prerecorded radio transcriptions, V-discs, and film soundtracks." Contains unissued material. Formats include audio cassettes. Organized by record label.

Illustrations; index (record labels).

7-88 Nielsen, Ole. *Jazz Records, 1942–80: A Discography.* **Vol. 6, Duke Ellington. Copenhagen: Stainless/Wintermoon, 1992. 613 pp.**

Covers 1942 to 1980. Includes unissued material, AFRS transcriptions, and live radio and TV broadcasts. List of record labels and matrix numbers.

Bibliography; indexes (compositions, song titles, musicians, venues, cities).

7-89 Timner, W. E. *Ellingtonia, 1923–1974: The Recorded Music of Duke Ellington and His Sidemen.* **4th ed. Studies in Jazz, no. 7. Lanham, MD: Scarecrow Press, 1996. 608 pp.**

Includes unissued material. Lists solos by Ellington.

Indexes (general, musicians, song titles).

7-90 Valburn, Jerry. *Duke Ellington on Compact Disc: An Index and Text of the Recorded Work of Duke Ellington on Compact Disc: An In-depth Study.* **Hicksville, NY: Marlor Productions, 1993. 253 pp.**

Covers Ellington's 1924 to 1971 recordings that have been released on compact disc. Organized by country. Includes film appearances and "dance dates."

Index (song titles).

Elman, Ziggy (trumpet/bandleader, U.S.)

7-91 Garrod, Charles, and Bill Korst. "Ziggy Elman and His Orchestra." In *Sonny Dunham and His Orchestra; Plus: Ziggy Elman and His Orchestra.* Zephyrhills, FL: Joyce Record Club Publication, 1990. 30 pp.
Not reviewed.
Index.

Elsdon, Alan (trumpet/bandleader, UK)

7-92 Bielderman, Gerard. *Alan Elsdon Discography.* 2nd ed. Eurojazz Discos, no. 37. Zwolle, Netherlands: Gerard Bielderman, 1998. 48 pp.
Covers 1955 to 1998, with a biography. Includes unissued material. First published in 1994.
Bibliography; indexes (musicians, releases, song titles); photographs.

Ennis, Skinnay (drums/singer/bandleader, U.S.)

7-93 Garrod, Charles. "Skinnay Ennis and His Orchestra." In *Sonny Burke and His Orchestra; Plus: Skinnay Ennis and His Orchestra.* Zephyrhills, FL: Joyce Record Club Publication, 1994, 42 pp.
Not reviewed.
Index

Erstrand, Lars (vibraphone/bandleader, Sweden)

7-94 Bielderman, Gerard. *Lars Erstrand Discography.* Eurojazz Discos, no. 91. Zwolle, Netherlands: Gerard Bielderman, 1999. 52 pp.
Covers 1964–1998, with a biography adapted from *Always in the Mood for Swing,* by D. Kjell Edgren. Includes unissued material.
Bibliography; indexes (musicians, releases, song titles); photographs.

Etté, Bernard (violin/bandleader, Germany)

7-95 Bergmeier, Horst, and Rainer E. Lotz. *Bernard Etté: A Biodiscography.* Sonderpublikation, no. 2. Dietramszell, Germany: Fox auf 78, 1995. 151 pp.
Not reviewed.
Photographs.

Fairweather, Al (trumpet/bandleader, UK)

7-96 Latham, John, and Gerard Bielderman. *Al Fairweather Discography.* Eurojazz Discos, no. 34. Zwolle, Netherlands: Gerard Bielderman, 1994. 60 pp.

Covers 1949 to 1993, with a biography and list of compositions. Includes unissued material.
Bibliography; illustrations; indexes (musicians, releases, song titles); photographs.

Fairweather, Digby (cornet/trumpet, UK)

7-97 Simpson, Norman, and Gerard Bielderman. *Digby Fairweather Discography*. Eurojazz Discos, no. 68. Zwolle, Netherlands: Gerard Bielderman, 1997. 40 pp.
Covers 1971 to 1997, with a biography. Includes unissued material.
Bibliography; indexes (musicians, releases, song titles).

Fallon, Jack (bass, Canada)

7-98 Bielderman, Gerard. *Jack Fallon Discography*. Eurojazz Discos, no. 87. Zwolle, Netherlands: Gerard Bielderman, 1998. 40 pp.
Covers 1946 to 1998, with a biography. Includes unissued material.
Bibliography; illustrations; indexes (musicians, releases, song titles); photographs.

Fawkes, Wally (clarinet/saxophone, UK)

7-99 Purser, Julian, and Gerard Bielderman. *Wally Fawkes Discography*. Eurojazz Discos, no. 90. Zwolle, Netherlands: Gerard Bielderman, 1999. 56 pp.
Covers 1945 to 1992. Includes unissued material.
Bibliography; indexes (musicians, releases, song titles); photographs.

Felix, Lennie (piano/bandleader, UK)

7-100 Simpson, Norman, and Bielderman, Gerard. *Lennie Felix Discography*. Eurojazz Discos, no. 77. Zwolle, Netherlands: Gerard Bielderman, 1998. 16 pp.
Covers 1947 to 1975, with a biography. Includes unissued material.
Illustrations; indexes (musicians, releases, song titles); photographs.

Fields, Shep (clarinet/saxophone, bandleader, U.S.)

7-101 Garrod, Charles. *Shep Fields and His Orchestra*. Revised edition. Zephyrhills, FL: Joyce Record Club Publication, 1994. 49 pp.
Not reviewed. First published in 1987.
Index.

Fitzgerald, Ella (singer, U.S.)

7-102 Garrod, Charles. "Ella Fitzgerald." In *Chick Webb and His Orchestra; Including: Ella Fitzgerald and Her Orchestra*. Zephyrhills, FL: Joyce Record Club Publication, 1993. 27 pp.
Not reviewed.
Index.

Flanagan, Ralph (piano/bandleader, U.S.)

7-103 Garrod, Charles. *Ralph Flanagan and His Orchestra*. Revised edition. Zephyrhills, FL: Joyce Record Club Publication, 1990. 46 pp.
Not reviewed. First published in 1985.
Index.

Forrest, Helen (singer, U.S.)

7-104 Garrod, Charles. *Helen Forrest*. Zephyrhills, FL: Joyce Record Club Publication, 1993. 45 pp.
Not reviewed.
Index.

Foster, Chuck (trumpet/bandleader, U.S.)

7-105 Garrod, Charles. *Chuck Foster and His Orchestra*. Zephyrhills, FL: Joyce Record Club Publication, 1992. 43 pp.
Not reviewed.
Index.

Foxley, Ray (piano/bandleader, UK)

7-106 Lee, Raymond. *Ray Foxley Discography*. Eurojazz Discos, no. 28. Zwolle, Netherlands: Gerard Bielderman, 1995. 36 pp.
Covers 1945 to 1999, with a biography. Includes unissued material. First published in 1992.
Bibliography; illustrations; indexes (musicians, releases, song titles); photographs.

Freetime Old Dixie Jassband (band, Netherlands)

7-107 Bielderman, Gerard. "Discography of the Freetime Old Dixie Jassband." In *Discography of Dutch Traditional Jazz Bands, vol. 2: Circus Square Jazz Band 1968–1995; Storyville Jassband 1968–1995; Freetime Old Dixie*

Jassband 1975–1995; Charlestown Jazzband 1971–1998. Eurojazz Discos, no. 93. Zwolle, Netherlands: Gerard Bielderman, 1999. pp. 24–31.
   Covers 1975 to 1995. Includes unissued material but no reissues.
   Bibliography; indexes (album titles, song titles); photographs.

Garber, Jan (violin/bandleader, U.S.)

7-108   Garrod, Charles. *Jan Garber and His Orchestra.* Zephyrhills, FL: Joyce Record Club Publication, 1992. 94pp.
   Not reviewed.
   Index.

Gentlemen of Jazz (band, Denmark)

7-109   Bielderman, Gerard. "Discography of the Gentlemen of Jazz." In *Discography of Danish Traditional Jazz Bands, vol. 1: Bourbon Street Jazzband 1975–1998; Gentlemen of Jazz 1989–1998; Pee Dee Jazzband 1988–1999; Vestre Jazzværk 1979–1997.* Eurojazz Discos, no. 103. Zwolle, Netherlands: Gerard Bielderman, 1999. pp. 12–17.
   Covers 1989 to 1998. Includes unissued material but no reissues.
   Indexes (album titles, song titles); photographs.

Gluskin, Lud (drums, U.S.)

7-110   Bergmeier, Horst, and Rainer E. Lotz. *Lud Gluskin: A Bio-Discography.* Sonderpublikation, no.1. Dietramszell, Germany: Fox auf 78, 1992. 136 pp.
   Covers 1924 to 1945. Annotated.
   Illustrations; photographs.

Goodman, Benny (clarinet/bandleader, U.S.)

7-111   Connor, D. Russell. *Benny Goodman: Wrappin' It Up.* Studies in Jazz, no. 23. Lanham, MD: Scarecrow Press, 1996. 179 pp.
   Covers 1929 to 1996, with annotations. Contains unissued material. Formats include video tapes. Lists film appearances. Includes "Savory Goodman Airchecks"; "Goodman Arrangements"; "Memorabilia Price Guide"; and "Necrology," a listing of Goodman's deceased associates.
   Index (song titles); photographs.

Gordon, Gray (clarinet/bandleader, U.S.)

7-112   Garrod, Charles. "Gray Gordon and His Orchestra." In *Del Courtney and His Orchestra; Plus: Gray Gordon and His Orchestra.* Zephyrhills: Joyce Record Club Publication, 1992. 34 pp.

Gray, Glen (saxophone/bandleader, U.S.)

7-113 Garrod, Charles, and Bill Korst. *Glen Gray & the Casa Loma Orchestra*. Revised edition. Zephyrhills, FL: Joyce Record Club Publication, 1993. 64 pp.
Not reviewed. First published in 1987.
Index.

Gray, Wardell (saxophone, U.S.)

7-114 Gazdar, Coover. *Easy Swing: The Wardell Gray Discography*. Bangalore, India: Coover Gazdar, 1997. 36 pp.
Covers 1944 to 1955. Contains unissued material. Lists solos. Formats include 78s.
Index (song titles); photographs.

Green, Brian (bandleader, UK)

7-115 Bielderman, Gerard. "Brian Green Discography." In *Discography of British Traditional Jazz Bands/Musicians, vol. 2: Black Bottom Stompers 1971–1982; Bill Brunskill's Jazzmen 1972–1986; Brian Green 1965–1968, 1994–1996; Colin Kingwell's Jazz Bandits 1964–1995*. Eurojazz Discos, no. 76. Zwolle, Netherlands: Gerard Bielderman, 1997. pp. 12–21.
Covers 1965 to 1994. No unissued material or reissues.
Bibliography; illustrations; indexes (album titles, song titles).

Greig, Stan (piano/drums/bandleader, UK)

7-116 Latham, John, and Raymond Lee. *Stan Greig Discography*. With Gerard Bielderman. Eurojazz Discos, no. 42. Zwolle, Netherlands: Gerard Bielderman, 1995. 56 pp.
Covers 1949 to 1993, with a biography and list of compositions. Includes unissued material.
Bibliography; illustrations; indexes (compositions, musicians, releases, song titles); photographs.

Hackett, Bobby (cornet/bandleader, U.S.)

7-117 Jones, Harold. *Bobby Hackett: A Bio-Discography*. Discographies, no. 80. Westport, CT: Greenwood Press, 1999. 290 pp.
Covers 1937 to 1976, with a biography. Includes unissued material.
Bibliography; indexes (musicians, releases, song titles).

Handy, George (piano/arranger/composer, U.S.)

7-118 Garrod, Charles, and Bill Korst. "George Handy." In *Boyd Raeburn and His Orchestra; Plus: Johnny Bothwell and George Handy*. Revised edition. Zephyrhills, FL: Joyce Record Club Publication, 1997. 39 pp.
Not reviewed. First published in 1985.
Index.

Handy, Capt. John (saxophone/clarinet, U.S.)

7-119 Lee, Raymond. *"Over the Waves": A Discography of Capt. John Handy*. Sounds of New Orleans, no. 1. Zwolle, Netherlands: Gerard Bielderman, 1995. 40 pp.
Covers 1958 to 1977, with a biography. Includes unissued material.
Bibliography; illustrations; indexes (musicians, releases, song titles).

Harbour Jazz Band (band, Netherlands)

7-120 Bielderman, Gerard. "Discography of the Harbour Jazz Band." In *Discography of Dutch Traditional Jazz Bands, vol. 1: Eric Krans' Dixieland Pipers 1950–1963; Bert de Kort's Dixieland Pipers 1977–1985; Harbour Jazz Band 1967–1996; Reunion Jazz Band 1966–1998; Revival Jassband 1977–1993*. Eurojazz Discos, no. 82. Zwolle, Netherlands: Gerard Bielderman, 1998. pp. 15–23.
Covers 1967 to 1996. Formats include audio cassettes. Contains unissued material.
Bibliography; indexes (album titles, song titles).

Harlem Ramblers (band, Switzerland)

7-121 Bielderman, Gerard. *Harlem Ramblers Discography*. Eurojazz Discos, no. 59. Zwolle, Netherlands: Gerard Bielderman, 1997. 20 pp.
Covers 1960 to 1996, with a band history. Includes unissued material. Lists band personnel, 1955 to 1997.
Indexes (album titles, song titles); photographs.

Hastings, Lennie (drums, UK)

7-122 Simpson, Norman, and Gerard Bielderman. *Lennie Hastings Discography*. Eurojazz Discos, no 51. Zwolle, Netherlands: Gerard Bielderman, 1996. 52 pp.
Covers 1951 to 1978, with a biography. Contains unissued material. Formats include audio cassettes.
Bibliography; illustrations; indexes (musicians, releases, song titles).

Hawdon, Dick (trumpet/bass, UK)

7-123 Bielderman, Gerard. *Dick Hawdon Discography*. Eurojazz Discos, no. 84. Zwolle, Netherlands: Gerard Bielderman, 1998. 32 pp.
  Covers 1949 to 1977, with a biography. Includes unissued material.
  Bibliography; indexes (musicians, releases, song titles); photographs.

Hawkins, Annie (bass, Australia)

7-124 Bielderman, Gerard, and Raymond Lee. *Annie Hawkins Discography*. Eurojazz Discos, no 96. Zwolle, Netherlands: Gerard Bielderman, 1999. 32 pp.
  Covers 1969 to 1998, with a biography. Includes unissued material.
  Bibliography; illustrations; indexes (album titles, musicians, song titles).

Hawkins, Erskine (trumpet/bandleader, U.S.)

7-125 Garrod, Charles. *Erskine Hawkins and His Orchestra*. Zephyrhills, FL: Joyce Record Club Publication, 1992. 24 pp.
  Not reviewed.
  Index.

Hayes, Tubby (saxophone, UK)

7-126 Schwartz, Barbara. *Tubby Hayes: A Discography*. Zurich: Black Press, 1990. 97 pp.
  Covers 1951 to 1967. Includes unissued material and film and TV work.
  Chronology; indexes (compositions by Tubby Hayes, musicians, releases, song titles).

Haymes, Dick (singer/bandleader, Argentina)

7-127 Garrod, Charles, and Denis Brown. *Dick Haymes and His Orchestra*. Zephyrhills, FL: Joyce Record Club Publication, 1990. 84 pp.
  Not reviewed.
  Index.

Heidt, Horace (bandleader, U.S.)

7-128 Garrod, Charles. *Horace Heidt and His Orchestra*. Zephyrhills, FL: Joyce Record Club Publication, 1993. 35 pp.
  Not reviewed.
  Index.

Herbeck, Ray (saxophone/clarinet/bandleader, U.S.)

7-129 Garrod, Charles. "Ray Herbeck and His Orchestra." In *Tiny Hill and His Orchestra; Plus: Ray Herbeck and His Orchestra*. Zephyrhills, FL: Joyce Record Club Publication, 1992. 35 pp.
Not reviewed.
Index.

Herman, Woody (clarinet/saxophone/bandleader, U.S.)

7-130 Morrill, Dexter. *Woody Herman: A Guide to the Big Band Recordings, 1936–1987*. Discographies, no. 40. New York: Greenwood Press, 1990. 129 pp.
Covers 1936 to 1987, with a biography and essay on "essential recordings." Lists solos. Includes "First Herd Repertoire."
Bibliography; indexes (musicians, record labels, song titles, alternative titles).

Hill, Tiny (singer/bandleader, U.S.)

7-131 Garrod, Charles. "Tiny Hill and His Orchestra." In *Tiny Hill and His Orchestra; Plus: Ray Herbeck and His Orchestra*. Zephyrhills, FL: Joyce Record Club Publication, 1992. 35 pp.
Not reviewed.
Index.

Himber, Richard (violin/vibraphone/bandleader, U.S.)

7-132 Garrod, Charles. *Richard Himber and His Orchestra*. Zephyrhills, FL: Joyce Record Club Publication, 1993. 31 pp.
Not reviewed.
Index.

Houlind, Doc (drums/singer/bandleader, Denmark)

7-133 Gruyters, Sjef, and Gerard Bielderman. *Doc Houlind Discography*. Eurojazz Discos, no 78. Zwolle, Netherlands: Gerard Bielderman, 1998. 36 pp.
Covers 1965–1997, with a biography. Contains unissued material.
Bibliography; indexes (musicians, releases, song titles).

Howard, Eddy (guitar/trombone/singer/bandleader, U.S.)

7-134 Garrod, Charles. *Eddy Howard and His Orchestra*. Revised edition. Zephyrhills, FL: Joyce Record Club Publication, 1994. 60 pp.
Not reviewed. First published in 1991.
Index.

Hübner, Abbi (cornet/trumpet/bandleader, Germany)

7-135 Elvers, Erwin, and Gerard Bielderman. *Abbi Hübner Discography.* 2nd ed. Eurojazz Discos, no. 16. Zwolle, Netherlands: Gerard Bielderman, 1995. 28 pp.

Covers 1958 to 1994, with a biography. Written in German and English. First published in 1988. Includes unissued material. Lists members of Abbi Hübner's Low Down Wizards.

Illustrations; indexes (musicians, releases, song titles); photographs.

Hudson, Dean (singer/bandleader, U.S.)

7-136 Garrod, Charles, and Bill Korst. "Dean Hudson and His Orchestra." In *Bobby Byrne and His Orchestra; Plus: Dean Hudson and His Orchestra.* Zephyrhills, FL: Joyce Record Club Publication, 1992.

Not reviewed.

Index.

Hudson, Will (arranger/composer/bandleader, U.S.)

7-137 Garrod, Charles. "Will Hudson and His Orchestra." In *Will Hudson and His Orchestra; The Hudson-Delange Orchestra; Eddie Delange and His Orchestra; George Paxton and His Orchestra; Bob Strong and His Orchestra.* Zephyrhills, FL: Joyce Record Club Publication, 1993. 39 pp.

Not reviewed.

Index

Humphrey, Willie (clarinet, U.S.)

7-138 Lee, Raymond. *New Orleans Clarinet: A Discography of Willie Humphrey.* Sounds of New Orleans, no. 2. Zwolle, Netherlands: Gerard Bielderman, 1996. 40 pp.

Covers 1926 to 1993, with a biography by Mike Hazeldine from the journal *New Orleans Music.* Includes unissued material.

Bibliography; illustrations; indexes (musicians, releases, song titles); photographs.

Hund, "Doggy" (trombone, Austria)

7-139 Lee, Raymond. *Discography of Gerhard "Doggy" Hund and the Maryland Jazz Band of Cologne.* Eurojazz Discos, no. 55. Zwolle, Netherlands: Gerard Bielderman, 1996. 40 pp.

Covers 1963 to 1996, with a biography in English and German. Includes unissued material.

Bibliography; indexes (musicians, releases, song titles); photographs.

Hunt, Fred (piano, UK)

7-140 Simpson, Norman, and Gerard Bielderman. *Fred Hunt Discography.* Eurojazz Discos, no. 80. Zwolle, Netherlands: Gerard Bielderman, 1998. 48 pp.

Covers 1951 to 1982, with a biography. Includes unissued material.

Bibliography; illustrations; indexes (musicians, releases, song titles); photographs.

Ibrahim, Abdullah (piano/saxophone, South Africa)

7-141 Rasmussen, Lars. *Abdullah Ibrahim: A Discography.* Copenhagen: The Booktrader, 1998. 239 pp.

Covers 1954 to 1998. Includes unissued material. Contains "List of Compositions"; "List of Musicians"; "Abdullah Ibrahim's Instruments"; and "Abdullah Ibrahim Compositions Recorded by Other Artists."

Bibliography; chronology; filmography/videography; index (releases).

Ingham, Keith (piano, UK)

7-142 Elvers, Erwin, and Gerard Bielderman. *Keith Ingham Discography.* Eurojazz Discos, no. 69. Zwolle, Netherlands: Gerard Bielderman, 1997. 52 pp.

Covers 1974 to 1996, with a biography. Includes unissued material.

Bibliography; illustrations; indexes (musicians, releases, song titles); photographs.

James, Harry (trumpet/bandleader, U.S.)

7-143 Garrod, Charles, and Peter Johnston. *Harry James and His Orchestra.* Vol. 1, *1937–1945.* Vol. 2, *1946–1954.* Vol. 3, *1955–1983.* Revised edition. Zephyrhills, FL: Joyce Record Club Publication, 1996. 88 pp. (vol. 1); 90 pp. (vol. 2); 83 pp. (vol. 3).

Not reviewed. First published in 1985.

Index.

Jones, Dill (piano, UK)

7-144 Griffiths, David. *Dill Jones Discography.* Eurojazz Discos, no. 46. Zwolle, Netherlands: Gerard Bielderman, 1996. 56 pp.

Covers 1947 to 1983, with a biography. Includes unissued material.

Bibliography; illustrations; indexes (musicians, releases, song titles); photographs.

Jones, Isham (piano/composer/bandleader, U.S.)

7-145 Garrod, Charles. *Isham Jones and His Orchestra*. Zephyrhills, FL: Joyce Record Club Publication, 1992. 33 pp.
Not reviewed.
Index.

Jordan, Louis (saxophone/singer/bandleader, U.S.)

7-146 Garrod, Charles. *Louis Jordan and His Orchestra*. Zephyrhills, FL: Joyce Record Club Publication, 1994. 28 pp.
Not reviewed.
Index.

Jurgens, Dick (composer/bandleader, U.S.)

7-147 Garrod, Charles. *Dick Jurgens and His Orchestra*. 2nd ed. Portland, OR: Joyce Record Club Publication, 1999. 62 pp.
Not reviewed. First published in 1988.
Index.

Kaatee, Frits (clarinet/saxophone, Netherlands)

7-148 Bielderman, Gerard. *Frits Kaatee Discography*. 4th ed. Eurojazz Discos, no. 23. Zwolle, Netherlands: Gerard Bielderman, 1996. 35 pp.
Covers 1956 to 1996, with a biography. Written in Dutch and English. Includes unissued material.
Bibliography; illustrations; indexes (musicians, releases, song titles); photographs.

Kaatee, George (trombone/bandleader, Netherlands)

7-149 Bielderman, Gerard. *George Kaatee Discography, Incorporating the New Orleans Syncopators*. Eurojazz Discos, no. 73. Zwolle, Netherlands: Gerard Bielderman, 1998. 40 pp.
Covers 1956–1995, with a biography in Dutch and English. Includes unissued material.
Bibliography; indexes (musicians, releases, song titles); photographs.

Kassel, Art (composer/singer/bandleader, U.S.)

7-150 Garrod, Charles. "Art Kassel and His Orchestra." In *Art Kassel and His Orchestra; Plus: Johnny Messner and His Orchestra*. Zephyrhills, FL: Joyce Record Club, 1993. 36 pp.

Not reviewed.
Index.

Kavelin, Al (bandleader, U.S.)

1-151 Garrod, Charles. "Al Kavelin and His Orchestra." In *Clyde Lucas and His Orchestra; Plus: Al Kavelin and His Orchestra; Carl Ravazza and His Orchestra; Ted Straeter and His Orchestra.* Zephyrhills, FL: Joyce Record Club Publication, 1995. 40 pp.
Not reviewed.
Index.

Keller, Werner (clarinet/bandleader, Switzerland)

7-152 Elvers, Erwin, and Gerard Bielderman. *Werner Keller—Tremble Kids Discography.* 2nd ed. Eurojazz Discos, no. 61. Zwolle, Netherlands: Gerard Bielderman, 1998. 32 pp.
Covers 1956 to 1997, with biography. Includes unissued material.
Bibliography; indexes (musicians, releases, song titles).

Kellin, Orange (clarinet, Sweden)

7-153 Lee, Raymond. *Orange Kellin Discography.* Eurojazz Discos, no. 54. Zwolle, Netherlands: Gerard Bielderman, 1996. 52 pp.
Covers 1961 to 1995. Includes unissued material. Interview with Claes Ringquist.
Illustrations; indexes (musicians, recordings, song titles); photographs.

Kenton, Stan (piano/arranger/bandleader, U.S.)

7-154 Garrod, Charles. *Stan Kenton and His Orchestra, vol. 1: 1940–1951.* Revised edition. Portland, OR: Joyce Record Club Publication, 1999. 81 pp.
Not reviewed. First published in 1984.
Index.

7-155 Garrod, Charles. *Stan Kenton and His Orchestra, vol. 3: 1960–1979.* Portland, OR: Joyce Record Club Publication, 1991. 66 pp.
Not reviewed.
Index.

King, Henry (piano/bandleader, U.S.)

7-156 Garrod, Charles. *Henry King and His Orchestra.* Zephyrhills, FL: Joyce Record Club Publication, 1994. 51 pp.

King, Wayne (saxophone, U.S.)

7-157 Garrod, Charles. *Wayne King and His Orchestra*. Zephyrhills, FL: Joyce Record Club Publication, 1994. 76 pp.
Not reviewed.
Index.

King Sisters (vocal group, U.S.)

7-158 Garrod, Charles, and Bill Korst. "The King Sisters." In *Alvino Rey and His Orchestra; Plus: The King Sisters 1939–1958*. Revised edition. Zephyrhills, FL: Joyce Record Club Publication, 1997. 37 pp.
Not reviewed. First published in 1986.
Index.

Colin Kingwell's Jazz Bandits (band, UK)

7-159 Bielderman, Gerard. "Discography of Colin Kingwell's Jazz Bandits." In *Discography of British Traditional Jazz Bands/Musicians, vol. 2: Black Bottom Stompers 1971–1982; Bill Brunskill's Jazzmen 1972–1986; Brian Green 1965–1968, 1994–1996; Colin Kingwell's Jazz Bandits 1964–1995*. Eurojazz Discos, no. 76. Zwolle, Netherlands: Gerard Bielderman, 1997. pp. 12–21.
Covers 1961 to 1995. No reissues. Formats include audio cassettes.
Bibliography; indexes (album titles, song titles); photographs.

Kirby, John (bass/bandleader, U.S.)

7-160 Garrod, Charles. *John Kirby and His Orchestra; Plus: Andy Kirk and His Orchestra*. Zephyrhills, FL: Joyce Record Club Publication, 1991. 37 pp.
Not reviewed.
Index.

Roy Kirby Paragon Jazz Band (band, UK)

7-161 Bielderman, Gerard. "Discography of the Roy Kirby Paragon Jazz Band." In *Discography of British Traditional Jazz Bands, vol. 4: Chez Chesterman 1960–1998; Mike Daniels' Delta Jazz Band 1948–1995; Roy Kirby Paragon Jazz Band; John Maddocks 1971–1998*. Eurojazz Discos, no. 89. Zwolle, Netherlands: Gerard Bielderman, 1998. pp. 24–30.
Covers 1975 to 1994. Formats include audio cassettes. No reissues.
Bibliography; indexes (album titles, song titles); photographs.

Kirk, Andy (saxophone/bandleader, U.S.)

7-162 Garrod, Charles. "Andy Kirk and His Orchestra." In *John Kirby and His Orchestra; Plus: Andy Kirk and His Orchestra*. Zephyrhills, FL: Joyce Record Club Publication, 1991. 37 pp.
  Not reviewed.
  Index.

Klein, Oscar (trumpet/cornet/clarinet/guitar, Austria)

7-163 Elvers, Erwin, and Gerard Bielderman. *Oscar Klein Discography*. 7th ed. Eurojazz Discos, no. 6. Zwolle, Netherlands: Gerard Bielderman, 1996. 72 pp.
  Covers 1953 to 1997, with a biography in German and English. Contains unissued material. Formats include videotapes. First published in 1986.
  Bibliography; indexes (releases, song titles); photographs.

Bert de Kort's Dixieland Pipers; *see* **Dixieland Pipers**

Eric Krans' Dixieland Pipers; *see* **Dixieland Pipers**

Krupa, Gene (drums/bandleader, U.S.)

7-164 Garrod, Charles. *Gene Krupa and His Orchestra*. Vol. 1, *1935–1946*. Vol. 2, *1947–1973*. Revised edition. Zephyrhills, FL: Joyce Record Club Publication, 1996. 70 pp. (vol. 1); 53 pp. (vol. 2).
  Not reviewed. First published in 1984.
  Index.

Kyser, Kay (bandleader, U.S.)

7-165 Garrod, Charles, and Raymond Hair. *Kay Kyser and His Orchestra*. 3rd ed. Portland, OR: Joyce Record Club Publication, 1999. 91 pp.
  Not reviewed. First published in 1986.
  Index.

Lane, Steve (cornet/bandleader, UK)

7-166 Capes, John S. *Steve Lane Discography, Incorporating the Famous Southern Stompers*. 2nd ed. Eurojazz Discos, no. 38. Zwolle, Netherlands: Gerard Bielderman, 1999. 64 pp.

Covers c. 1950—1998, with a biography. Also contains recordings by one of Lane's bands, the Famous Southern Stompers. Includes unissued material. First published in 1994.

Bibliography; illustrations; indexes (musicians, releases, song titles); photographs.

Laurie, Cy (clarinet/bandleader, UK)

7-167 Bielderman, Gerard. *Cy Laurie Discography*. **4th ed. Eurojazz Discos, no. 8. Zwolle, Netherlands: Gerard Bielderman, 1995. 28 pp.**

Covers 1950 to 1995, with a biography. Formats include audio cassettes. Contains unissued material. First published in 1986.

Bibliography; illustrations; indexes (album titles, musicians, song titles); photographs.

Lawrence, Denise (UK)

7-168 Bielderman, Gerard. "Discography of Denise Lawrence & Storyville Tickle." In *Discography of British Traditional Jazz Bands/Musicians, vol. 3: Denise Lawrence & Storyville Tickle 1984–1997; The Savannah Jazz Band 1988–1997; Jim Shelley's (Frisco) Jazz Band 1976–1997*. **Eurojazz Discos, no. 79. Zwolle, Netherlands: Gerard Bielderman, 1997. pp. 3–12.**

Covers 1984 to 1997. No unissued material or reissues. Formats include audio cassettes.

Illustrations; indexes (album titles, song titles); photographs.

Lawrence, Elliot (piano/arranger/bandleader, U.S.)

7-169 Garrod, Charles. *Elliot Lawrence and His Orchestra*. **Revised edition. Zephyrhills, FL: Joyce Record Club Publication, 1996. 46 pp.**

Not reviewed. First published in 1986.

Index.

Lay, Pete (drums, UK)

7-170 Bielderman, Gerard. *Pete Lay Discography*. **Eurojazz Discos, no. 92. Zwolle, Netherlands: Gerard Bielderman, 1999. 28 pp.**

Covers 1971 to 1999. Includes unissued material.

Indexes (musicans, releases, song titles); photographs.

Lemon, Brian (piano, UK)

7-171 Simpson, Norman, and Gerard Bielderman. *Brian Lemon Discography*. Eurojazz Discos, no. 53. Zwolle, Netherlands: Gerard Bielderman, 1996. 60 pp.

Covers 1957 to 1996, with a biography. Includes unissued material.
Illustrations; indexes (musicians, releases, song titles); photographs.

Lewis, Ted (clarinet/bandleader, U.S.)

7-172 Garrod, Charles. *Ted Lewis and His Orchestra*. Zephyrhills, FL: Joyce Record Club Publications, 1994. 38 pp.

Not reviewed.
Index.

Ley, Eggy (saxophone, UK)

7-173 Bielderman, Gerard. *Eggy Ley Discography*. 2nd ed. Eurojazz Discos, no. 12. Zwolle, Netherlands: Gerard Bielderman, 1995. 20 pp.

Covers 1956 to 1986, with a biography. Includes unissued material. First published in 1987.
Bibliography; indexes (musicians, records, song titles).

Lightfoot, Terry (clarinet/bandleader, UK)

7-174 Bielderman, Gerard. *Terry Lightfoot Discography*. 3rd ed. Eurojazz Discos, no. 24. Zwolle, Netherlands: Gerard Bielderman, 1998. 36 pp.

Covers 1956 to 1997, with a biography. Includes unissued material. First published in 1991.
Bibliography; illustrations; indexes (musicians, releases, song titles); photographs.

Lindgren, Ole "Fessor" (trombone/bandleader, Denmark)

7-175 Elvers, Erwin, and Gerard Bielderman. *Fessor Discography*. 4th ed. Eurojazz Discos, no. 30. Zwolle, Netherlands: Gerard Bielderman, 1997. 56 pp.

Covers 1956 to 1997, with an essay by Lindgren entitled "About 'Fessor' and his Music." Includes unissued material. List of compositions. First published in 1993.
Bibliography; illustrations; indexes (musicians, releases, song titles); photographs.

Litton, Martin (piano, UK)

7-176 Bielderman. Gerard. *Martin Litton Discography.* 2nd ed. Eurojazz Discos, no. 50. Zwolle, Netherlands: Gerard Bielderman, 1999. 40 pp.

Covers 1979 to 1999, with a biography. Includes unissued materials. First published in 1996.

Bibliography; indexes (musicians, releases, song titles); photographs.

Long, Johnny (violin/bandleader, U.S.)

7-177 Garrod, Charles, and Bill Korst. *Johnny Long and His Orchestra.* Revised edition. Zephyrhills, FL: Joyce Record Club Publication, 1993. 39 pp.

Not reviewed. First published in 1984.

Index.

Lopez, Vincent (piano/bandleader, U.S.)

7-178 Garrod, Charles. *Vincent Lopez and His Orchestra.* Zephyrhills, FL: Joyce Record Club Publication, 1994. 61 pp.

Not reviewed.

Index.

Lucas, Clyde (trombone/singer/bandleader, U.S.)

7-179 Garrod, Charles. "Clyde Lucas and His Orchestra." In *Clyde Lucas and His Orchestra; Plus: Al Kavelin and His Orchestra; Carl Ravazza and His Orchestra; Ted Straeter and His Orchestra.* Zephyrhills, FL: Joyce Record Club Publication, 1995. 40 pp.

Not reviewed.

Index.

Lunceford, Jimmie (saxophone/bandleader, U.S.)

7-180 Garrod, Charles. *Jimmie Lunceford and His Orchestra.* Zephyrhills, FL: Joyce Record Club Publication, 1990. 31 pp.

Not reviewed.

Index.

7-181 Lyttkens, Bertil. *The Jimmie Lunceford Legacy on Records.* Stockholm: Bertil Lyttkens, 1996. 100 pp.

Covers 1927 to 1947. Contains unissued material. Formats include 45s and 78s. Lists of transcriptions, films, and radio broadcasts.

Bibliography; illustrations; indexes (musicians, releases, song titles); photographs.

Luter, Claude (clarinet/bandleader, France)

7-182 Elvers, Erwin, and Gerard Bielderman. *Claude Luter Discography.* Eurojazz Discos, no. 57. Zwolle, Netherlands: Gerard Bielderman, 1997. 60 pp.

Covers 1944 to 1991, with a biography. Includes unissued material. Formats include 78s. List of unidentified recordings with Luter.

Bibliography; illustrations; indexes (releases, song titles); photographs.

Lyman, Abe (drums/bandleader, U.S.)

7-183 Garrod, Charles. *Abe Lyman and His Orchestra.* Zephyrhills, FL: Joyce Record Club Publication, 1995. 28 pp.

Not reviewed.

Index.

Maddocks, John (clarinet/saxophone/singer/bandleader, UK)

7-184 Bielderman, Gerard. "John Maddocks Discography." In *Discography of British Traditional Jazz Bands, vol. 4: Chez Chesterman 1960–1998; Mike Daniels' Delta Jazz Band 1948–1995; Roy Kirby Paragon Jazz Band; John Maddocks 1971–1998.* Eurojazz Discos, no. 89. Zwolle, Netherlands: Gerard Bielderman, 1998. pp. 31–43.

Covers 1971 to 1998. Formats include audio cassettes. No unissued material.

Bibliography; indexes (album titles, song titles).

Maltby, Richard (cornet/arranger/bandleader, U.S.)

7-185 Garrod, Charles. *Richard Maltby and His Orchestra.* Zephyrhills, FL: Joyce Record Club Publication, 1994. 27 pp.

Not reviewed.

Index.

Manne, Shelly (drums, U.S.)

7-186 Brand, Jack. *Shelly Manne: Sounds of the Different Drummer.* Discography/filmography by Bill Korst. Edited by Vince Danca. Transcriptions by Robert DeVita. Rockford, IL: Percussion Express, 1997. 187 pp.

Annotated bio-discography covering 1940 to 1984. Includes unissued material. Filmography; musical transcriptions; photographs.

Manone, Wingy (trumpet/singer/bandleader, U.S.)

7-187 Garrod, Charles. *Wingy Manone and His Orchestra*. Zephyrhills, FL: Joyce Record Club Publication, 1994. 26 pp.
Not reviewed.
Index.

Marks, Roger (trombonist/bandleader, UK)

7-188 Bielderman, Gerard. *Roger Marks Discography*. 2nd ed. Eurojazz Discos, no. 62. Zwolle, Netherlands: Gerard Bielderman, 1999. 24 pp.
Covers 1977 to 1999, with a biography. Includes unissued material. Formats include audio cassettes and videotapes. First published in 1997.
Bibliography; indexes (musicians, releases, song titles); photographs.

Marquet, Alain (clarinet, France)

7-189 Bielderman, Gerard. *Alain Marquet Discography*. Eurojazz Discos, no. 106. Zwolle, Netherlands: Gerard Bielderman, 1999. 28 pp.
Covers 1965 to 1999, with a biography. Includes unissued material.
Bibliography; indexes (musicians, releases, song titles); photographs.

Marterie, Ralph (bandleader, Italy)

7-190 Brethour, Ross, Charles Garrod, and Edward Novitsky. *Ralph Marterie and His Orchestra*. Zephyrhills, FL: Joyce Record Club Publication, 1992. 71 pp.
Not reviewed.
Index.

Martin, Freddy (saxophone/bandleader/arranger/composer, U.S.)

7-191 Garrod, Charles. *Freddy Martin and His Orchestra*. 2 vols. Revised edition. Zephyrhills, FL: Joyce Record Club Publication, 1996. 71 pp. (vol. 1); 68 pp. (vol. 2).
Not reviewed. Volume 1 covers 1931 to 1947 and volume 2 covers 1947 to 1967. First published in 1987.
Index.

Maryland Jazz Band of Cologne; *see* **Hund, "Doggy"**

Mason, Phil (cornet, UK)

7-192 Bielderman, Gerard, and Raymond Lee. *Phil Mason Discography.* Eurojazz Discos, no. 104. Zwolle, Netherlands: Gerard Bielderman, 1999. 36 pp.

Covers 1971 to 1999, with a biography. Includes unissued material. Formats include audio cassettes.

Bibliography; indexes (musicians, releases, song titles); photographs.

Mason, Rod (cornet/trumpet/bandleader, UK)

7-193 Bielderman, Gerard. *Rod Mason Discography.* 7th ed. Eurojazz Discos, no. 7. Zwolle, Netherlands: Gerard Bielderman, 1998. 44 pp.

Covers 1961 to 1998, with a biography. Includes unissued material. First published in 1986.

Bibliography; illustrations; indexes (musicians, releases, song titles); photographs.

May, Billy (trumpet/bandleader/composer/arranger, U.S.)

7-194 Garrod, Charles. *Billy May and His Orchestra.* Zephyrhills, FL: Joyce Record Club Publication, 1991. 45 pp.

Not reviewed.

Index.

7-195 Mirtle, Jack. *The Music of Billy May: A Discography.* Foreword by Alan Livingston. Westport, CT: Greenwood Press, 1998. 568 pp.

Bio-discography covering 1943 to 1998. Organized into the following categories: "Leader, Arranger, Composer, 1944–1998"; "Sideman and Arranger for Others"; "Radio, Film, Television and International Appearances"; and "The Road Band from 1951." Includes unissued material. Formats include 78s. List of transcriptions. Appendixes include "Recordings and Arrangements Erroneously Credited to Billy May" and "May's Charlie Barnet and Glenn Miller Arrangements."

Bibliography; indexes (broadcasts, musicians, releases, song titles); photographs.

McCoy, Clyde (trumpet/bandleader, U.S.)

7-196 Garrod, Charles. "Clyde McCoy and His Orchestra." In *Henry Busse and His Orchestra; Plus: Clyde McCoy and His Orchestra.* Zephyrhills, FL: Joyce Record Club Publication, 1990. 53 pp.

Covers 1931 to 1966.
Index (song titles).

McIntyre, Hal (saxophone/clarinet/bandleader, U.S.)

7-197 Garrod, Charles. *Hal McIntyre and His Orchestra.* **Revised edition. Zephyrhills, FL: Joyce Record Club Publication, 1999. 45 pp.**
Not reviewed. First published in 1974.
Index.

McRae, Carmen (singer, U.S.)

7-198 Brown, Denis. *Carmen McRae: A Discography.* **Birmingham, UK: Denis Brown, 1996. 69 pp.**
Not reviewed.
Index.

Melly, George (singer, UK)

7-199 Bielderman, Gerard. *George Melly Discography, Incorporating Mick Mulligan's Jazz Band.* **2nd ed. Eurojazz Discos, no. 33. Zwolle, Netherlands: Gerard Bielderman, 1997. 36 pp.**
Covers 1950 to 1995, with a biography. Includes unissued material. First published in 1993.
Bibliography; indexes (musicians, releases, song titles).

Ian Menzies & the Clyde Valley Stompers (band, UK)

7-200 Bielderman, Gerard. **"Discography of Ian Menzies & the Clyde Valley Stompers."** In *Discography of British Traditional Jazz Bands/Musicians, vol. 1: Avon Cities Skiffle Group 1956–1958; Avon Cities [Jazz Band] 1956–1997; Dick Charlesworth 1957–1994; Clyde Valley Stompers 1956–1983; Saints Jazz Band 1956–1983.* **2nd ed. Eurojazz Discos, no. 72. Zwolle, Netherlands: Gerard Bielderman, 1999. pp. 22–30.**
Covers 1956 to 1983. Includes unissued material. First published in 1997.
Bibliography; indexes (album titles, song titles); photographs.

Merseysippi Jazz Band (band, UK)

7-201 Bielderman, Gerard. *Merseysippi Jazz Band Discography.* **Eurojazz Discos, no. 60. Zwolle, Netherlands: Gerard Bielderman, 1997. 24 pp.**

Covers 1946 to 1996, with a band profile. Includes unissued material. Formats include audio cassettes. List of "Band Personnel, 1949–1997."
Bibliography; illustrations; indexes (releases, song titles); photographs.

Messner, Johnny (bandleader/clarinet/singer, U.S.)

7-202 Garrod, Charles. "Johnny Messner and His Orchestra." In *Art Kassel and His Orchestra; Plus: Johnny Messner and His Orchestra*. Zephyrhills, FL: Joyce Record Club Publication, 1993. 36 pp
Not reviewed.
Index.

Meyer, Peter "Banjo" (banjo/guitar, Germany)

7-203 Bielderman, Gerard. *Peter "Banjo" Meyer Discography*. 2nd ed. Eurojazz Discos, no. 67. Zwolle, Netherlands: Gerard Bielderman, 1998. 44 pp.
Covers 1963 to 1998, with a biography in German and English. Includes unissued material. First published in 1997.
Bibliography; illustrations; indexes (musicians, releases, song titles); photographs.

Miller, Glenn (trombone/bandleader, U.S.)

7-204 Garrod, Charles. *Glenn Miller and His Orchestra*. 3 vols. Zephyrhills, FL: Joyce Record Club Publication, 1995. 104 pp. (vol. 1); 94 pp. (vol. 2); 72 pp. (vol. 3).
Not reviewed. Volume 1 covers 1935 to 1940; volume 2 covers 1941 to 1942; and volume 3 ("The Air Force Band") covers 1943 to 1944.
Index.

Millinder, Lucky (bandleader, U.S.)

7-205 Garrod, Charles. "Lucky Millinder and His Orchestra." In *Tiny Bradshaw and His Orchestra; Plus: Lucky Millinder and His Orchestra*. Zephyrhills, FL: Joyce Record Club Publication, 1994. 31 pp.
Not reviewed.
Index.

Mills Brothers (vocal quartet, U.S.)

7-206 Garrod, Charles. *Mills Brothers*. Zephyrhills, FL: Joyce Record Club Publication, 1994. 39 pp.
Not reviewed.
Index.

Monroe, Vaughn (trumpet/singer/bandleader, U.S.)

7-207 Garrod, Charles. *Vaughn Monroe and His Orchestra.* Revised edition. Zephyrhills, FL: Joyce Record Club Publication, 1996. 93 pp.
Not reviewed. First published in 1986.
Index.

Mooney, Joe (accordion/piano, U.S.)

7-208 Salemann, Dieter. *Joe Mooney, 1911–1975: A Sunshine Boy? The Story of an Underrated Jazzman.* Berlin: Dieter Salemann, 1998. 47 pp.
Annotated bio-discography, covers 1927 to 1965. Contains unissued material.
Bibliography; illustrations; index (general); photographs.

Morel, Jean-Pierre (cornet/bandleader, France)

7-209 Bielderman, Gerard, and Aart van de Munt. *Jean-Pierre Morel Discography.* Alternate title: *Charquet & Co.* 3rd ed. Eurojazz Discos, no. 11. Zwolle, Netherlands: Gerard Bielderman, 1995. 16 pp.
Covers 1967 to 1978, with a bibliographic essay. Includes unissued material. First published in 1987.
Illustrations; indexes (releases, song titles).

Morgan, Russ (trombone/bandleader/arranger, U.S.)

7-210 Garrod, Charles. *Russ Morgan and His Orchestra.* Revised edition. Zephyrhills, FL: Joyce Record Club Publication, 1993. 83 pp.
Not reviewed.
Index.

Morks, Jan (clarinet/bandleader, Netherlands)

7-211 Bielderman, Gerard. *Jan Morks Discography.* 3rd ed. Eurojazz Discos, no. 9. Zwolle, Netherlands: Gerard Bielderman, 1996. 36 pp.
Covers 1950 to 1984, with a biography in Dutch in English. Includes unissued material. First published in 1986.
Illustrations; indexes (musicians, releases, song titles).

Morris, Sonny (cornet/trumpet/singer, UK)

7-212 Lee, Raymond. *Sonny Morris Discography.* Eurojazz Discos, no. 102. Zwolle, Netherlands: Gerard Bielderman, 1999. 36 pp.
Covers 1949 to 1999, with a biography. Contains unissued material. Formats include 78s.
Bibliography; indexes (musicians, releases, song titles); photographs.

Morrow, Buddy (trombone/bandleader, U.S.)

7-213 Garrod, Charles. *Buddy Morrow and His Orchestra*. Zephyrhills, FL: Joyce Record Club Publication, 1995. 48 pp.
   Not reviewed.
   Index.

Mulligan, Gerry (saxophone/bandleader/arranger, U.S.)

7-214 Klinkowitz, Jerome. *Listen: Gerry Mulligan; An Aural Narrative in Jazz*. New York: Schirmer Books, 1991. 306 pp.
   Annotated bio-discography covering 1945 to 1989. Includes unissued material.
   Bibliography; illustrations; index (song titles); photographs.

Mick Mulligan's Jazz Band; *see* **Melly, George**

Murphy, Rose (piano/singer, U.S.)

7-215 Brethour, Ross. *Rose Murphy Discography*. Aurora, Ontario, Canada: Ross Brethour, 1996. 18 pp.
   Covers 1942 to 1980, annotated, with a biography. Contains unissued material, transcriptions, films, and radio broadcasts. Formats include 45s.
   Illustrations; index (song titles); photographs.

Nelson, Ozzie (bandleader/reeds/singer, U.S.)

7-216 Garrod, Charles, and Bill Korst. *Ozzie Nelson and His Orchestra*. Zephyrhills, FL: Joyce Record Club Publication, 1991. 23 pp.
   Not reviewed.
   Index.

New Black Eagle Jazz Band; *see* **Pringle, Tony**

Nicholas, Albert (clarinet/saxophone, U.S.)

7-217 Dürr, Klaus-Uwe. *The Recordings of Albert Nicholas*. [Hamburg: n.p., 1994]. 47 pp.
   Not reviewed.
   Discography.

Nichols, Keith (piano, UK)

7-218 Purser, Julian, and Gerard Bielderman. *Keith Nichols Discography*. 2nd ed. Eurojazz Discos, no. 18. Zwolle, Netherlands: Gerard Bielderman, 1996. 68 pp.

Covers 1965 to 1995, with a biography by James Asman and Digby Fairweather. Includes unissued material. First published in 1993.

Bibliography; illustrations; indexes (musicians, releases, song titles); photographs.

Nichols, Red (cornet/bandleader, U.S.)

7-219 Evans, Philip R., Stanley Hester, Stephen Hester, and Linda Evans. *The Red Nichols Story: After Intermission, 1942–1965*. Studies in Jazz, no. 22. Lanham, MD: Scarecrow Press, 1997. 746 pp.

Annotated bio-discography from 1942 to 1965. Contains unissued material. Formats include 78s. Lists AFRS transcriptions and radio and television broadcasts.

Indexes (musician, song titles); photographs.

Noble, Ray (bandleader/arranger/composer, UK)

7-220 Garrod, Charles. *Ray Noble and His Orchestra*. Zephyrhills, FL: Joyce Record Club Publication, 1991. 79 pp.

Not reviewed.

Index.

Noone, Jimmie (clarinet/bandleader, U.S.)

7-221 Behncke, Bernhard H., and Klaus-Uwe Dürr. *Jimmie Noone*. Hamburg: Klaus-Uwe Dürr, 1996. 20 pp.

Bio-discography covering 1923 to 1944. Includes unissued material. "Based upon handwritten notes and a discography by the late Harm Sagawe."

Bibliography; photographs.

O'Day, Anita (singer, U.S.)

7-222 Wölfer, Jürgen. *Anita O'Day: An Exploratory Discography*. Zephyrhills, FL: Joyce Record Club Publication, 1990. 45 pp.

Covers 1941 to 1980. Includes unissued material. Contains radio broadcasts.

Bibliography; index (song titles).

Oliver, King (cornet/bandleader, U.S.)

7-223 Dürr, Klaus-Uwe. *The Recordings of Joe "King" Oliver.* Revised by Bernhard H. Behncke. Hamburg: Klaus-Uwe Dürr, 1997. 26 pp.

Covers 1923 to 1931, with biographical information based on Laurie Wright's 1984 book *"King" Oliver.* Includes unissued material. First published in 1989.

Illustrations; musical transcriptions; photographs.

Oliver, Sy (trumpet/singer/bandleader/arranger, U.S.)

7-224 Garrod, Charles. *Sy Oliver and His Orchestra.* Zephyrhills, FL: Joyce Record Club Publication, 1993. 42 pp.

Not reviewed.

Index.

Örnberg, Tomas (piano/reeds, Sweden)

7-225 Bielderman, Gerard, and Aart van de Munt. *Tomas Örnberg/Bent Persson.* Eurojazz Discos, no. 44. Zwolle, Netherlands: Gerard Bielderman, 1996. 80 pp.

Covers 1970 to 1996, with a biography. Includes unissued material.

Bibliography; illustrations; indexes (musicians, recordings, song titles); photographs.

Ory, Kid (trombone, U.S.)

7-226 Bailey, Sid. *"Greatest Slideman Ever Born": A Discography of Edward "Kid" Ory.* Foreword by Floyd Levin. West Sussex, UK: Sid Bailey, 1996. 167 pp.

Covers 1922 to 1971. Includes "Thoughts on Ory Compositions," by Geoff Cole, and interviews of George Probert and Teddy Buckner. Contains unissued material. Formats include audio cassettes and 78s.

Bibliography; illustrations; indexes (musicians, "recording sidemen," song titles); photographs.

Osborne, Will (bandleader/singer, Canada)

7-227 Garrod, Charles. *Will Osborne and His Orchestra.* Zephyrhills, FL: Joyce Record Club Publication, 1991. 28 pp.

Not reviewed.

Index.

Parker, Charlie (saxophone, U.S.)

7-228 Bregman, Robert, Leonard Bukowski, and Norman Saks. *Charlie Parker Discography.* Redwood, NY: Cadence Jazz Books, 1993. 88 pp.
   Covers 1940 to 1954. Contains unissued material. Lists radio and television broadcasts.
   Indexes.

7-229 Komara, Edward M. *The Dial Recordings of Charlie Parker: A Discography.* Westport, CT: Greenwood Press, 1998. 232 pp.
   Covers 1946 to 1947, annotated. Provides analysis of the ten sessions Parker made with Dial Records. Includes "the repertory, original issues and reissues, titles and notated transcriptions, and analyses of performances. Commentary explains many of the titles to Parker's pieces and collates the various recordings in which he performed his Dial repertory outside the confines of the Dial studios." Contains unissued material.
   Bibliography; indexes (names, song titles, transcriptions); musical transcriptions.

Parker, Evan (saxophone, UK)

7-230 Martinelli, Francesco. *Evan Parker Discography.* Pisa, Italy: Bandecchi and Vivaldi editore, 1994. 57 pp.
   Covers 1968 to 1994. Formats include EPs. Contains unissued material.
   Bibliography; indexes (musicians, releases).

Parker, Johnny (piano, UK)

7-231 Bielderman, Gerard. *Johnny Parker Discography.* 2nd edition. Eurojazz Discos, no. 10. Zwolle, Netherlands: Gerard Bielderman, 1994. 60 pp.
   Covers 1950 to 1994, with a biography. Includes unissued material. First published in 1987.
   Bibliography; illustrations; indexes (musicians, releases, song titles); photographs.

Pastor, Tony (saxophone/singer/bandleader, U.S.)

7-232 Garrod, Charles. *Tony Pastor and His Orchestra.* Revised edition. Zephyrhills, FL: Joyce Record Club Publication, 1997. 52 pp.
   Not reviewed.
   Index.

Paxton, George (saxophone/bandleader, U.S.)

7-233 Garrod, Charles. "George Paxton and His Orchestra." In *Will Hudson and His Orchestra; The Hudson-Delange Orchestra; Eddie Delange and His Orchestra; George Paxton and His Orchestra; Bob Strong and His Orchestra.* Zephyrhills, FL: Joyce Record Club Publication, 1993. 39 pp.
  Not reviewed.
  Index.

Pee Dee Jazzband (band, Denmark)

7-234 Bielderman, Gerard, and Erwin Elvers. "Discography of the Pee Dee Jazz Band." In *Discography of Danish Traditional Jazz Bands, vol. 1: Bourbon Street Jazzband 1975–1998; Gentlemen of Jazz 1989–1998; Pee Dee Jazzband 1988–1999; Vestre Jazzværk 1979–1997.* Eurojazz Discos, no. 103. Zwolle, Netherlands: Gerard Bielderman, 1999. pp. 18–24.
  Covers 1988 to 1999. Includes unissued material but no reissues.
  Indexes (album titles, song titles); photographs.

Persson, Bent (cornet, Sweden)

7-235 Bielderman, Gerard, and Aart van de Munt. *Tomas Örnberg/Bent Persson.* Eurojazz Discos, no. 44. Zwolle, Netherlands: Gerard Bielderman, 1996. 80 pp.
  Covers 1970 to 1996, with a biography. Includes unissued material.
  Bibliography; illustrations; indexes (musicians, releases, song titles); photographs.

Peruna Jazzmen (band, Denmark)

7-236 Bielderman, Gerard, and Aart van de Munt. *Discography Peruna Jazzmen.* Eurojazz Discos, no. 52. Zwolle, Netherlands: Gerard Bielderman, 1997. 28 pp.
  Covers 1963 to 1996, with a band profile. Includes unissued material.
  Bibliography; indexes (musicians, releases, song titles).

Petters, John (drums, UK)

7-237 Bielderman, Gerard. *John Petters Discography.* Eurojazz Discos, no. 58. Zwolle, Netherlands: Gerard Bielderman, 1999. 28 pp.
  Covers 1977 to 1999, with a biography. Contains unissued material. First published in 1997.
  Illustrations; indexes (musicians, releases, song titles); photographs.

Pettiford, Oscar (bass, U.S.)

7-238 Gazdar, Coover. *First Bass: The Oscar Pettiford Discography.* Bangalore, India: Coover Gazdar, 1991. 84 pp.

Annotated discography covering 1940 to 1960. Contains unissued material. Includes "Pettiford on Film."

Bibliography; indexes (musicians, song titles); photographs.

Pointon, Mike (trombone/singer, UK)

7-239 Bielderman, Gerard. *Mike Pointon Discography.* Eurojazz Discos, no. 95. Zwolle, Netherlands: Gerard Bielderman, 1999. 32 pp.

Covers 1960 to 1998, with a biography. Contains unissued material. Formats include audio cassettes and videotapes.

Bibliography; indexes (musicians, releases, song titles); photographs.

Powell, Bud (piano/composer, U.S.)

7-240 Smith, Carl. *Bouncing with Bud: All the Recordings of Bud Powell.* Brunswick, ME: Biddle Publishing, 1997. 175 pp.

Annotated discography covering 1944 to 1966, with a biography by Mark Gardner. Includes "A Tribute to Bud," by Francis Paudras.

Bibliography; index (recordings).

Powell, Teddy (guitar/bandleader, U.S.)

7-241 Garrod, Charles, and Bill Korst. *Teddy Powell and His Orchestra.* Revised edition. Zephyrhills, FL: Joyce Record Club Publication, 1990. 30 pp.

Not reviewed. First published in 1974.

Index.

Prima, Louis (trumpet/singer/bandleader, U.S.)

7-242 Garrod, Charles. *Louis Prima and His Orchestra.* Zephyrhills, FL: Joyce Record Club Publication, 1991. 40 pp.

Not reviewed.

Index.

Pringle, Tony (cornet/bandleader, UK)

7-243 Lee, Raymond, and Gerard Bielderman. *Tony Pringle Discography, Incorporating the New Black Eagle Jazz Band.* 3rd edition. Eurojazz Discos, no. 31. Zwolle, Netherlands: Gerard Bielderman, 1999. 40 pp.

Covers 1971 to 1998, with a biography. Contains unissued material. Formats include audio cassettes and videotapes. First published in 1993.
 Bibliography; illustrations; indexes (musicians, releases, song titles).

Raeburn, Boyd (saxophone/bandleader, U.S.)

7-244 Garrod, Charles, and Bill Korst. "Boyd Raeburn and His Orchestra." In *Boyd Raeburn and His Orchestra; Plus: Johnny Bothwell and George Handy.* Revised edition. Zephyrhills, FL: Joyce Record Club Publication, 1997. 39 pp.
 Not reviewed. First published in 1985.
 Index.

Randall, Freddy (trumpet/cornet, UK)

7-245 Bielderman, Gerard, and Ray Stansby. *Freddy Randall Discography.* 3rd ed. Eurojazz Discos, no. 14. Zwolle, Netherlands: Gerard Bielderman, 1995. 28 pp.
 Covers 1944 to 1982, with a biography. Includes unissued material.
 Bibliography; illustrations; indexes (musicians, releases, song titles); photographs.

Ravazza, Carl (violin/singer/bandleader, U.S.)

7-246 Garrod, Charles. "Carl Ravazza and His Orchestra." In *Clyde Lucas and His Orchestra; Plus: Al Kavelin and His Orchestra; Carl Ravazza and His Orchestra; Ted Straeter and His Orchestra.* Zephyrhills, FL: Joyce Record Club Publication, 1995. 40 pp.
 Not reviewed.
 Index.

Reunion Jazz Band (band, Netherlands)

7-247 Bielderman, Gerard. "Discography of the Reunion Jazz Band." In *Discography of Dutch Traditional Jazz Bands, vol. 1: Eric Krans' Dixieland Pipers 1950–1963; Bert de Kort's Dixieland Pipers 1977–1985; Harbour Jazz Band 1967–1996; Reunion Jazz Band 1966–1998; Revival Jassband 1977–1993.* Eurojazz Discos, no. 82. Zwolle, Netherlands: Gerard Bielderman, 1998. 1:25–31.
 1966–1998. Includes unissued material.
 Bibliography; indexes (album titles, song titles); photographs.

Revival Jassband (band, Netherlands)

7-248 Bielderman, Gerard. "Discography of the Revival Jassband." In *Discography of Dutch Traditional Jazz Bands, vol. 1: Eric Krans' Dixieland Pipers 1950–1963; Bert de Kort's Dixieland Pipers 1977–1985; Harbour Jazz Band 1967–1996; Reunion Jazz Band 1966–1998; Revival Jassband 1977–1993.* Eurojazz Discos, no. 82. Zwolle, Netherlands: Gerard Bielderman, 1998. pp. 32–39.

Covers 1977 to 1993. Includes unissued material but no reissues.

Bibliography; indexes (album titles, song titles); photographs).

Rey, Alvino (bandleader/guitar, U.S.)

7-249 Garrod, Charles, and Bill Korst. "Alvino Rey and His Orchestra." In *Alvino Rey and His Orchestra; Plus: The King Sisters 1939–1958.* Revised edition. Zephyrhills, FL: Joyce Record Club Publication, 1997. 37 pp.

Not reviewed. First published in 1986.

Index.

Rich, Buddy (drums, U.S.)

7-250 Meriwether, Doug. *Mister, I Am the Band! Buddy Rich, His Life and Travels.* Discography by Clarence C. Hintze. North Bellmore, NY: National Drum Association, 1998. 435 pp.

Bio-discography covering 1930 to 1987. Contains unissued material. Formats include audio cassettes and videocassettes. Lists transcriptions.

Index; photographs.

Richards, Johnny (arranger, U.S.)

7-251 Hartley, Jack, and Jürgen Wölfer. *Johnny Richards: The Definitive Bio-Discography.* Lake Geneva, WI: Balboa Books, 1998. 116 pp.

Covers 1937 to 1968, with a short biography. Includes recordings of Richards' music by others from 1971 to 1998, and recordings of "Young at Heart" from 1953 to 1998. Contains unissued material.

Bibliography; illustrations; index (song titles); notes.

Rimington, Sammy (clarinet/saxophone, UK)

7-252 Bielderman, Gerard. *Sammy Rimington Discography.* 6th ed. Eurojazz Discos, no. 2. Zwolle, Netherlands: Gerard Bielderman, 1998. 76 pp.

Covers 1959 to 1997, with a short biography from John Chilton's *Who's Who of British Jazz.*

Bibliography; illustrations; indexes (musicians, releases, song titles); photographs.

Roberscheuten, Frank (reeds, Netherlands)

7-253 Bielderman, Gerard. *Frank Roberscheuten Discography.* Eurojazz Discos, no. 85. Zwolle, Netherlands: Gerard Bielderman, 1998. 32 pp.
 Covers 1984 to 1998, with a biography in English and Dutch. Includes unissued material.
 Bibliography; illustrations; indexes (musicians, releases, song titles); photographs.

Robinson, Jim (trombone, U.S.)

7-254 Lee, Raymond. *Big Jim: A Discography of Jim Robinson.* Sounds of New Orleans, no. 4. Zwolle, Netherlands: Gerard Bielderman, 1998. 104 pp.
 Covers 1927 to 1976, with a biography by Brian Wood. Contains unissued material. Formats include videotapes.
 Illustrations; indexes (musicians, releases, song titles).

Robison, Willard (piano/bandleader, U.S.)

7-255 Boyd, Brian G. *Willard Robison and His Piano: A Discography.* Toronto: Brian G. Boyd, 1990. 34 pp.
 Covers 1924 to 1937, with a biographical sketch. Includes unissued material.
 Bibliography; illustrations; notes; photographs.

Rosolino, Frank (trombone, U.S.)

7-256 Decaens, Jean-Loup. *Frank Rosolino: une discographie/A Discography.* Saint-Leu-d'Esserent, France: J.-L. Decaens, 1998. 446 pp.
 Covers 1949 to 1978. In French and English.
 Bibliography; index.

Russell, Pee Wee (clarinet, U.S.)

7-257 Hilbert, Robert. *Pee Wee Speaks: A Discography of Pee Wee Russell.* With David Niven. Studies in Jazz, no. 13. Metuchen, NJ: Scarecrow Press, 1992. 377 pp.
 Covers 1922 to 1968. Includes unissued material. Lists film soundtracks, radio and TV broadcasts, and concerts.
 Illustrations; index; photographs.

Saints Jazz Band (band, UK)

7-258 Bielderman, Gerard. "Saints Jazz Band Discography." In *Discography of British Traditional Jazz Bands/Musicians, vol. 1: Avon Cities Skiffle Group 1956–1958; Avon Cities [Jazz Band] 1956–1997; Dick Charlesworth 1957–1994; Clyde Valley Stompers 1956–1983; Saints Jazz Band 1956–1983*. 2nd ed. Eurojazz Discos, no. 72. Zwolle, Netherlands: Gerard Bielderman, 1999.

Covers 1950 to 1962. Includes unissued material. First published in 1997.

Bibliography; indexes (album titles, song titles).

Sarpila, Antti (clarinet/saxophone, Finland)

7-259 Westerberg, Hans. *The Swinging Beginning: An Antti Sarpila Bio/Discography; Recordings 1981–1998*. Introduction by Risto Ennekari. Helsinki: Hans Westerberg, 1999. 193 pp.

Bio-discography covering 1981 to 1998, in Finnish and English. Lists radio and TV broadcasts.

Index.

Savannah Jazz Band (band, UK)

7-260 Bielderman, Gerard. "Discography of the Savannah Jazz Band." In *Discography of British Traditional Jazz Bands/Musicians, vol. 3: Denise Lawrence & Storyville Tickle 1984–1997; The Savannah Jazz Band 1988–1997; Jim Shelley's (Frisco) Jazz Band 1976–1997*. Eurojazz Discos, no. 79. Zwolle, Netherlands: Gerard Bielderman, 1997. pp. 13–23.

Covers 1988 to 1997. Contains unissued material but no reissues. Formats include audio cassettes.

Bibliography; illustrations; indexes (album titles, song titles).

Savitt, Jan (violin/singer/bandleader/arranger, Russia)

7-261 Hall, George. *Jan Savitt and His Orchestra*. Revised by Charles Garrod. Zephyrhills, FL: Joyce Record Club Publication, 1992. 35 pp.

Not reviewed. First published in 1974.

Index.

Scott, Raymond (composer/bandleader, U.S.)

7-262 Garrod, Charles. *Raymond Scott and His Orchestra*. Revised edition. Portland, OR: Joyce Record Club Publication, 1999. 56 pp.

Not reviewed. First published in 1988.

Index.

Semple, Archie (cornet/clarinet/bandleader, UK)

7-263 Simpson, Norman, and Gerard Bielderman. *Archie Semple Discography*. Eurojazz Discos, no. 66. Zwolle, Netherlands: Gerard Bielderman, 1997. 40 pp.

Covers 1951 to 1964, with a biography. Includes unissued material.

Bibliography; indexes (musicians, releases, song titles); photographs.

Jim Shelley's Jazz Band & Frisco Jazz Band (band, UK)

7-264 Bielderman, Gerard. "Discography of Jim Shelley's Jazz Band & Frisco Jazz Band." In *Discography of British Traditional Jazz Bands/Musicians, vol. 3: Denise Lawrence & Storyville Tickle 1984–1997; The Savannah Jazz Band 1988–1997; Jim Shelley's (Frisco) Jazz Band 1976–1997*. Eurojazz Discos, no. 79. Zwolle, Netherlands: Gerard Bielderman, 1997. pp. 24–26.

Covers 1976 to 1995. Contains unissued material but no reissues. Formats include audio cassettes.

Bibliography; indexes (album titles, song titles).

Shepherd, Dave (clarinet, UK)

7-265 Stanley, Ray, and Gerard Bielderman. *Dave Shepherd Discography*. Eurojazz Discos, no. 48. Zwolle, Netherlands: Gerard Bielderman, 1996. 24 pp.

Covers 1951 to 1994, with a biography.

Bibliography; indexes (musicians, releases, song titles); photographs.

Sherwood, Bobby (bandleader/trumpet, U.S.)

7-266 Garrod, Charles, and Bill Korst. "Bobby Sherwood." In *Bobby Sherwood and His Orchestra; Also Randy Brooks and His Orchestra*. 2nd ed. Portland, OR: Joyce Record Club Publication, 1999. 43 pp.

Not reviewed. First published in 1999.

Index.

Shoffner, Bob (trumpet, U.S.)

7-267 Dürr, Klaus-Uwe. *The Recordings of Bob Shoffner*. 2nd edition. Hamburg: Klaus-Uwe Dürr, 1997. 15 pp.

Covers 1925 to 1965. Contains unissued material. Includes "A Conversation with Bob Shoffner."

Notes; photographs.

Sims, Ken (trumpet/cornet, UK)

7-268 Bielderman, Gerard. *Ken Sims Discography.* Eurojazz Discos, no. 101. Zwolle, Netherlands: Gerard Bielderman, 1999. 28 pp.

Covers 1957 to 1999, with a biography. Contains unissued material. Formats include audio cassettes.

Bibliography; indexes (musicians, releases, song titles); photographs.

Sinatra, Frank (singer, U.S.)

7-269 Garrod, Charles. *Frank Sinatra, 1952–1981: Vol. 2.* Zephyrhills, FL: Joyce Record Club Publication, 1990. 93 pp.

Covers 1952 to 1981. Lists radio and TV broadcasts. Contains unissued material. Volume 1 (1935–1951) published in 1989.

Index (song titles).

7-270 Sayers, Scott P., and Ed O'Brien. *Sinatra: The Man and His Music; The Recording Artistry of Francis Albert Sinatra, 1939–1992.* Austin, TX: TSD Press, 1992. 303 pp.

Covers 1939 to 1992. Contains unissued material. Includes "Sinatra Conducts." Lists V Discs and films.

Illustrations; index (song titles); photographs.

Slack, Freddie (piano/bandleader, U.S.)

7-271 Garrod, Charles. "Freddie Slack and His Orchestra." In *Will Bradley and His Orchestra; Plus: Freddie Slack and His Orchestra.* [not reviewed]. First Published in 1926. Revised edition. Zephyrhills, FL: Joyce Record Club Publication, 1997. 32 pp.

Index.

Smith, Jabbo (cornet/trumpet/singer, U.S.)

7-272 Dürr, Klaus-Uwe. *The Recordings of Jabbo Smith.* 2nd edition. Hamburg: Klaus-Uwe Dürr, 1997. 22 pp.

Covers 1926 to 1983. Includes reminiscences by Smith. Includes unissued material. First published in 1995.

Photographs.

Smith, Keith (trumpet, UK)

7-273 Bielderman, Gerard. *Keith Smith Discography.* Eurojazz Discos, no. 45. Zwolle, Netherlands: Gerard Bielderman, 1995. 32 pp.

Covers 1960 to 1991, with a biography. Contains unissued material.
Bibliography; illustrations; indexes (musicians, releases, song titles); photographs.

Smith, Ray (piano, UK)

7-274 Bielderman, Gerard. *Ray Smith Discography.* 3rd ed. Eurojazz Discos, no. 26. Zwolle, Netherlands: Gerard Bielderman, 1996. 44 pp.
Covers 1961 to 1996. Includes unissued materials. First published in 1992.
Bibliography; indexes (musicians, releases, song titles); photographs.

Smith, Stuff (violin, U.S.)

7-275 Barnett, Anthony. *Desert Sands: The Recordings & Performances of Stuff Smith; An Annotated Discography & Biographical Source Book.* Lewes, UK: Allardyce, Barnett, 1996. 348 pp.
Covers 1932 to 1967, annotated. Includes unissued material. Appendixes detail Smith's unrecorded compositions and recordings of his compositions by other musicians.
Bibliography; illustrations; indexes (musicans, song titles); musical transcriptions; photographs.

7-276 ———. *Up Jumped the Devil: The Supplement to Desert Sands; The Recordings & Performances of Stuff Smith; An Annotated Discography & Biographical Source Book.* Lewes, UK: Allardyce, 1998. 94 pp.
"Corrections and additions to *Desert Sands.*"
Illustrations; photographs.

7-277 McNeil. W. K., and Louis Hatchett. *Stuff Smith Discography.* Portland, OR: Joyce Record Club Publication, 1999. 73 pp.
Not reviewed.
Index.

Snow, Michael (piano/trumpet/composer, Canada)

7-278 Snow, Michael, ed. *Music/Sound, 1948–1993: The Performed and Recorded Music/Sound of Michael Snow, Solo and with Various Ensembles, His Sound-Films and Sound Installations; Improvisation/Composition from 1948 to 1993.* Discography by Raymond Gervais. Toronto: Alfred A. Knopf Canada, [1994]. 302 pp.
Bio-discography.
Photographs.

South, Eddie (violin, U.S.)

7-279 Barnett, Anthony. *Black Gypsy: The Recordings of Eddie South; An Annotated Discography & Itinerary.* Foreword by Leroy Jenkins. Lewes, UK: Allardyce, 1999. 123 pp.
Covers 1923 to 1959, annotated. Includes unissued material.
Bibliography; indexes (musicians, song titles); musical transcriptions; photographs.

Spanier, Muggsy (cornet, U.S.)

7-280 Whyatt, Bert. *Muggsy Spanier, the Lonesome Road: A Biography and Discography.* New Orleans: Jazzology Press, 1995. 236 pp.
Bio-discography covering 1924 to 1964. Includes unissued material. Appendixes: "Listing of Muggsy Spanier Composer Credits" and "Example of Band Arrangements."
Indexes (bands, musicians, song titles); musical transcriptions; photographs.

Spivak, Charlie (bandleader/trumpet, U.S.)

7-281 Garrod, Charles. *Charlie Spivak and His Orchestra.* Revised edition. Zephyrhills, FL: Joyce Record Club Publication, 1996. 63 pp.
Not reviewed. First published in 1972.
Index.

Stacy, Jess (piano, U.S.)

7-282 Coller, Derek. *Jess Stacy: The Quiet Man of Jazz; A Biography and Discography.* New Orleans: Jazzology Press, 1997. 298 pp.
Bio-discography from 1926 to 1982. Lists recordings, radio and TV broadcasts. Contains unissued material. Appendixes include "Listing of Stacy Associates"; "The Stacy Style," by John Steiner; "Compositions."
Indexes (discography, biography); photographs.

Storyville Jassband (band, Netherlands)

7-283 Bielderman, Gerard. "Discography of the Storyville Jassband." In *Discography of Dutch Traditional Jazz Bands, vol. 2: Circus Square Jazz Band 1968–1995; Storyville Jassband 1968–1995; Freetime Old Dixie Jassband 1975–1995; Charlestown Jazzband 1971–1998.* Eurojazz Discos, no. 93. Zwolle, Netherlands: Gerard Bielderman, 1999. pp. 15–23.
Covers 1968 to 1995. Includes unissued material.
Bibliography; indexes (album titles, song titles).

Straeter, Ted (piano/bandleader, U.S.)

7-284 Garrod, Charles. "Ted Straeter and His Orchestra." In *Clyde Lucas and His Orchestra; Plus: Al Kavelin and His Orchestra; Carl Ravazza and His Orchestra; Ted Straeter and His Orchestra.* Zephyrhills, FL: Joyce Record Club Publication, 1995. 40 pp.
   Not reviewed.
   Index.

Strandberg, Paul (cornet/trumpet, Sweden)

7-285 Bielderman, Gerard. *Paul Strandberg Discography.* Eurojazz Discos, no. 75. Zwolle, Netherlands: Gerard Bielderman, 1997. 24 pp.
   Covers 1977 to 1997, with a biography. Formats include audio cassettes. No unissued material.
   Bibliography; indexes (musicians, releases, song titles); photographs.

Strange, Pete (trombone, UK)

7-286 Simpson, Norman. *Pete Strange Discography.* Eurojazz Discos, no. 81. Zwolle, Netherlands: Gerard Bielderman, 1998. 44 pp.
   Covers 1956 to 1998, with a biography. Includes unissued material.
   Bibliography; illustrations; indexes (musicians, releases, song titles); photographs.

Strong, Bob (saxophone/bandleader, U.S.)

7-287 Garrod, Charles. "Bob Strong and His Orchestra." In *Will Hudson and His Orchestra; The Hudson-Delange Orchestra; Eddie Delange and His Orchestra; Bob Strong and His Orchestra.* Zephyrhills, FL: Joyce Record Club Publication, 1993. 39 pp.
   Not reviewed.
   Index

Sun Ra (keyboards/bandleader/composer, U.S.)

7-288 Campbell, Robert L. *The Earthly Recordings of Sun Ra.* Redwood, NY: Cadence Jazz Books, 1994. 252 pp.
   Covers Sun Ra as "leader, arranger, or sideman" from 1946 to 1993. Formats include singles, audio cassettes, videocassettes. Lists films, TV, and radio broadcasts.
   Bibliography; indexes (film/video, musicians, releases, song titles).

7-289 Geerken, Hartmut, and Bernhard Hefele. *Omniverse Sun Ra: Comprehensive Pictorial and Annotated Discography*. Wartaweil, Germany: Waitawhile, 1994. 250 pp.

Covers 1946 to 1992, annotated, with biography. Contains essays by Robert L. Campbell, Sigrid Hauff, Chris Cutler, Robert Lax, Salah Ragab, Karl Heinz Kessler, and Gabi Geist. Includes unissued material.

Bibliography; filmography; indexes (compositions, instruments, musicians, releases); photographs; tapeography.

Sunshine, Monty (clarinet/bandleader, UK)

7-290 Bielderman Gerard. *Monty Sunshine Discography*. 2nd edition. Eurojazz Discos, no. 36. Zwolle, Netherlands: Gerard Bielderman, 1995. 68 pp.

Covers 1949 to 1994, with a biography. Contains unissued material. First published in 1994.

Bibliography; illustrations; indexes (musicians, releases, song titles); photographs.

Swift, Duncan (trombone, UK)

7-291 Griffiths, David. *Duncan Swift Discography*. Eurojazz Discos, no. 88. Zwolle, Netherlands: Gerard Bielderman, 1998. 32 pp.

Covers 1961 to 1996, with a biography by Bev Pegg and Roy Hubbard. Formats include audio cassettes. Lists radio and TV broadcasts. Contains unissued material.

Bibliography; indexes (musicians, releases, song titles); photographs.

Swiss Dixie Stompers (band, Switzerland)

7-292 Elvers, Erwin, and Gerard Bielderman. *Discography Swiss Dixie Stompers*. Eurojazz Discos, no. 47. Zwolle, Netherlands: Gerard Bielderman, 1997. 24 pp.

Covers 1964 to 1997, with a band history by Walter Hesse in Swiss and English. No unissued material. Formats include audio cassettes.

Bibliography; indexes (musicians, releases, song titles); photographs.

Teagarden, Jack (trombone/bandleader, U.S.)

7-293 Garrod, Charles. *Jack Teagarden and His Orchestra*. Zephyrhills, FL: Joyce Record Club Publication, 1993. 47 pp.

Covers 1930 to 1963, with a brief biography. Lists airchecks. Contains unissued material.
Index (song titles).

Thornhill, Claude (piano/composer/arranger/bandleader, U.S.)

7-294 Garrod, Charles. *Claude Thornhill and His Orchestra.* Revised edition. Zephyrhills, FL: Joyce Record Club Publication, 1996. 49 pp.
Not reviewed. First published in 1985.
Index.

Timmons, Bobby (piano/composer, U.S.)

7-295 Schlouch, Claude. *Bobby Timmons: A Discography.* Marseilles, France: Claude Schlouch, 1999.
Covers 1956 to 1998. Lists radio broadcasts.
Indexes (musicians, releases, song titles).

Tremble Kids; *see* Keller, Werner

Trumbauer, Frank (saxophone, U.S.)

7-296 Evans, Philip R., and Larry F. Kiner. *Tram: The Frank Trumbauer Story.* With William Trumbauer. Studies in Jazz, no. 18. Metuchen, NJ: Scarecrow Press, 1994. 821 pp.
Bio-discography from 1923 to 1937. Lists airchecks and radio broadcasts. Contains unissued material.
Bibliography; chronology; index (song titles); photographs.

Tucker, Orrin (bandleader/saxophone, U.S.)

7-297 Garrod, Charles. *Orrin Tucker and His Orchestra.* Zephyrhills, FL: Joyce Record Club Publication, 1992. 27 pp.
Not reviewed.
Index.

Tucker, Tommy (bandleader/piano/singer, U.S.)

7-298 Garrod, Charles. *Tommy Tucker and His Orchestra.* Zephyrhills, FL: Joyce Record Club Publication, 1990. 29 pp.
Not reviewed.
Index.

Turnock, Brian (bass, UK)

7-299 Lee, Raymond. *Brian Turnock Discography.* Eurojazz Discos, no. 97. Zwolle, Netherlands: Gerard Bielderman, 1999. 52 pp.
Discography.

Vaughan, Sarah (singer, U.S.)

7-300 Brown, Denis. *Sarah Vaughan: A Discography.* Discographies, no. 47. Westport, CT: Greenwood Press, 1991. 167 pp.
Covers 1944 to 1988. Formats include 78s, 45s, EPs. Contains unissued material.
Bibliography; index (musicians).

Venuti, Joe (violin /bandleader, U.S.)

7-301 Garrod, Charles. *Joe Venuti and His Orchestra.* Zephyrhills, FL: Joyce Record Club Publication, 1993. 41 pp.
Not reviewed.
Index.

Vestre Jazzværk (band, Denmark)

7-302 Elvers, Erwin, and Gerard Bielderman. "Discography of Vestre Jazzværk." In *Discography of Danish Traditional Jazz Bands, vol. 1: Bourbon Street Jazzband 1975–1998; Gentlemen of Jazz 1989–1998; Pee Dee Jazzband 1988–1999; Vestre Jazzværk 1979–1997.* Eurojazz Discos, no. 103. Zwolle, Netherlands: Gerard Bielderman, 1999. pp. 25–32.
Covers 1979 to 1992. No unissued material or reissues.
Indexes (album titles, song titles).

Waller, Fats (piano/singer/composer, U.S.)

7-303 Wright, Laurie. *"Fats" in Fact: With a Memoir by Ernie Anderson.* Chigwell, UK: Storyville Publications, 1992. 552 pp.
Bio-discography. Lists onlys 78-rpm issues. Includes list of Waller's compositions.
Illustrations; indexes (musicians, song titles); musical transcriptions; photographs.

Wallis, Bob (trumpet, UK)

7-304 Bielderman, Gerard. *Bob Wallis Discography.* 3rd ed. Eurojazz Discos, no. 27. Zwolle, Netherlands: Gerard Bielderman, 1998. 28 pp.

Covers 1955 to 1985, with a biography. Formats include 78s. First published in 1992.

Bibliography; illustrations; indexes (musicians, releases, song titles); photographs.

Webb, Chick (bandleader/drums, U.S.)

7-305 Garrod, Charles. "Chick Webb." In *Chick Webb and His Orchestra: Including Ella Fitzgerald and Her Orchestra*. Zephyrhills, FL: Joyce Record Club Publication, 1993. 27 pp.

Not reviewed.

Index.

Webster, Ben (saxophone, U.S.)

7-306 Langhorn, Peter, and Thorbjørn Sjøgren. *Ben: The Music of Ben Webster; A Discography*. Copenhagen: JazzFormats, 1996. 288 pp.

Covers 1931 to 1973. Lists radio broadcasts and films. Includes unissued material.

Indexes (musicians, song titles).

Weems, Ted (bandleader/trombone/violin, U.S.)

7-307 Garrod, Charles. *Ted Weems and His Orchestra*. Contributions by Bill Binder. Zephyrhills, FL: Joyce Record Club Publication, 1993. 27 pp.

Not reviewed.

Index.

Welsh, Alex (trumpet, UK)

7-308 Bielderman, Gerard. *Alex Welsh Discography*. 3rd ed. Eurojazz Discos, no. 20. Zwolle, Netherlands: Gerard Bielderman, 1997. 36 pp.

Covers 1952 to 1977, with a biography by Norman Simpson. Includes unissued material. First published in 1990.

Bibliography; illustrations; indexes (musicians, releases, song titles); photographs.

West Jesmond Rhythm Kings; *see* Durham, Mike

White, Brian (clarinet/bandleader, UK)

7-309 Bielderman, Gerard. *Brian White Discography*. Eurojazz Discos, no. 56. Zwolle, Netherlands: Gerard Bielderman, 1996. 28 pp.

Covers 1956 to 1993, with a biography. Formats include 78s and audio cassettes. Contains unissued material.
Bibliography; indexes (musicians, releases, song titles); photographs.

Wiley, Lee (singer, U.S.)

7-310 Selk, Len, and Gus Kuhlman. *Lee Wiley: A Bio-Discography.* Riverdale, NY: Len Selk, 1997. 68 pp.
Covers 1931 to 1972. Includes unissued material. Lists radio and TV broadcasts. Includes previously published material.
Index (general).

Williams, Roy (trombone/singer, UK)

7-311 Simpson, Norman, and Gerard Bielderman. *Roy Williams Discography, 1956–1997.* 3rd ed. Eurojazz Discos, no. 22. Zwolle, Netherlands: Gerard Bielderman, 1998. 68 pp.
Covers 1956 to 1997, with a biography. Includes unissued material. First published in 1991.
Bibliography; indexes (musicians, releases, song titles); photographs.

Young, Lester (saxophone, U.S.)

7-312 Büchmann-Møller, Frank. *You Got to Be Original, Man! The Music of Lester Young.* Foreword by Lewis Porter. Discographies, no. 33. Westport, CT: Greenwood Press, 1990. 528 pp.
Annotated solography, with in-depth solo analysis, from 1936 to 1958. Includes unissued material. Lists concerts and radio and TV broadcasts.
Indexes (transcribed solos, song titles); musical transcriptions.

7-313 Koster, Piet, and Harm Mobach. *Lestorian Notes: A Discography and Bibliography of Lester Young.* Amsterdam: Micrography, 1998. 487 pp.
Covers 1936 to 1959, with a brief biographical sketch. Contains unissued material. Formats include 78s. Lists radio and TV broadcasts.
Bibliography; indexes (musicians, releases, song titles).

Zenith Hot Stompers (band, UK)

7-314 Hubbard, Roy, and Gerard Bielderman. *Zenith Hot Stompers Discography.* 2nd ed. Eurojazz Discos, no. 64. Zwolle, Netherlands: Gerard Bielderman, 1998. 24 pp.
Covers 1966 to 1998, with band profile. Includes unissued material. First published in 1997.
Indexes (releases, song titles).

COMPREHENSIVE

7-315 Bruyninckx, Walter. *70 Years of Recorded Jazz.* 39 vols. Mechelen, Belgium: Walter Bruyninckx, 1991.

Discography, alphabetical by artist. Coverage extends into the 1990s, depending on the volume. Contains unissued material.

Index (published separately).

7-316 Lord, Tom. *The Jazz Discography.* 22 vols. West Vancouver, British Columbia, Canada: Lord Music Reference, 1992–1999.

Covers 1896 to 1999. Arranged alphabetically by musician or band. Contains unissued material. Available on CD-ROM as well as online subscription, at www.lordisco.com.

7-317 Raben, Erik, ed. *Jazz Records 1942–80.* Vol. 4, *Cla–Da.* Vol. 5, *Dav–El.* Vol. 7, *Ell–Fra.* Copenhagen: JazzFormats, 1993–1999. 854 pp. (vol. 4); 854 pp. (vol. 5); 655 pp. (vol. 7).

Volume 4 spans the Clayton Brothers to Mel Davis. Volume 5 spans Michael "Rambler" Davis to Roddy Elias. Volume 7 spans Harvey Ellington to Simon Frazier. Lists live recordings, broadcasts, and transcriptions. Includes "Selective Listing of Basic Original Issued Albums." For volume 6, which is dedicated entirely to Duke Ellington, *see* "Ellington, Duke" in this chapter above.

Bibliography; index (musicians).

GEOGRAPHICAL

7-318 Bergh, Johs, and Jan Evensmo. *Jazz Tenor Saxophone in Norway, 1917–1959.* Oslo: Norwegian Jazz Archives, 1996. 90 pp.

Formats include audio cassettes, reel-to-reel tapes, 78s, and 45s. Lists airshots. Contains unissued material. Includes "Norwegian Tenor Saxophone Appearances on LP" and "Norwegian Tenor Saxophone Appearances on CD."

7-319 Brard, Olivier, and Daniel Nevers. *Le jazz en France: Jazz and Hot Dance Music Discography.* Selection 3. Translated by Laurel R. Wright. Paris: Musiques Archives Documents, 1991. [unpaged].

Covers 1907 to 1985, in English and French, with notes in English. Alphabetical by artist. Includes unissued material. Selections (volumes) 1 and 2 published in 1989.

7-320 Huggard, Dennis O. *Catalogue of the National Jazz Festival Recordings, Tauranga.* 3rd ed. Auckland, New Zealand: Dennis O. Huggard, 1997. 31 pp.

Covers the National Jazz Festival held in Tauranga, New Zealand, from 1964 to 1987.
Illustrations; photographs.

7-321 ———. *Discographical Listing of Jazz Recordings of New Zealand, 1930–1980.* **3rd ed. Auckland, New Zealand: Dennis O. Huggard, 1997. 62 pp.**
Alphabetical by artist. Formats include acetates and audio cassettes. No unissued material or reissues.
Illustrations.

7-322   Pernet, Robert. *Belgian Jazz Discography.* **Brussels: Robert Pernet, 1999. 832 pp.**
Covers 1897 to 1999. Alphabetical by musician. Includes a list of Belgian jazz compositions from the 1920s and 1930s. Contains unissued material.
Bibliography; illustrations; index (musicians).

7-323   Suzuki, Naoki. *Jazz on Japanese TV: Jan.–Dec. 1990.* **Fujieda-shi, Japan: Naoki Suzuki, 1990. 58 pp.**
Covers foreign jazz programs broadcast on Japanese TV in 1990. Alphabetical by artist.
Index.

RECORDING COMPANIES

Debut

7-324   Weiler, Uwe. *The Debut Label: A Discography.* **Norderstedt, Germany: Uwe Weiler, 1994. 286 pp.**
Covers 1951 to 1997. Arranged in chronological order. Formats include audio cassettes. Contains unissued material.
Bibliography; illustrations; index (song titles); notes.

Saba/MPS

7-325   Fischer, Klaus-Gotthard. *Jazzin' the Black Forest.* **Berlin: Crippled Library, 1999. 323 pp.**
History-discography from the early 1960s to 1983.
Photographs.

Splasc(h)

7-326 Fini, Francesco. *Splasc(h) Records: A Label Discography; The Most Complete Documentation about the New Italian Jazz*. **Imola, Italy: Fini Editions, 1997. 175 pp.**

Covers 1981 to 1996. Includes live performances. Arranged by numerical series.

Index (musicians).

Vogue

7-327 Ruppli, Michel. *Vogue Productions*. **With Charles Delaunay. 2 vols. Paris: AFAS (Association Française des Déteneurs de Documents Audiovisuels et Sonores), 1992. 226 pp.**

Covers 1945 to 1984, in French and English. Volume 1 covers recording sessions; volume 2 has numerical listings. Includes 78s and 45s. Contains unissued material.

Index (musicians).

Miscellaneous

7-328 Crawford, Richard, and Jeffrey Magee. *Jazz Standards on Record, 1900–1942: A Core Repertory*. **CBMR Monographs, no. 4. Chicago: Center for Black Music Research, 1992. 94 pp.**

Discography arranged alphabetically by song title. Includes unissued material.

Bibliography; notes.

7-329 Evensmo, Jan. *History of Jazz Tenor Saxophone: Black Artists*. **4 vols. Norwegian Jazz Archives publication nos. 7–9, 11. Oslo: Norsk Jazzarchiv, 1996–1999. 141 pp. (vol. 1); 171 pp. (vol. 2); 220 pp. (vol. 3); 438 pp. (vol. 4).**

Solography, 1917 to 1949. Formats include 78s. Lists transcriptions.

Chronology; statistics.

7-330 Kiner, Larry F., and Harry MacKenzie. *Basic Musical Library, "P" Series, 1–1000*. **Discographies, no. 39. New York: Greenwood Press, 1990. 326 pp.**

Covers the first 1000 recordings of the "P" Popular Series issued by the Armed Forces Radio Service, 1941 to 1947. Arranged numerically by series number. No unissued recordings or reissues.

Bibliography; illustrations; indexes (musicians, song titles).

7-331   Laird, Ross. *Tantalizing Tingles: A Discography of Early Ragtime, Jazz, and Novelty Syncopated Piano Recordings, 1889–1934.* **Discographies, no. 59. Westport, CT: Greenwood Press, 1995. 258 pp.**

Covers all non-classical recordings, with the exception of ethnic recordings. Arranged alphabetically by artist. Appendix: "Non-Solo Instrumental Recordings by Selected Pianists."

Bibliography; illustrations; index (song titles).

7-332   MacKenzie, Harry. *Command Performance, USA! A Discography.* **Discographies, no. 64. Westport, CT: Greenwood Press, 1996. 255 pp.**

Covers 1942 to 1949. Includes Armed Forces Radio Services programs "Command Performance," "Mail Call," and "GI Journal."

Bibliography; chronology; illustrations; indexes (musicians on "Command Performance," musicians on "Mail Call"); photographs.

7-333   MacKenzie, Harry, and Lothar Polomski. *One Night Stand Series, 1–1001.* **Discographies, no. 44. New York: Greenwood Press, 1991. 326 pp.**

Covers U.S. Armed Forces Radio Service transcriptions for programs that include live broadcasts or remotes. Includes the Regular Series (September 1943 to May 1946) up to 1001 ("to round off a mastering week"); the Fill Series (December 1943 to 1946); the Popular Music Replacement Series (1944 to 1946); and "Unidentified Programmes." Arranged numerically by transcription number. Entries include the off-the-air recording date, location, song titles, and names of musicians, composers, and announcers. Appendixes include "Directory of Band Leaders"; "[Band] Themes"; and "Commercial Issues" (by country of origin).

Bibliography; illustrations; indexes (musicians); photographs.

7-334   Wheeler, Geoffrey. *Jazz by Mail, 1936 to 1958: Including Complete Discographies for Jazztone & Dial Records.* **Manassas, VA: Hillbrook Press, 1999. 507 pp.**

History and annotated discography, covering 1936 to 1958. Includes U.S. and European Jazztone record club discographies.

Bibliography.

8
Record Guides

Only a handful of jazz record guides were published in the 1990s. These were designed to help buyers sort through the burgeoning number of CD issues, offering critical ratings and, in some cases, more in-depth essays.

8-1   Cook, Richard, and Brian Morton. *The Penguin Guide to Jazz on CD.* **4th ed. New York: Penguin Books, 1998. 1745 pp.**
Listings for more than 10,000 CDs, with full personnel, critical ratings. musical descriptions, and biographical details. Does not include blues musicians.
Index.

8-2   Fordham, John. *Jazz on CD: The Essential Guide.* **London: K. Cathie, 1991. 392 pp.**
Organized by historical period, then alphabetically by artist. Includes biographical information. Does not include blues musicians.
Index.

8-3   Gayford, Martin. *The Best of Jazz: The Essential CD Guide.* **San Francisco: Collins Publishers, 1993. 144 pp.**
Brief biographies of artists followed by CD listings.
Index; photographs.

8-4   Holtje, Steve, and Nancy Ann Lee, eds. *MusicHound Jazz: The Essential Album Guide.* **Detroit: Visible Ink Press, 1998. 1390 pp.**
Biographies, suggested purchases (plus "what to buy next," "what to avoid," "worth searching for"), and lists of compilation albums, books/magazines/newsletters, websites, record labels, radio stations, and music festivals.
Bibliography; indexes (highest-rated CDs, musicians); photographs.

8-5   Kernfeld, Barry, ed. *Blackwell Guide to Recorded Jazz.* 2nd ed. Cambridge, MA: Blackwell, 1995. 587 pp.

Musicological essays and discographies. Contributors include James Lincoln Collier, Digby Fairweather, Mike Hazeldine, Mark Gardner, and Ekkehard Jost.

Discographies; indexes (musicians, song titles).

8-6   Knopper, Steve, ed. *MusicHound Swing! The Essential Album Guide.* Detroit: Visible Ink Press, 1999. 461 pp.

Biographies, suggested purchases (plus "what to buy next," "what to avoid," "worth searching for"), and lists of compilation albums, books/magazines/newsletters, websites, record labels, and radio stations.

Bibliography; indexes (highest-rated CDs, musicians); photographs.

8-7   Piazza, Tom. *The Guide to Classic Recorded Jazz.* Iowa City: University of Iowa Press, 1995. 391 pp.

Musicological study of classic recordings that "have formed or that exemplify the definitive elements of the jazz style" from the 1920s to about 1970. After a chronological survey, the book is organized by instrument.

Index.

8-8   Stroff, Stephen M. *Discovering Great Jazz: A New Listener's Guide to the Sounds and Styles of the Top Musicians and Their Recordings on CDs, LPs, and Cassettes.* New York: Newmarket Press, 1991. 179 pp.

History of jazz and its notable musicians from its "prehistory" until the 1990s. Organized as a running narrative of biographical entries with recommended recordings and listening guidance.

Bibliography; discography; glossary; index; photographs.

8-9   Swenson, John, ed. *The Rolling Stone Jazz and Blues Album Guide.* New York: Random House, 1999. 781 pp.

Brief critical biographies on jazz and blues musicians, with album ratings. Includes list of anthologies. Small portions previously published in *The Rolling Stone Jazz Record Guide* (Random House, 1985) and *The Rolling Stone Album Guide* (Random House, 1992).

8-10   Umphred, Neal. *Goldmine's Price Guide to Collectible Jazz Albums, 1949–1969.* 2nd ed. Iola, WI: Krause Publications, 1994. 592 pp.

Listings of first and later pressings of LPs issued from 1948 to 1969. Includes "Record Company Label Directory"; "Jazz at the Philharmonic"; and "Various Artists Compilations and All-Star Sessions." Appendixes include "David Stone Martin and the Art of Jazz" and "Jazz and the Audiophile." First published in 1992.

Bibliography; illustrations; photographs.

8-11 **Wynn, Ron, Michael Erlewine, et al., eds.** *All Music Guide to Jazz: The Best CDs, Albums & Tapes.* **San Francisco: Miller Freeman Books, 1994. 752 pp.**

Arranged alphabetically by artist. Annotated discographies include "essential recordings" and "first purchases." Also includes Mark C. Gridley's introduction to jazz styles, and "music maps" by style and instrument.

Bibliography; index.

9
Pictorial

Pictorial works published in the 1990s included collections of album covers, posters and photography by William Claxton, William Gottlieb, Carol Friedman, and Milt Hinton.

PHOTOGRAPHY

9-1 Abe, K (Katsuji). *50 Jazz Greats from Heaven.* **Tokyo: Shinko, 1995. 177 pp.**
Includes Cannonball Adderley, Georgie Auld, Eddie Condon, John Coltrane, Wild Bill Davison, Duke Ellington, Thad Jones, Thelonious Monk, Joe Pass, Zoot Sims, Sarah Vaughan, and Mary Lou Williams. Text in Japanese.

9-2 ———. *Jazz Street.* **Tokyo: Libro Porto, [1990]. [unpaged.]**
Collection of photographs of jazz musicians. Includes Art Pepper, Bud Powell, Don Cherry, Chet Baker, Miles Davis, Donald Byrd, Punch Miller, Anita O'Day, Bill Crow, Bill Evans, Billie Holiday, Thelonious Monk, Dexter Gordon, Louis Armstrong, Duke Ellington, Lester Young, Erroll Garner, Art Blakey, Kenny Dorham, Horace Silver, Hank Mobley, John Coltrane, Eric Dolphy, Clifford Brown, Dizzy Gillespie, Ernie Henry, Earl Hines, Jimmy Archey, Muggsy Spanier, Earl Watkins, Lionel Hampton, Al Haig, Stan Getz, Tommy Potter, Charlie Parker. Descriptions of photos in Japanese and English.

9-3 Avery, Ray. *Stars of Jazz.* **Copenhagen: JazzMedia ApS, 1998. 160 pp.**
Photos of guest stars on the "Stars of Jazz" TV show, taken by host Avery. Includes Chet Baker, Ray Brown, Dave Brubeck, June Christy, Herb Ellis, Billie

Holiday, Harry James, Art Pepper, Oscar Peterson, Frank Rosolino, and Mel Tormé. Essays include "Variations on a Tired Theme," by Harry Siders.
Index.

9-4 Brask, Ole. *Ole Brask: Photographs; Jazz.* **Text by Milt Hinton. Kiel, Germany: Nieswand, 1995. [unpaged.]**
Photos taken from 1959 to 1976. Includes Ben Webster, Slam Stewart, Wild Bill Davison, Red Allen, Anthony Braxton, Ornette Coleman, Coleman Hawkins, J. J. Johnson, Mary Lou Williams, Lionel Hampton, and Dizzy Gillespie. Text in German and English.

9-5 Claxton, William. *Claxography: The Art of Jazz Photography.* **Text by William Claxton and James Gavin. Kiel, Germany: Nieswand Verlag, 1995. 129 pp.**
Includes photos of Miles Davis, John Coltrane, and Billy Strayhorn.

9-6 Claxton, William. *Jazz Seen.* **Köln, Germany: Taschen, 1999. 287 pp.**
Includes photos of John Coltrane, Nat King Cole, Maynard Ferguson, Joe Williams, Ornette Coleman, Duke Ellington, Diana Krall, Sylvia Syms, Gerry Mulligan, Ben Webster, Sonny Rollins, Gil Evans, Miles Davis, Frank Sinatra, Cassandra Wilson, and Jacky Terrasson.

9-7 Friedlander, Lee. *The Jazz People of New Orleans.* **New York: Pantheon Books, 1992. 119 pp.**
Photos taken from 1957 to 1974. Includes Johnny St. Cyr, Punch Miller, Fess Manetta, Kid Thomas Valentine, and Willie Humphrey. Afterword ("Mecca, LA") by Whitney Balliett.

9-8 Friedman, Carol. *The Jazz Pictures.* **Santa Fe, NM: Tondo, 1999. 203 pp.**
Includes photos of Sarah Vaughan, Ornette Coleman, Chet Baker, Max Roach, Hank Jones, Elvin Jones, Thad Jones, Cecil Taylor, Jimmy Heath, Eubie Blake, Mose Allison, Zoot Sims, Lionel Hampton, Nina Simone, Art Farmer, Kenny Barron, Archie Shepp, Dexter Gordon, and Joe Lovano.

9-9 Gottlieb, William P. *The Golden Age of Jazz: Text and Photographs.* **Revised and expanded. San Francisco: Pomegranate Artbooks, 1995. 162 pp.**
Includes photos of Willie "The Lion" Smith, James P. Johnson, Freddie Moore, Fess Williams, Louis Armstrong, Red Allen, J. C. Higginbotham, Benny Goodman, Vido Musso, Sid Catlett, Harry James, Ella Fitzgerald, Dizzy Gillespie, Miles Davis, and John Hammond. First published in 1979.
Index.

9-10 Hinton, Milt, et al. *Overtime: The Jazz Photographs of Milt Hinton.* **San Francisco: Pomegranate Artbooks, 1991. 164 pp.**

Photos by bass player Milt Hinton. Includes Louis Armstrong, Louie Bellson, Eubie Blake, Kenny Burrell, Benny Carter, Doc Cheatham, Roy Eldridge, Pee Wee Erwin, Lionel Hampton, Coleman Hawkins, Billie Holiday, Dick Hyman, Milt Jackson, Jo Jones, Charles Mingus, and Dinah Washington.

9-11 Hughes, Ralph, ed. *The Jazz Family Album.* **5 vols. East Stroudsburg, PA: East Stroudsburg University Music Dept., 1992–1997.**

All photos are from the Al Cohn Memorial Jazz Collection at East Stroudsburg University. Includes vol. 1: Charlie Parker, Coleman Hawkins, Bucky Pizzarelli, Lester Young, Herb Ellis; vol. 2: Dizzy Gillespie, Count Basie, Joe Turner, Sonny Rollins, Cannonball Adderley, Joe Williams; vol. 3: Sarah Vaughan, Buck Clayton, Dave Liebman, Leonard Feather, Charlie Parker, John Coltrane, Stan Getz; vol. 4: Lionel Hampton Orchestra, Dexter Gordon, Dick Wellstood, Shorty Rogers, Art Pepper. Volume 5 not reviewed.

9-12 Latxague, Robert. *Jazz: La Photographie.* **Translated into English and adapted by Christophe Marchand-Kiss and Laird Hunt. Chambéry, France: Editions Comp'Act, 1996. 253 pp.**

Collection of essays in French and English and photographs of Jazz á Vienne (Jazz in Vienne). Topics include Eddy Louiss, Ernie Watts's "Latin Music at the Festival," and Sonny Rollins.

9-13 Lowe, Jacques. *Jazz: Photographs of the Masters.* **Text by Cliff Preiss. New York: Artisan, 1995. 252 pp.**

Photographs of over 200 musicians. Includes Dave Brubeck, Benny Carter, Jon Faddis, Herbie Hancock, Milt Jackson, Pat Metheny, McCoy Tyner, Betty Carter, and Shirley Horn.

9-14 Motion, Tim. *Jazz Portraits: An Eye for the Sound; Images of Jazz and Jazz Musicians.* **London: Salamander, 1995. 128 pp.**

Collection of photographs by 23 photographers, including Bill Gottlieb (1940s); Herman Leonard (1950s and 1960s); and Daniel Ferri and Jonathan Oppong-Wiafe (1990s). Subjects include Jimmy McGriff, Big Sid Catlett, Bunk Johnson, Art Tatum, Billie Holiday, Lester Young, Charlie Parker, Slam Stewart, Gerry Mulligan, Shelly Manne, and Art Pepper.

Index.

9-15 Persson, Jan. *Jazz Portraits.* **Foreword by Dan Morgenstern. Copenhagen: Tiderne Skifter, 1996. 143 pp.**

Photos taken from 1963 to 1996. Includes Louis Armstrong, Zutty Singleton, Arvell Shaw, Trummy Young, Duke Ellington, Johnny Hodges, Paul Gonsalves, Harry Carney, Barney Bigard, Ben Webster, and Clark Terry.

Bibliography; discography; index.

9-16   Redfern, David. *The Unclosed Eye: The Music Photography of David Redfern.* **London: Sanctuary Music Library, 1999. 175 pp.**

Photos of rock and jazz musicians. Jazz subjects include Louis Armstrong, Miles Davis, Duke Ellington, Roy Ayers, Kenny Ball, Chris Barber, Count Basie, Art Blakey, Dave Brubeck, Ornette Coleman, John Coltrane, Ed Currie's Jazz Band, Bill Evans, Erroll Garner, Stan Getz, and Stephane Grappelli.

Index.

9-17   Spilka, Bill. *Chops.* **New York: New York Brass Conference for Scholarships, 1990. 77 pp.**

Photos of jazz and symphonic brass players. Includes Cat Anderson, Doc Cheatham, Sonny Cohn, Dizzy Gillespie, Thad Jones, Ed Lewis, Jimmy Owens, Dave Stahl, and Marvin Stamm.

Index.

9-18   Spitzer, David D. *Jazz: Photographs.* **Foreword by Ira Gitler. San Francisco: Woodford Press, 1994. 159 pp.**

Includes Jon Hendricks, Charles Mingus, Dave Brubeck, Chet Baker, Betty Carter, Nancy Wilson, Sonny Fortune, Ella Fitzgerald, and Mary Lou Williams.

Index.

9-19   Tanner, Lee. *Jazz Address Book.* **San Francisco: Pomegranate Calendars & Books, 1990. 121 pp.**

Includes Jimmy Rushing, Budd Johnson, Eric Dolphy, Milt Jackson, Art Blakey, Ray Nance, Chet Baker, Roy Haynes, and Art Farmer.

9-20   van der Elsken, ed. *Jazz.* **Amsterdam: Fragment Uitgeverij, 1991. [unpaged.]**

Includes Louis Armstrong, Modern Jazz Quartet, Lester Young, Miles Davis, Chet Baker, Kid Ory, Count Basie, Oscar Peterson, Ella Fitzgerald, Art Blakey, Illinois Jacquet, Gene Krupa, Stan Getz, Zoot Sims, Erroll Garner, Wilbur Little, Elvin Jones, and Stuff Smith.

ALBUM COVERS

9-21   Marsh, Graham, et al., eds. *Blue Note: The Album Cover Art.* **San Francisco: Chronicle Books, 1991. 127 pp.**

"Features the cover art of Reid Miles, who designed almost 500 record sleeves for Blue Note over a 15-year period." Contains "History of Blue Note Records"; "Unissued Sessions Released in Japan"; "Back Covers"; "Cover Versions"; and "Promotional Material." Includes covers of albums by John Coltrane, Miles Davis, Sonny Rollins, Thelonious Monk, Herbie Hancock, Art Blakey, and Ornette Coleman.

Index.

9-22 **Marsh, Graham, and Glyn Callingham, eds.** *Blue Note 2: The Album Cover Art.* **San Francisco: Chronicle Books, 1997. 110 pp.**

Contains a biography of Reid Miles. Includes albums by Sonny Rollins, John Coltrane, Thelonious Monk, Charles Mingus, Don Cherry, Ornette Coleman, and Wayne Shorter.

9-23 ———, **eds.** *New York Hot: East Coast Jazz of the 50s & 60s; The Album Cover Art.* **San Francisco: Chronicle Books, 1993. 110 pp.**

Cover art for Prestige, Riverside, and Atlantic Records. Includes records by Miles Davis, Sonny Rollins, Mal Waldron, John Coltrane, Thelonious Monk, Modern Jazz Quartet, Charlie Mingus, Cannonball Adderley, and Bill Evans.

POSTERS

9-24 **Troxler, Niklaus.** *Jazzplakate/Jazz Posters/Affiches de jazz.* **Schaftlach, Germany: Oreos, 1991. 240 pp.**

Posters designed by Troxler for Switzerland's "Jazz in Willisau" festivals, which began in 1975. Includes Cecil Taylor, Dexter Gordon, Keith Jarrett, and McCoy Tyner.

10
Reference Works

Reference works published in the 1990s ranged from the scholarly *New Grove Dictionary of Jazz* to the *Rough Guide to Jazz*, addressing a more general readership.

BIBLIOGRAPHIES

10-1 Carner, Gary. *Jazz Performers: An Annotated Bibliography of Biographical Materials.* **Foreword by John Chilton. New York: Greenwood Press, 1990. 364 pp.**

Annotated bibliography of jazz books, theses, dissertations, and scholarly journal articles "published in all languages from 1921 to 1990." Arranged alphabetically by author. Includes a supplemental bibliography of general books, collections, histories, textbooks, illustrated books, and reference works.

Indexes (author, subject).

10-2 Gray, John. *Fire Music: A Bibliography of the New Jazz, 1959–1990.* **New York: Greenwood Press, 1991. 515 pp.**

Annotated bibliography of the "New Jazz" (also known as "free jazz," "avant-garde," etc.) and its many developments from 1959 to 1991. Sources listed are books, dissertations, periodical and newspaper articles, film, videos, and audiotapes. Includes list of archives and research centers.

Indexes (musicians, author, subject).

10-3   Meadows, Eddie S. *Jazz Research and Performance Materials: A Select Annotated Bibliography.* **2nd ed. New York: Garland Publishing, 1995. 806 pp.**

Revised edition. Covers materials published from 1920 to 1995. Includes sections on jazz research libraries; biographies and autobiographies; collective biographies; theses and dissertations; and technical materials.

Indexes (author, subject).

DICTIONARIES AND ENCYCLOPEDIAS

10-4   Carr, Ian, Digby Fairweather, and Brian Priestley. *Jazz: The Rough Guide; The Essential Companion to Artists and Albums.* **London: Rough Guides, 1995. 754 pp.**

Arranged alphabetically by musician, with almost 2000 biographical entries accompanied by suggested recordings. "Completely revised edition of the *Essential Guide to Jazz.*"

Glossary; photographs.

10-5   Feather, Leonard, and Ira Gitler. *The Biographical Encyclopedia of Jazz.* **New York: Oxford University Press, 1999. 718 pp.**

Based in part on earlier reference books: Leonard Feather's *Encyclopedia of Jazz*, *The New Encyclopedia of Jazz*, and *The Encyclopedia of Jazz in the Sixties*, and Leonard Feather and Ira Gitler's *The Encyclopedia of Jazz in the Seventies.* Emphasis on musicians from the U.S.

Bibliography; discography; filmography.

10-6   Kernfeld, Barry. *The New Grove Dictionary of Jazz.* **2nd ed. New York: St. Martin's Press, 1994. 1358 pp.**

Covers musicians, musical instruments, associations and non-profits, record producers, record labels, nightclubs, festivals, libraries, archives, and topics/terms. Originally published in two volumes in 1988.

Bibliography; discography; musical transcriptions; photographs; tables.

10-7   Larkin, Colin. *The Guinness Who's Who of Jazz.* **2nd ed. Enfield, UK: Guinness Publishing, 1995. 508 pp.**

Includes musicians, composers, arrangers, and labels, and ranges from New Orleans traditional jazz to the present. "Forms a part of the multi-volume *Guinness Encyclopedia of Popular Music.*" First published in 1992.

Bibliography; discography; photographs.

10-8   Powell, Neil. *The Language of Jazz.* **Manchester, UK: Carcanet, 1997. 151 pp.**

"Lexicon of words and phrases associated with jazz." Includes "ordinary words with special meanings in jazz"; "names and nicknames of outstanding jazz musicians"; "place-names associated with movements in jazz"; jazz record labels; and jazz venues.

Bibliography; discography.

11
Miscellaneous

This chapter includes conference proceedings and books on a wide variety of subjects: ephemera, disposing of your jazz collection, radio transcripts from France for a New York radio station, the connection between modern jazz and American poetry, and writers who have expressed an affinity for jazz.

CONFERENCE PROCEEDINGS

11-1   Baker, David N., ed. *New Perspectives on Jazz: Report on a National Conference Held at Wingspread, Racine, Wisconsin, September 8–10, 1986.* **Washington, DC: Smithsonian Institution Press, 1990. 133 pp.**

Includes four commissioned papers and a response to each. "The purpose of the conference was to reexamine the jazz field for those involved in it, explain it for those not familiar with it, and direct it for those responsible for its future." Includes "The Influence of Jazz on the History and Development of Concert Music" (Gunther Schuller, presenter; Olly Wilson, respondent); "The Evolution of Jazz" (Gary Giddins, presenter; Dan Morgenstern, respondent); "Jazz Criticism and Its Effect on the Art Form" (Amiri Baraka, presenter; Stanley Crouch, respondent); "Jazz in the Contemporary Marketplace: Professional and Third-Sector Economic Strategies for the Balance of the Century" (Billy Taylor, presenter; Jimmy Lyons and George Butler, respondents). Sponsored by the National Jazz Service Organization and other organizations in cooperation with Indiana University School of Music and the National Endowment for the Arts.

11-2   Oliphant, Dave, ed. *The Bebop Revolution in Words and Music.* **Austin: Harry Ransom Humanities Research Center, The University of Texas at Austin, 1994. 227 pp.**

Papers and discussion from a symposium held in 1992 in conjunction with an exhibition "mounted by the Harry Ransom Humanities Research Center to showcase the wealth of jazz-related materials in its archive of [jazz historian] Ross Russell." Includes "Symposium Keynote Address," by Ross Russell; "The Bebop Revolution in Words and Music: An Exhibition"; "Charlie Parker: An Overview," by Gary Giddins; "The Dial Recordings of Charlie Parker," by Edward Komara; "The Bop Aesthetic and Black Intellectual Tradition," by Lorenzo Thomas; "Langston Hughes as Bop Ethnographer in 'Trumpet Player: 52nd Street'", by Nicholas M. Evans; "A Short Stay in the Sun: The Reception of Bebop, 1944–1950," by Bernard Gendron; "Donna Lee and the Ironies of Bebop," by Douglass Parker; "The Bebop Tradition in South America," by José Hosiasson; and "Bebop in the 1990s: A Panel Discussion." Originally published in the journal the *Library Chronicle of the University of Texas at Austin*, vol. 24, nos. 1–2.

Illustrations; musical transcriptions; photographs.

OTHER

11-3   Godbolt, Jim. *The World of Jazz: In Printed Ephemera and Collectibles.* **London: Studio Jazz, 1990. 160 pp.**

"Stages of jazz's development in words and contemporary ephemera" that reflect "not only the music but the social and racial mores that attended its history." Contains magazine articles, posters, song sheets, album covers, and cartoons.

Bibliography; illustrations; index; photographs.

11-4   Goldenberg, David, ed. *Assessing, Insuring, and Disposing of Jazz Record Collections.* **IAJRC monograph series, no. 1. Bel Air, MD: The International Association of Jazz Record Collectors, 1990. 84 pp.**

Discussion of how to properly dispose of a jazz record collection, through auction, sale, or donation to an institution. Includes "Appraising Your Collection: Basic Principles," by Russ Shor; "Appraising Your Collection for Donation to an Institution," by Jerry Atkins; "Appraising Your Collection to Sell," by Frederick Cohen; "Donating Your Collection to an Institution," by Jerry Atkins; "Disposing of Microgroove Record Collections," by Frederick Cohen; and "Disposing of 78 rpm Record Collections" by Robert Hilbert. Appendixes include "Institutions and Archives"; "Dealers/Appraisers"; "Jazz Publications"; and "Determining Value of Donated Property: The Glenn Miller Air Force Tape Collection."

Bibliography; photographs.

11-5   Hartman, Charles O. *Jazz Text: Voice and Improvisation in Poetry, Jazz, and Song.* **Princeton, NJ: Princeton University Press, 1991. 192 pp.**

Study of the connection between modern jazz and American poetry. Includes "Lee Konitz: All the Things 'All the Things You Are' is on Bands"; "Ornette Coleman: The Shapes of Jazz"; and "Jazz, Song, Poetry: Toward Speaking For."
Bibliography; discography; illustrations; notes.

11-6   Jarrett, Michael. *Drifting on a Read: Jazz as a Model for Writing.* Albany, NY: State University of New York Press, 1999. 227 pp.

Exploration of the work of writers, such as Ralph Ellison and Michael Ondaatje, who have "expressed an affinity for jazz" and "brought jazz into language."
Bibliography; annotated discography; illustrations; index.

11-7   Liebman, David. *The Art of Recording.* New Albany, IN: Jamey Aebersold Jazz, 1995. 59 pp.

Focuses primarily on the jazz musician. Includes "Live Performing"; "The Studio"; "Why Record"; "The Producer's Role"; "The Engineer"; "Two-Track vs. Multi-Track"; "Musical Preparation/Repertoire"; "Arrangements, Parts, Rehearsal"; "Set Up"; "Pacing"; "Post Production"; and "My Ten Favorite Jazz Recordings." The book is drawn from articles that first appeared in the *Saxophone Journal.*

11-8   Vian, Boris. *Jazz in Paris: Chroniques de jazz pour la station de radio WNEW, New York (1948–1949).* Discography by Claude Rameil. Paris: Pauvert, 1997. 237 pp.

Transcriptions of radio broadcasts made by Boris Vian for WNEW radio in New York City from 1948 to 1949. In English and French.
Bibliography; discography; photographs.

Subject Index

Note: The numbers following each subject listing indicate the chapter and entry number; for example, "Adams, Pepper, 1–205" indicates chapter 1, entry number 205. Boldfaced entry numbers indicate that the subject is the principal focus of the book in question.

AACM, 2–33
Abrams, Muhal Richard, 2–33
Adams, Pepper, 1–219
Adderley, Cannonball, 4–42, 9–1, 9–11, 9–23
Adler, Larry, **1–1**
Afro-Cuban music, **2–4**. *See also* Latin jazz
Ahola, Sylvester, **1–2**
Air Force Band, 7–204
Akiyoshi, Toshiko, 1–186
Alabama State Teachers College, 1–227
Alcorn, Alvin, 6–35
Alden, Howard, 1–210
Alexander, Van, **7–1**
"All of Me" (composition), 5–6
"All the Things You Are" (composition), 11–5
Allen, Henry "Red," 9–4, 9–9
Allen, Pete, **7–2**
Allison, Mose, **1–3**, 1–190, 9–8
Ambrose, 1–225
Anderson, Cat, 9–17
Anderson, Ernestine, 6–52
Anderson, Ivie, 1–200

Andrews, Ernie, 1–205
Andrews Sisters, 1–197, 1–200, **7–3**
Andriessen, Louis, 6–10
Anthony, Ray, 1–197, 1–204
Antolini, Charly, **7–4**
Archey, Jimmy, **1–4**, 9–2
Armed Forces Radio Service (U.S.), **7–330**, **7–332**, **7–333**
Armstrong, Louis, **1–5**, **1–6**, **1–7**, **1–8**, **1–9**, **1–10**, **1–11**, **1–12**, **1–13**, 1–134, 1–146, 1–182, 1–183, 1–195, 1–200, **1–202**, 1–214, 1–215, 1–217, 1–223, 2–1, 2–13, 2–22, 2–39, 4–5, 4–6, 4–11, **4–19**, 4–20, 4–31, 6–36, **7–5**, 9–2, 9–9, 9–10, 9–15, 9–16, 9–20
Art Ensemble of Chicago, 2–33
Ashby, Harold, 1–186
Asher, Don, **1–14**
Ashman, Mickey, **7–6**
Association for the Advancement of Creative Musicians. *See* AACM
Auld, Georgie, **7–7**, 9–1
Australian Jazz Quartet, 6–3
avant-garde jazz, 1–209, 1–220, 2–6, 2–28, 2–33, 4–33, 10–2

Avon Cities Jazz Band, **7–8**
Avon Cities Skiffle Group, **7–8**
Ayers, Roy, 9–16
Ayler, Albert, 1–42, 1–218, 1–220, 2–33, 4–19
Ayres, Mitchell, **7–9**

Bagneris, Vernel, 1–187
Bailey, Benny, 6–42
Bailey, Donald "Duck," 1–213
Bailey, Judy, 1–210
Bailey, Mildred, 1–194
Bailey, Pearl, 4–4
Baker, Chet, **1–15**, **1–16**, **1–17**, 1–194, 1–215, 1–216, 6–24, 9–2, 9–3, 9–8, 9–18, 9–19, 9–20
Baker, Josephine, 1–232
Baker, Kenny, **1–18**
Ball, Kenny, **7–10**, 9–16
Bama State Collegians, **1–227**
Bamford, Johnny, 6–3
Bana OK, 1–77
Bang, Billy, 1–220
Barbarin, Paul, 6–36
Barber, Chris, **7–11**, 9–16
Barda, Daniel, **7–12**
Barker, Danny, 4–22
Barlow, Dale, 1–210
Barnes, Emile, 6–35
Barnes, John, **7–13**
Barnes, Paul "Polo," 6–35
Barnet, Charlie, 1–204, 1–226, 2–26, **7–14**, 7–195
Barrelhouse Jazzband, **7–15**
Barrett, Dan, 1–187
Barrett, Sweet Emma, 6–36
Barron, Kenny, 9–8
Basie, Count, 1–142, 1–197, 1–201, 1–204, 1–217, 1–226, 2–13, 2–21, 2–27, 4–3, 4–4, 4–23, 4–40, 6–48, 9–11, 9–16, 9–20
bass guitar, 3–1
Bata-Kusai Jazz Singers, 5–12
Beal, Eddie, 6–19
bebop, 1–80, 1–82, 1–180, 1–194, **2–28**, **2–29**, **2–30**, 2–31, 4–9, 4–12, 4–16, 4–18, 4–20, 4–31, 4–33, 4–40, 6–43, **11–2**
Bechet, Leonard, 6–35
Bechet, Sidney, 1–179, 1–214, 1–218, 2–1, 2–13, 3–11, 4–20, 4–23, 4–40
Beecham, John, **7–16**
Beiderbecke, Bix, 1–188, 1–217, 1–221, 2–1, 4–20, 4–21, 4–24, **6–30**, **7–17**
Bellson, Louie (Louis), 1–68, 1–180, 3–6, 9–10
Beneke, Tex, **7–18**
Benkó Dixieland Band, **7–19**
Bennett, Tony, **1–19**, **1–20**, 1–197, 1–201, 1–215
Bennink, Han, 6–10
Benson, George, 2–34, 2–36
Benson, Gil, 6–42
Benson, Ivy, 1–225
Berigan, Bunny, **1–21**, 1–221
Berklee College of Music, 2–38
Bernie, Ben, **7–20**
Bertles, Bob, 1–210
big band jazz. *See* swing
Big Band Jump (periodical), 1–204
Bigard, Alex, 6–35
Bigard, Barney, 9–15
Bilk, Acker, **7–21**
Billett, Cuff, **7–22**
Black Bottom Stompers, **7–23**
Black, Brown, and Beige (composition), 1–66
Black, James, 3–5
Black and Tan (film), 2–39
"Black and Tan Fantasy" (composition), 1–66
Blake, Eubie, 1–141, 9–8, 9–10
Blakey, Art, 1–190, 1–219, 2–31, 3–6, 4–42, 9–2, 9–16, 9–19, 9–20, 9–21
Bley, Paul, 5–2, **7–24**
Blount, Chris, **7–25**
Blowers, Johnny, **1–22**
Blue Note (record company), **9–21**, **9–22**
blues, 1–58, 1–65, 1–207, 1–230, 2–10, 2–19, 4–6, 4–7, 4–35, 5–4, 6–19, 6–43, 8–9
"Blutopia" (composition), **1–207**
Bobo, Willie, 1–142

Bocage, Peter, 6–35
Bockemuehl, Eugene, **1–23**
Bockey, Gene. *See* Bockemuehl, Eugene
"Body and Soul" (composition), 4–21
Boeren, Eric, 6–10
Boland, Francy, **1–33**
Bolden, Buddy, **1–24, 1–25,** 1–214, 4–14, 6–34
boogie-woogie, 4–38
Boone, Lester, 1–196
bop. *See* bebop
bossa nova, 2–37
Boswell, Connee, 1–194, 1–200, 1–221
The Boswell Sisters, 1–200, 1–221
Bothwell, Johnny, **7–26**
Bouliane, Denys, 4–41
Bourbon Street Jazz Band, **7–27**
Bowden, Colin, **7–28**
Bowie, Lester, 1–216, 2–33
Bradley, Will, **7–29**
Bradshaw, Tiny, **7–30**
Braff, Ruby, 1–180, 1–190
Brantley, Tiny, 6–23
Braud, Wellman, 6–36
Braxton, Anthony, **1–26, 1–27, 1–28, 1–29,** 1–190, **1–207,** 2–33, 4–12, 4–20, 9–4
Brennan, Dave, **7–31**
Brewer, Teresa, 1–232
Brokenska, Jack, 1–210
Brooklyn Academy of Music, 6–43
Brookmeyer, Bob, 1–190
Brooks, Randy, **7–32**
Brotherhood of Breath, **1–116**
Brown, Charles, 1–219
Brown, Clifford, 2–31, 9–2
Brown, Lawrence, 1–189
Brown, Les, 1–198, 1–201
Brown, Ray, 9–3
Brown, Sandy, **7–33**
Browne, Samuel Rodney, 6–23
Browning, Ivan Harold, 6–23
Brubeck, Dave, **1–30, 1–31,** 1–183, 1–190, 1–205, 1–218, 6–24, 6–48, 9–3, 9–13, 9–16, 9–18
Bruff, Larry, **1–121**
Brunis, George, 6–36

Brunskill, Bill, **7–34**
Bryant, Clora, 6–22
Bryant, David, 6–22
Bryant, Ray, 1–190
Bryant, Rusty, 6–46
Bryden, Beryl, **7–35**
Buckner, Teddy, 6–23, 7–226
Bue, Papa, **7–36**
Burbank, Albert, **7–37**
Burke, Raymond, 6–36
Burke, Sonny, **7–38**
Burrell, Kenny, 9–10
Burrows, Don, 1–210, 6–3
Bushell, Garvin, **1–32,** 1–213
Busse, Henry, **7–39**
Byas, Don, 1–222
Byrd, Donald, 9–2
Byrne, Bobby, **7–40**
Byron, Don, 4–12

cabaret card law (New York), 6–44
Café Society, 6–45
Calloway, Cab, 1–80, 4–20
Camero, Candido, 1–142
Cameron, Jay, 1–213
Campi, Gigi, **1–33**
Candido, 1–142
Carle, Frankie, 1–204
Carmichael, Hoagy, 2–39, **6–30**
Carney, Harry, 9–15
Carter, Benny, 1–186, 1–218, 4–12, 9–10, 9–13
Carter, Betty, 1–208, 1–210, 1–219, 9–13, 9–18
Carter, John, 6–51
Carter, Ron, 1–222
Catlett, Big Sid, 3–4, 9–9, 9–14
Chaix, Henri, **7–41**
Challis, Bill, 1–185, 4–39
Chaloff, Serge, 7–42
"Chant of the Weed" (composition), 5–6
Charles, Ray, 1–215, 6–52
Charlestown Jazzband, **7–43**
Charlesworth, Dick, **7–44**
Charquet & Co. *See* Morel, Jean-Pierre
Cheatham, Adolphus "Doc," **1–34,** 1–184, 1–185, 4–3, 4–39, 9–10, 9–17

Cherry, Don, 1–219, 1–222, 2–33, 4–39, 9–2, 9–22
Chescoe, Laurie, **7–45**
Chester, Bob, **7–46**
Chesterman, Chez, **7–47**
Chisholm, George, **7–48**
Chittison, Herman, **7–49**
Christian, Charlie, 2–22, 3–7, 3–8, 6–41, **7–50**
Christophe, Harold, 6–35
Christy, June, 1–215, 9–3
Circus Square Jazz Band, **7–51**
Clark, Buddy, **7–52**
Clark, Mahlon, 1–185
Clark, Sonny, 2–31
Clarke-Boland Big Band, **1–33**
Clarke, Kenny, 1–33, 1–179
Clayton, Buck, 4–20, 9–11
Clinton, Larry, **7–53**
Clooney, Rosemary, **1–35**, 1–232
Clyde Valley Stompers. *See* Menzies, Ian
Coetzee, Basil, 6–2
Cohn, Al, 9–11
Cohn, Sonny, 9–17
Cola, Kid Sheik, 1–196, 6–35, **7–5**
Cole, Geoff, **7–55**
Cole, Lorenza Jordan, 6–23
Cole, Nat "King," **1–36**, 1–195, 1–199, 1–215, 2–39, **7–56**, 9–6
Cole, Paddy, 1–37
Coleman, Bill, **1–38**
Coleman, Earl, 4–14
Coleman, Ornette, **1–39**, **1–40**, 1–214, 1–218, 1–220, 1–222, 2–3, 2–13, 2–33, 4–6, 4–13, 4–35, 4–36, 4–42, 6–51, 9–4, 9–6, 9–8, 9–16, 9–21, 9–22, 11–5
Coleman, Steve, 1–211
collectibles (jazz), 11–3
Collette, Buddy, 6–22, 6–23
Collie, Max, **7–57**
Coltrane, John, **1–41**, **1–42**, **1–43**, **1–44**, **1–45**, 1–183, 1–192, 1–195, 1–209, 1–214, 1–216, 1–218, 1–220, 2–1, 2–13, 2–31, 2–33, 3–11, 4–19, 4–20, 4–35, 4–36, 4–42, **7–58**, 9–1, 9–2, 9–5, 9–6, 9–11, 9–16, 9–21, 9–22, 9–23
Colyer, Ken, **7–59**

Command Performance (radio program), **7–332**
"Concerto for Cootie" (composition), 1–65
Condon, Eddie, 1–57, 4–4, 4–10, 4–11, 4–20, 9–1
Conzo, Joe, 1–140
Cook, Will Marion, 6–48
cool jazz, 2–28, 2–35, 6–3. *See also* West Coast jazz
Coryell, Larry, 1–190, 1–211
Courtney, Del, **7–60**
Cowens, Kat, 1–196
Craig, Frank, 6–50
Crane River Jazz Band. *See* Colyer, Ken
Creole Band, 6–16
Crosby, Bing, **1–46**, 1–194, 1–199, 1–200, 1–223
Crosby, Bob, **7–61**
Crow, Bill, 9–2
Cugat, Xavier, **7–62**
Currie, Ed, 9–16

Dailey, Joe, 6–42
Dameron, Tadd, **1–47**, 6–48
Daniels, Mike, **7–63**
Dankworth, John, **1–48**, 1–225
Dauner, Wolfgang, 5–2
Davies, John R. T., **7–64**
Davis, Eddie "Lockjaw," 1–213, 1–222
Davis, Eddy, 1–187
Davis, Harry, 1–225
Davis, Joe, **1–49**
Davis, Miles, **1–50**, **1–51**, **1–52**, **1–53**, **1–54**, **1–55**, 1–99, 1–136, 1–142, 1–183, 1–184, 1–185, **1–206**, 1–209, 1–214, 1–216, 1–222, 2–1, 2–3, 2–13, 2–31, 2–35, 2–36, 4–6, 4–9, 4–13, **4–19**, 4–20, 4–29, 4–35, 6–18, **7–65**, 9–2, 9–5, 9–6, 9–9, 9–16, 9–20, 9–21, 9–23
Davis, Nathan, 1–213
Davison, Wild Bill, **1–56**, **1–57**, 4–39, 9–1, 9–4
Dawn, Dolly, 1–232, 4–39
Dawson, Eddie, 6–35
Day, Doris, 1–232, **7–66**
Debut (record company), **7–324**
Déczi, Laco, 6–11

Subject Index

DeFranco, Buddy, 1–180, 6–48, **7–67**
Dejan, Harold, 6–35, 6–37
Dejan, Leo, 6–35
Delaney, Eric, 1–225
Delange, Eddie, **7–68**
Delay, Mike, 6–35
Dentici, Sal, 1–196
Desmond, Paul, 1–180, 4–20
Dial Records, 7–229, **7–334**, 11–2
Dibango, Manu, **1–58**, 4–36
Dickenson, Vic, 1–186, 4–2, 4–10, **7–69**
Dickie, Neville, **7–70**
Dillard, Bill, 1–185
Dilworth, Arthur, 6–27
Dilworth, Bobby, 6–27
Dittamo, Fred, 6–42
Dixieland jazz, **2–19**, **4–43**, **6–17**
Dixieland Pipers, **7–71**
Dixon, Bill, **7–72**
Dodds, Baby, **1–59**, 1–146, 3–5, 3–6, 6–36
Dodds, Johnny, 6–30
Doerner, George G. Jr., 6–27, 6–28
Dolphy, Eric, 1–179, 4–42, 9–2, 9–19
Dominique, Natty, 1–146, 6–36
Donahue, Al, **7–73**
Donahue, Sam, 7–74
Donegan, Dorothy, 1–180, 1–231, 4–4
Dones, Bessie Williams, 6–23
"Donna Lee" (composition), 11–2
Donner, Otto, 6–6
Dorham, Kenny, 6–51, 9–2
Dorough, Bob, 1–213
The Dorsey Brothers. *See* Dorsey, Jimmy and Dorsey, Tommy
Dorsey, Jimmy, 1–23, 2–27, 1–198, 1–221, 1–226, 4–20, **7–75**, **7–76**
Dorsey, Tommy, 1–160, 1–198, 1–221, 1–226, 2–27, 4–11, 4–20, **7–75**, **7–77**
Douglass, Bill, 6–22
Down Beat (periodical), 1–109, **4–1**
Down Town Jazz Band, **7–78**
Draper, Barclay, 1–196
Drummond, Ray, 4–36
drums, **3–2**, **3–3**, **3–4**, **3–5**, **3–6**
Duffy, Al, 4–39
Duhé, Lawrence, 6–36

Dunbar, Kate, 1–210
Dunham, Sonny, **7–79**
Durham, Eddie, 6–51
Durham, Mike, **7–80**
Dutch Swing College Band, **7–81**
Duvivier, George, **1–60**
Dyani, Johnny, 6–2

Eager Beavers, 5–12
Ecklund, Peter, 1–187
Eckstine, Billy, 1–80, 1–200, 1–215, **7–82**
Ehrlich, Marty, 4–36
Eldridge, Roy, 1–195, 9–10
Elgart, Larry, 1–197, **7–83**
Elgart, Les, **7–84**
Ellington, Duke, **1–61**, **1–62**, **1–63**, **1–64**, **1–65**, **1–66**, **1–67**, **1–68**, **1–69**, **1–70**, **1–71**, 1–166, 1–179, 1–183, 1–184, 1–189, 1–195, 1–198, 1–200, **1–202**, **1–207**, 1–214, 1–217, 1–226, 2–1, 2–13, 2–21, 2–26, 2–27, 2–39, 4–3, 4–4, 4–10, 4–11, 4–14, 4–19, 4–20, 4–22, 4–23, 4–24, 4–35, 6–38, **7–85**, **7–86**, **7–87**, **7–88**, **7–89**, **7–90**, 9–1, 9–2, 9–6, 9–15, 9–16
Ellington, Mercer, 1–184, 1–190
Ellis, Herb, 9–3, 9–11
Ellison, Ralph, 11–5
Elman, Ziggy, **7–91**
Elsdon, Alan, **7–92**
Ennis, Skinnay, **7–93**
Entwistle, John, 3–1
Erstrand, Lars, **7–94**
Erwin, Pee Wee, 9–10
ethnomusicology, 5–5
Etté, Bernard, 7–95
Europe, James Reese, **1–72**, 1–191, 4–5, 4–33
Evans, Bill, **1–73**, 1–190, 1–218, 2–13, 4–2, 9–2, 9–16, 9–23
Evans, Gil, 1–53, 1–190, 1–219, 9–6
Evans, Herschel, 6–51

Faddis, Jon, 9–13
Fagen, Donald, 1–219
Fairweather, Al, **7–96**

Fairweather, Digby, **7–97**
Fallon, Jack, **7–98**
Falson, Ron, 6–3
Famous Southern Stompers, **7–166**
Farmer, Art, 1–85, 1–213, 6–22, 9–8, 9–19
Fawkes, Wally, **7–99**
Feather, Leonard, 9–11
Felix, Lennie, **7–100**
Ferbos, Lionel, 6–35
Ferguson, Maynard, **1–74**, 4–3, 9–6
Ferguson, Otis, 4–2
Feza, Mongezi, 6–2
Fields, Shep, **7–101**
15th Infantry Regiment Band, 1–72
52nd Street (New York City), 1–81, 6–45, 11–2
Fitzgerald, Andy, 6–42
Fitzgerald, Ella, **1–75**, **1–76**, 1–182, 1–183, 1–184, 1–192, 1–193, 1–194, 1–200, 1–212, 1–215, 1–223, 1–232, 4–3, **7–102**, 9–9, 9–18, 9–20
Five Spot (club), 4–20
"Flamingo" (composition), 1–68
Flanagan, Ralph, 7–103
Flanagan, Tommy, 1–190
"Fontainebleau" (composition), 1–47
Forrest, Helen, 1–201, 1–232, 7–104
Fortune, Sonny, 9–18
Foster, Chinee, 6–36
Foster, Chuck, 7–105
Foster, Pops, 6–36
Foster, Teddy, 1–225
Fox, Jo Brooks, **1–193**
Fox, Jules, **1–193**
Fox, Roy, 1–225
Foxley, Ray, **7–106**
Franco, **1–77**
Frazier, Cié, 6–35
"Free" (composition), 1–39
free jazz. *See* avant-garde jazz
freebop, 2–35
Freeman, Bud, 1–188, 1–213, 1–221
Freetime Old Dixie Jassband, **7–107**
funeral rites and ceremonies, **6–39**
funk music, 2–37

fusion jazz, 2–3, 2–6, 2–28, 2–35, 2–36, 2–37, 4–33, 6–43

G, Kenny, 2–36
Gaillard, Slim, 4–10
Gallaud, Louis, 6–35
Garbarek, Jan, **1–78**, 1–99
Garber, Jan, **7–108**
Garland, Edward, 6–36
Garland, Red, 6–51
Garner, Erroll, 1–222, 2–22, 4–10, 9–2, 9–16, 9–20
Gaskin, Leonard, 1–142
gender. *See* women and jazz
Gennett Studios, **6–30**
Gentlemen of Jazz, **7–109**
Geraldo, 1–225
Gerhardt, Ladislav, 6–11
Getz, Stan, **1–79**, 1–142, 1–183, 1–218, 4–10, 9–2, 9–11, 9–16, 9–20
GI Journal (radio program), 7–332
Gibbs, Terry, 4–10
Gillespie, Dizzy, **1–80**, **1–81**, **1–82**, 1–136, 1–180, 1–183, 1–190, 1–192, 1–209, 1–216, 1–222, 2–30, 4–11, 4–19, 4–29, 6–38, 9–2, 9–4, 9–9, 9–11, 9–17
Giordano, Vince, 1–187
Giuffre, Jimmy, 6–51
Gleason, Ralph, 6–26
Gluskin, Lud, **7–110**
Goldkette, Jean, 1–221
Goldstein, Linda, 1–231
Golson, Benny, 1–205, 4–31
Gonella, Nat, 1–225
Gonsalves, Paul, 4–2, 9–15
González, Jerry, 1–140
"Goodbye Old Gal Goodbye" (composition), 1–103
Goodman, Benny, **1–83**, 1–179, 1–180, 1–183, 1–217, 1–221, 1–226, 2–21, 2–22, 2–26, 2–27, 4–3, 4–4, 4–20, 4–21, 6–48, **7–111**, 9–9
Gordon, Dexter, 1–222, 6–24, 9–2, 9–8, 9–11, 9–24
Gordon, Gray, **7–112**
Gordon, Max, 1–205

Subject Index 179

gospel music, 2–35
Grabowsky, Paul, 1–210
Granz, Norman, 4–22
Grappelli, Stephane, 1–179, 9–16
Gray, Glen, **7–113**
Gray, Wardell, **7–114**
Green, Bill, 6–22
Green, Brian, **7–115**
Green, Freddie, 1–186
Green, Grant, **1–84**
Green, Johnny, 1–201
Greer, Sonny, 4–2, 4–20
Greig, Stan, **7–116**
Griffin, Chris, 4–39
Griffin, Johnny, 1–222
Grosz, Marty, 1–187
Gruntz, George, **1–228**
Gryce, Gigi, **1–85**
Guarnieri, Johnny, 3–10
Guesnon, George, 1–196, 6–35, 6–36
guitar, **3–7**, **3–8**, **3–9**

Hackett, Bobby, 1–221, 4–39, 6–49, **7–117**
Haden, Charlie, 1–216
Haggart, Bob, 1–185, 1–204, 4–3
Haig, Al, 9–2
Haines, Connie, 1–232
Hairston, Jester, 6–23
Halcox, Pat, 7–11
Half Note (club), 4–10
Hall, Edmond, 6–36
Hall, Fred, 1–201
Hamburg Swingers, 6–8
Hamilton, Chico, 1–190
Hamilton, Scott, 4–13
Hammond, John, 4–20, 9–9
Hampton, Lionel, 1–179, 2–27, 4–20, 9–2, 9–4, 9–8, 9–10, 9–11
Hancock, Herbie, 1–216, 1–219, 9–13, 9–21
Handy, George, **7–118**
Handy, Capt. John, 6–35, **7–119**
Handy, Sylvester, 6–35
Hanna, Jake, 1–185
Harbour Jazz Band, **7–120**

hard bop, 2–6, 2–28, **2–31**, 2–35
Hargrove, Rich, **1–202**
Harlem, 6–45
Harlem Group of Frankfurt, 6–8
Harlem Ramblers, **7–121**
Harrell, Tom, 4–36
Hastings, Lennie, **7–122**
Hawdon, Dick, **7–123**
Hawes, Hampton, 4–20
Hawkins, Annie, **7–124**
Hawkins, Coleman, **1–86**, 1–183, 1–217, 2–1, 2–29, 3–11, 4–20, 9–4, 9–10, 9–11
Hawkins, Erskine, 1–185, 1–191, 1–204, **7–125**
Hayes, Tubby, **7–126**
Haymes, Dick, **7–127**
Haynes, Roy, 9–19
Heath, Jimmy, 9–8
Heath, Moira, **1–203**
Heath, Ted, **1–87**, **1–203**, 1–225
Heidt, Horace, **7–128**
Henderson, Fletcher, 1–217, 1–218, 1–226, 2–26
Henderson, Joe, 1–211
Henderson, Leora, 4–20
Hendricks, Jon, 1–213, 1–219, 9–18
Henry, Ernie, 9–2
Herbeck, Ray, **7–129**
Herman, Woody, **1–88**, **1–89**, **1–90**, **1–91**, 1–193, 1–226, 2–26, 2–27, 3–11, 7–42, **7–130**
Heywood, Eddie, **1–92**
Heywood, Evelyn, 1–92
Hi-De-Ho (club), 4–20
Higginbotham, J. C., 9–9
Hill, Andrew, 5–2
Hill, Tiny, **7–131**
Himber, Richard, **7–132**
Hines, Earl, 1–80, 1–183, 4–2, 4–42, 6–26, 9–2
Hodes, Art, 1–93, 4–3, 4–20
Hodges, Johnny, **1–202**, 4–24, 9–15
Holiday, Billie, 1–179, 1–182, 1–183, 1–194, 1–208, 1–215, 1–217, 1–223, **1–230**, 2–1, 4–18, 4–19, 4–20, 4–21,

4–22, 4–24, 4–39/4–42, 9–2, 9–3, 9–10, 9–14
Honda, Helen, 5–13
Hope, Elmo, 2–31
Hopkins, Claude, **1–94**
Horn, Paul, **1–95**
Horn, Shirley, 1–231, 9–13
Horne, Lena, 1–183, 1–232
Houlind, Doc, **7–133**
Howard, Eddie, **7–134**
Howard, Nappy, 1–196
Howard, Thomas, 6–46
Hübner, Abbi, **7–135**
Hudson, Dean, **7–136**
Hudson, Will, **7–137**
Hueting, Roefie, 7–78
Hughes, Dick, **1–96**
Hughes, Langston, 11–2
Humphrey, Percy, 6–35
Humphrey, Willie, **7–138**, 9–7
Hund, Doggy, **7–139**
Hunt, Fred, **7–140**
Hurte, Leroy, 6–23
Húščava, Dušan, 6–11
Hylton, Jack, 1–225
Hyman, Dick, 1–185, 3–10, 9–10

Ibrahim, Abdullah, 1–208, 1–219, 6–2, **7–141**
Igawa, George, 5–13
Igoe, Sonny, 1–185
improvisation, 4–7, 4–16, 4–17, 4–31, 4–40, 4–43, 5–1, 5–2, 5–3, 5–4, 5–5, 6–43
Ingham, Keith, **7–142**
International Sweethearts of Rhythm, 4–6, 4–20
"Interstellar Space" (composition), 1–41
Italian Instabile Orchestra, 1–229

Jackson, Estella, 6–27
Jackson, Milt, 9–10, 9–13, 9–19
Jackson, Oliver, 1–185
Jacquet, Illinois, 1–186, 9–20
Jamal, Ahmad, 4–42
James, Etta, **1–97**

James, Harry, **1–97**, 1–197, 1–198, 1–201, **7–143**, 9–3, 9–9
Janssen, Guus, 6–10
Japanese Sandmen, 5–13
Jarman, Joseph, 2–33
Jarrett, Keith, **1–99**, 1–211, 1–214, 1–218, 1–219, 9–24
Jarvis, Jane, 4–39
Jazz á Vienne (festival), 9–12
Jazz and Blues Festival (Brooklyn, NY), **6–43**
Jazz at Lincoln Center, 1–61, 1–113, 4–32
Jazz at the Philharmonic, 2–6, 8–10
Jazz in Willisau (festival, Switzerland), 9–24
Jazz Oral History Project, 1–60
jazz-rock. *See* fusion jazz
The Jazz Singer (film), 2–39
Jazztone (record company), **7–334**
Jefferson, Blind Lemon, 6–51
Jeffries, Herb, 1–68, 1–191, 1–201
Jeter-Pillars Orchestra, 1–191
jive music, 1–212
Johansson, Jan, **1–100**
Johansson, Markku, 6–6
Johnson, Budd, 1–197, 9–19
Johnson, Bunk, 1–146, 4–38, 6–36, 9–14
Johnson, Freita Shaw, 6–23
Johnson, J. C., 1–141
Johnson, James P., 1–141, 3–10, 4–20, 4–38, 9–9
Johnson, J. J., **1–101**, 1–179, 9–4
Jonáš, Gabriel, 6–9
Jones, Dill, **7–144**
Jones, Elvin, 1–42, 9–8, 9–20
Jones, Hank, 9–8
Jones, Isham, **7–145**
Jones, Jo, 3–4, 3–6, 9–10
Jones, Jonah, 1–186
Jones, Philly Joe, 1–222
Jones, Quincy, **1–102**, 6–52
Jones, Thad, 4–18, 9–1, 9–8, 9–17
Joplin, Scott, **1–103**, **1–104**, 1–179, 6–51
Jordan, Louis, **1–105**, 1–212, 1–218, **7–146**
Jordan, Steve, **1–106**

"Junior Hop" (composition), 1–65
Jurgens, Dick, **7–147**

Kaatee, Frits, **7–148**
Kaatee, George, **7–149**
Kallen, Kitty, 1–232
Kanerva, Markku, 6–5
Kassel, Art, **7–150**
Kaune, Amos, 6–42
Kavelin, Al, **7–151**
Kaye, Sammy, 2–27
Keane, Helen, 1–231
Keller, Werner, **7–152**
Kelley, Peck, 4–2
Kellin, Orange, 1–187, **7–153**
Kelly, Emma, 6–24
Kelly, George, 1–185
Kelly, Jack, 6–35
Kelly, Wynton, 2–31
Kelso, Jackie, 6–22
Kenton, Stan, **1–107**, 1–198, 1–218, 4–3, **7–154, 7–155**
Keppard, Louis, 6–36
Kerouac, Jack, 4–9
King, Henry, **7–156**
King Sisters, 1–201, **7–158**
King, Wayne, **7–157**
Kingwell, Colin, **7–159**
Kirby, John, 1–108, 7–160
Kirby, Roy, 7–161
Kirk, Andy, 1–191, **7–162**
Kirk, Rahsaan Roland, 6–46
Klein, Oscar, **7–163**
Knepper, Jimmy, 1–180
Knights of Harlem, 6–16
Koglmann, Franz, 4–41
Kohlman, Freddie, 3–5
Koivistoinen, Eero, 6–6
"Koko" (composition), 1–65
Konitz, Lee, 1–190, 11–5
Korner, Alexis, 2–36
Krall, Diana, 1–232, 9–6
Krivin, Dr. Martin, 6–42
Krupa, Gene, **1–109**, 1–218, 3–4, **7–164,** 9–20
Kuhn, Joachim, 5–2

Kuhn, Steve, 4–42
Kyser, Kay, **7–165**

LaFaro, Scott, 4–42
Lahti, Pentti, 6–6
Laine, Frankie, 1–197
Laine, Reino, 6–6
Lambert, Dave, 4–10
Lamond, Don, **1–110**
Lane, Steve, **7–166**
Lang, Eddie, 3–8
Langford, Frances, 1–232
Larkins, Ellis, 1–186, 4–4
Latin jazz, 1–140, 2–4, 2–37, 5–10, 9–12
Laurie, Cy, **7–167**
Lawrence, Denise, **7–168**
Lawrence, Elliott, **7–169**
Lawrence, Syd, 1–225
Lawson, Yank, 1–204
Lay, Pete, **7–170**
Lee, David, 3–5
Lee, Peggy, 1–215 1–232, 4–4
Lemon, Brian, **7–171**
Lennon Sisters, 1–232
Leonard, Harlan, 1–191
Lewis, Ed, 9–17
Lewis, John, 4–19, 4–42
Lewis, Mel, 4–18
Lewis, Ted, **7–172**
Lewis, Vic, 1–225
Ley, Eggy, **7–173**
Liebman, Dave, **1–206,** 9–11
Lightfoot, Terry, **7–174**
Lincoln, Abbey, 4–36
Lincoln Center. *See* Jazz at Lincoln Center
Lindgren, Ole "Fessor," **7–175**
Lindy hop, 2–20
liner notes, 2–40
Lingle, Paul, 1–128
Linkola, Jukka, 6–6
Linnavalli, Esko, 6–6
Lipa, Peter, 6–11
Liston, Melba, 6–22
Little, Wilbur, 9–20
Litton, Martin, **7–176**
Lloyd, Charles, 1–99

Lomax, Alan, 6–32
Long, Johnny, **7–177**
Lopez, Vincent, **7–178**
Loss, Joe, 1–225
Louiss, Eddy, 9–12
Lovano, Joe, 4–36, 6–48, 9–8
Love, Preston, **1–111**
"Lovin' Babe" (composition), 1–103
Low Down Wizards, 7–135
Lucas, Clyde, **7–179**
Lucas, Nick, 3–8
Lunceford, Jimmie, 4–19, 4–20, 6–48, **7–180**, **7–181**
Luter, Claude, **7–182**
Lyman, Abe, **7–183**
Lyons, Jimmy, 6–26

Machito, 1–142
Mackintosh, Ken, 1–225
Maddocks, John, **7–184**
Mail Call (radio program), 7–332
Maltby, Richard, **7–185**
Manetta, Fess, 1–146, 9–7
Manetta, Manuel, 6–36
Manne, Shelly, **7–186**, 9–14
Manone, Wingy, **7–187**
marabi, **6–1**
Marable, Fate, 1–191
Marks, Roger, **7–188**
Marquet, Alain, **7–189**
Marquette, Pee Wee, 4–10
Marrero, Lawrence, 6–36
Marsalis, Branford, 1–112, 1–211, 4–13
Marsalis, Delfeayo, 1–210
Marsalis, Ellis Louis Jr., **1–112**
Marsalis, Wynton, 1–112, **1–113**, **1–114**, 1–211, 1–214, 1–216, 1–218, 2–3, 2–30, 2–34, 4–32
Marterie, Ralph, **7–190**
Martin, David Stone, 8–10
Martin, Freddy, **7–191**
Maryland Jazz Band of Cologne. *See* Hund, Doggy
Mason, Phil, **7–192**
Mason, Rod, **7–193**
Masso, George, 4–39
Mayerl, Billy, **1–115**

Mayhew, Virginia, 1–231
Mays, Billy, **7–194**, **7–195**
McCoy, Clyde, **7–196**
McGehee, Deedie, 6–23
McGregor, Chris, **1–116**, 6–2
McGriff, Jimmy, 9–14
McIntyre, Hal, **7–197**
McKenna, Dave, 6–49
McKinley, Ray, 1–185, 1–204, 3–4, 4–3, 4–4
McKinney's Cotton Pickers, 1–191
McLaughlin, John, **1–117**, 1–211
McNeely, Big Jay, **1–118**, 6–22
McNeil, Albert, 6–23
McPartland, Jimmy, 1–188
McPartland, Marian, 1–231, 4–10
McRae, Carmen, 1–182, 1–222, 4–19, 4–22, **7–198**
McShann, Jay, 1–219, 6–40
Melly, George, **7–199**
Melody Kings, 6–16
Melody Maker (periodical), 1–215
Menzies, Ian, **7–200**
Mercer, Johnny, 6–28
Mercer, Mabel, 1–223
Merseysippi Jazz Band, **7–201**
Messner, Johnny, **7–202**
Metheny, Pat, 3–7, 9–13
Metropole (club), 4–4
Meyer, Peter "Banjo," **7–203**
Mezzrow, Mezz, **1–119**
Miles, Lizzie, 1–196
Miles, Reid, 9–21, 9–22
Miller, Glenn, **1–120**, **1–121**, **1–122**, 1–168, 1–198, 1–226, 2–21, 2–26, 2–27, 7–195, **7–204**
Miller, Marcus, 3–1
Miller, Punch, 9–2, 9–7
Millinder, Lucky, **7–205**
Mills Brothers, **7–206**
Mince, Johnny, 1–185, 4–39
Mingus, Charles, 1–179, 1–190, 1–209, 1–214, 1–218, 1–220, 2–31, 2–33, 2–40, 4–1, 4–6, 4–22, 4–35, 4–36, 9–10, 9–18, 9–22, 9–23
Minton's (club), 4–20
Mintzer, Bob, 1–210

Mitchell, Red, 1–213
Mitchell, Roscoe, 2–33
Mo' Better Blues (film), 4–17
Mobley, Hank, 9–2
modal jazz, 1–209, 2–28
Modern Jazz Quartet, 1–183, 4–19, 9–20, 9–23
Moeketsi, Kippie, 6–2
Moholo, Louis, 6–2
Mole, Miff, 1–221
Monk, Thelonious, **1–123, 1–124, 1–125,** 1–183, 1–192, 1–209, 1–222, 2–30, 2–31, 4–10, 4–20, 4–22, 4–23, 4–32, 4–35, 4–36, 4–42, 9–1, 9–2, 9–21, 9–22, 9–23
Monroe, Vaughn, **7–207**
Monterey Jazz Festival, **6–26**
Montgomery, Wes, 1–192, 3–7
Moondoc, Jemeel, 1–220
Mooney, Jess, 6–28
Mooney, Joe, **7–208**
Moore, Freddie, 1–188, 9–9
Moore, Oscar, 3–8
Morehouse, Chauncey, 4–39
Morel, Jean-Pierre, **7–209**
Morello, Joe, 3–6
Morgan, Andrew, 6–35
Morgan, Frank, 1–219, 4–18
Morgan, Lee, 2–31
Morgan, Russ, **7–210**
Morks, Jan, **7–211**
Morris, Sonny, **7–212**
Morrow, Buddy, 1–185, **7–213**
Morton, Jelly Roll, **1–126,** 1–217, 1–218, 4–20, 4–384–42, **6–30**
Mosby, Esvan, 6–23
Motian, Paul, 3–6
MPS (record company), **7–325**
"Mr. J. B. Blues" (composition), 1–65
Mulligan, Gerry, 1–183, 1–192, 1–218, 4–2, 4–10, **7–214,** 9–6, 9–14
Mulligan, Mick. *See* Melly, George
Muranyi, Joe, 1–187
Murphy, Mark, 1–213
Murphy, Rose, **7–215**
Murray, David, 1–211, 2–3, 2–34
Murray, Sunny, 1–208

Musician (periodical), 1–216
Musso, Vido, 9–9

Nance, Ray, 9–19
Nanton, "Tricky Sam," 1–189
Napodano, John, 6–42
Narita, Cobi, 1–231
National Jazz Festival (Tauranga, New Zealand), **7–320**
Navarro, Fats, 1–209
Nazi Germany, **6–7, 6–8**
NDR Bigband, 4–41
Nelson, Ozzie, **7–216**
New Black Eagle Jazz Band. *See* Pringle, Tony
New Orleans jazz, 3–5. *See also* Dixieland jazz
New Orleans Jazz and Heritage Festival, **6–38**
New York, New York (film), 2–39
Nicholas, Albert, 7–217
Nichols, Herbie, 1–209, 4–42
Nichols, Keith, **7–218**
Nichols, Red, **1–127,** 1–221, **7–219**
Nick's (club), 6–45
Noble, Ray, 4–39, **7–220**
Nock, Mike, 1–210
Noone, Jimmie, **7–221**
Norman, Fred, 4–39
Norris, Walter, 1–180
Norvo, Red, 1–198, 1–221, 4–2

O'Casey, Hots, 1–128
O'Connell, Helen, 1–201, 1–204, 1–232
O'Day, Anita, 1–194, 1–215, 1–232, 9–22
O'Farrill, Chico, 1–195
OK Jazz, **1–77**
Oliver, King, 1–179, 2–1, 4–20, 4–24, 6–27, 6–30, **7–223**
Oliver, Shirley, 6–16
Oliver, Sy, **7–224**
Olson, Cliff, 1–196
Ondaatje, Michael, 11–6
One Night Stand (radio program), **7–333**
Örnberg, Tomas, **7–225**
Ory, Kid, 6–36, **7–226,** 9–20
Osborne, Will, **7–227**

Owens, Jimmy, 9–17
Oxtot, Dick, **1–128**

Page, Hot Lips, 6–51
Page, Patti, 1–232
Palmer, Roy, 6–36
Paragon Jazz Band. *See* Kirby, Roy
Parker, Chan, 1–129
Parker, Charlie, 1–80, 1–129, **1–130**, **1–131**, 1–136, 1–142, 1–180, 1–183, 1–186, 1–195, 1–209, 1–214, 1–217, 2–13, 2–30, 3–11, 4–10, 4–11, 4–12, **4–19**, 4–20, 4–21, 4–22, 4–35, **5–4**, **7–228**, **7–229**, 9–2, 9–11, 9–14, 11–2
Parker, Evan, **7–230**
Parker, Johnny, **7–231**
Pass, Joe, 1–190, 3–7, 3–8, 9–1
Pastor, Tony, **7–232**
Pastorius, Jaco, **1–132**, 1–216, 3–1
Patitucci, John, 3–1
Paudras, Francis, 1–138
Paul, Emanuel, 1–196
Pavageau, "Slow Drag," 6–36
Paxton, George, **7–233**
Peacock, Gary, 4–42
Pearce, Arthur, **1–133**
Pee Dee Jazzband, **7–234**
Pelosi, Art, 6–49
Peplowski, Ken, 1–185
Pepper, Art, 4–12, 4–42, 9–2, 9–3, 9–11, 9–14
Persson, Bent, **7–235**
Peruna Jazzmen, **7–236**
Peterson, Oscar, **1–134**, 1–183, 4–24, 4–42, 6–16, 6–18, 9–3, 9–20
Petters, John, **7–237**
Pettiford, Oscar, **7–238**
Pettis, Jack, 4–39
Phillips, Sid, 7–10
piano, **3–10**, 7–331
Pierce, Billie, 6–35
Pierce, DeDe, 6–35
Pierce, Nat, 1–186
Pizzarelli, Bucky, **1–135**, 1–185, 9–11
Pizzarelli, John, 1–135, 1–185
Playboy Club (New York), 4–10
Pointon, Mike, **7–239**
Polcer, Ed, 1–187

Pollack, Ben, 1–221
Porter, Bob, 1–142
Porter, Roy, **1–136**
poststructuralism, 5–5
Potter, Tommy, 9–2
Powell, Bud, **1–137**, **1–138**, 1–209, 1–218, 4–32, **7–240**, 9–2
Powell, Mel, 1–180
Powell, Teddy, **7–241**
"Powerhouse" (short story), 4–17
Preservation Hall (New Orleans), **6–32**
Prestige (record company), 1–50, 9–23
Price, Sammy, **1–139**
Prima, Louis, **7–242**
Pringle, Tony, **7–243**
Probert, George, 7–226
Puente, Tito, **1–140**
Pukwana, Dudu, 6–2
Pullen, Don, 4–36
Purvis, Jack, 1–221

Queens Museum of Art, 1–11
Quill, Gene, 4–10

R & B. *See* rhythm and blues
Ra, Sun. *See* Sun Ra
Rabin, Oscar, 1–225
Rachabane, Barney, 6–2
race, 1–205, **5–7**, **5–8**, **5–9**, **5–10**, **5–11**, **5–12**
Raeburn, Boyd, **7–244**
ragtime, 1–72, 2–3, 2–19, 3–5, 4–43, **7–331**
Rainey, Gertrude "Ma," **1–230**
Randall, Freddy, **7–245**
Randolph, Popsie, 4–10
Ravazza, Carl, **7–246**
Raymond, Al, **1–224**
Razaf, Andy, **1–141**
record collections, 11–4
recording studios and industry, 11–7
Red Feather (club), 1–193
Reeves-Phillips, Sandra, 1–187
Reig, Teddy, **1–142**
Reinhardt, Django, **1–143**, 1–179, 3–7, 3–8, 4–35, 6–48
"Reminiscing in Tempo" (composition), 1–61

Reunion Jazz Band, **7–247**
Revival Jazz Band, **7–248**
Rey, Alvino, 1–201, **7–249**
rhythm and blues, 2–31, 4–36, 6–27
rhythm section, 5–5
Rich, Buddy, **1–144**, 3–4, 3–6, **7–250**
Richards, Johnny, **7–251**
Rimington, Sammy, **7–252**
Ringquist, Claes, 7–153
Riverside (record company), 9–23
Roach, Max, 1–208, 1–209, 1–218, 1–219, 1–222, 3–6, 9–8
Roberscheuten, Frank, **7–253**
Roberts, Luckey, 3–10
Roberts, Lynn, 1–232
Robinson, Jim, **7–254**
Robinson, Smokey, 3–5
Robison, Willard, **7–255**
Rodney, Red, 1–205, 1–219
Rogers, Shorty, 9–11
Rohde, Bryce, 1–210
Rollins, Sonny, 1–183, 1–186, 1–209, 1–216, 1–218, 2–31, 3–11, 4–13, 4–40, 9–6, 9–11, 9–12, 9–21, 9–22, 9–23
Ronnie Scott's (club), 1–148
Roomful of Blues, 6–49
Roppolo, Leon, 6–30
Rosenkrantz, Timme, 1–163
Rosolino, Frank, **7–256**, 9–3
Ross, Annie, 1–200, 1–215
Rousseau, Walter Robert, 6–23
Rowles, Jimmy, 1–180
Roy, Harry, 1–225
Royal, Marshal, 6–22, 6–23
Rubin, Stan, 1–187
Ruff, Willie, **1–145**, 1–219
Rugolo, Pete, 4–41
Ruiz, Hilton, 1–140
Rushing, Jimmy, 4–6, 9–19
Russell, Bill, **1–146**
Russell, George, 1–218
Russell, Pee Wee, **1–147**, 1–221, 4–10, 4–39, **7–257**
Russell, Ross, 4–42, 11–2

Saba (record company), **7–325**
St. Cyr, Johnny, 6–36, 9–7
Saints Jazz Band, **7–258**

Salazar, Max, 1–140
salsa music, 2–4
Sample, Joe, 1–219
San Sebastián Jazz Festival, 6–13
Sanborn, David, 1–211, 2–36
Sanchez, Poncho, 1–140
Santos, Ray, 1–140
Sarpila, Antti, 6–6, **7–259**
Savannah Jazz Band, **7–260**
Savannah Jazz Festival, 6–28
Savitt, Jan, **7–261**
Savoy Records, 1–142
saxophone, **3–11**, **7–318**, **7–329**
Sayles, Emanuel, 1–196, 6–35
Schwedler, Charlie, 6–7
Scobey, Bob, 1–128
Scofield, John, 2–34
Scott, Raymond, **7–262**
Scott, Ronnie, **1–148**
Sellitti, Joseph, 6–42
Semple, Archie, **7–263**
"Sepia Panorama" (composition), 1–61
Service bands, 2–25
Sesma, Chico, 1–140
Setzer, Brian, 1–212
Sharrock, Sonny, **1–149**, 4–12
Shaw, Artie, **1–150**, 1–198, 1–204, 1–210, 1–221, 1–226, 2–27, 4–3
Shaw, Arvell, 1–197, 9–15
Shearing, George, 1–180, 4–42
Shelley, Jim, **7–264**
Shepherd, Dave, **7–265**
Shepp, Archie, 1–218, 1–219, 2–33, 9–8
Sherwood, Bobby, **7–266**
Shoffner, Bob, **7–267**
Short, Bobby, **1–151**
Short Cuts (film), 2–39
Shorter, Wayne, 1–216, 2–36, 9–22
Silver, Horace, 1–205, 1–219, 2–31, 9–2
Simeon, Omer, 6–36
Simone, Nina, 1–215, 1–218, 1–222, 9–8
Sims, Ken, **7–268**
Sims, Zoot, 4–11, 9–1, 9–8, 9–20
Sinatra, Frank, **1–152**, **1–153**, **1–154**, **1–155**, **1–156**, **1–157**, **1–158**, **1–159**, **1–160**, **1–161**, **1–162**, 1–199, 1–215, 7–269, 7–270, 9–6
Singleton, Zutty, 3–6, 9–15

Sissle, Noble, 1–191, 6–48
skiffle music, **2–10**
Slack, Freddie, **7–271**
Smith, Beasley, 6–50
Smith, Bessie, **1–194**, 1–217, **1–230**, 1–232, 4–11, **4–19**, 4–20
Smith, Buster, 6–51
Smith, Carrie, 1–187
Smith, Fletcher, 6–22
Smith, Huey "Piano," 1–212
Smith, Jabbo, 1–186, 1–188, **7–272**
Smith, Jimmy, 1–211
Smith, Keith, **7–273**
Smith, Marion Downs, 6–23
Smith, Ray, **7–274**
Smith, Stuff, 1–163, **7–275**, **7–276**, **7–277**, 9–20
Smith, Tommy, 1–179
Smith, W. O., **1–164**
Smith, Willie "The Lion," **3–10**, 4–20, 4–29, 9–9
Smock, Ginger, 6–23
"Snoring Sampson" (composition), 1–103
Snow, Michael, **7–278**
Solal, Martial, 4–42
Šošoka, Jozef, 6–11
"Soulphony" (composition), 1–47
South, Eddie, **7–279**
"Space Is the Place" (composition), 4–20
Spanier, Muggsy, 1–128, 6–30, **7–280**, **9–2**
Spargo, Tony, 4–39
Spivak, Charlie, **2–281**
Splasc(h) (record company), **7–326**
Stacy, Jess, **7–282**
Stafford, Jo, 1–232
Stahl, Dave, 9–17
Stamm, Marvin, 9–17
Starr, Kay, 1–201, 4–4
Stars of Jazz (television show), 1–57, 9–3
Stephenson, Kool, 6–37
Stewart, Rex, **1–165**
Stewart, Sammy, 6–46
Stewart, Slam, 9–4, 9–14
Still, Verna Arvey, 6–23
Still, William Grant, 6–23
Stitt, Sonny, 1–190

Stone, Lew, 1–225
Storyville Jassband, **7–283**
Storyville (New Orleans), 1–24
Storyville Tickle. *See* Lawrence, Denise
Straeter, Ted, **7–284**
Strandberg, Paul, **7–285**
"Strange Fruit" (composition), 1–230
Strange, Pete, **7–286**
Strayhorn, Billy, 1–68, 1–166, 1–195, 9–5
stride piano, 3–10
Strong, Bob, **7–287**
"Subtle Slough" (composition), 1–65
"Such Sweet Thunder" (composition), 4–24
Sudhalter, Richard, 1–187
Summers, Eddie, 6–35
Sun Ra, **1–167**, 1–184, **1–207**, 1–208, 1–218, 2–1, 2–33, 4–12, 4–20, 4–35, **7–288**, **7–289**
Sunshine, Monty, **7–290**
Sutton, Ralph, 3–10, 4–3
Swallow, Steve, 4–42
Swift, Duncan, **7–291**
swing (style), 1–80, 1–197, 1–198, 1–225, 2–3, **2–18**, **2–21**, **2–22**, **2–24**, **2–25**, 2–29, 2–35, 2–37, **3–4**, 3–7, 4–13, 4–20, 4–33, 4–40
Swiss Dixie Stompers, **7–292**
Syms, Sylvia, 4–20, 9–6
Szabó, Gábor, 1–190

tango music, 2–37
Tanner, Paul, **1–168**
Tapscott, Horace, 1–208, 6–22
Tarto, Joe, 1–188
Tatum, Art, **1–169**, 1–183, 1–195, 2–22, 4–11, 4–21, 4–32, 6–48, 9–14
Taylor, Cecil, 1–218, 1–220, 2–33, 4–20, 9–8, 9–24
Teagarden, Jack, 1–194, 1–221, 6–51, **7–293**
television, 7–323
Terrasson, Jacky, 9–6
territory bands, 2–18
Terry, Clark, 1–68, 1–190, 9–15
Thielemans, Toots, 1–179
Thigpen, Ed, 3–6

Thomas, Hersal, 6–51
Thomas, Kid, 1–196
Thomas, Leon, 1–222
Thornhill, Claude, 1–180, 4–10, **7–294**
Threadgill, Henry, 1–190, 4–13
Timmons, Bobby, **7–295**
Tipton, Billy, **1–170**
Tizol, Juan, 1–189
Tolliver, Charles, 1–222
Tormé, Mel, 1–194, 1–199, 1–204, 1–215, 1–223, 9–3
Tough, Dave, 3–4
township jazz, **6–2**
Tremble Kids. See Keller, Werner
Trent, Alphonso, 1–191
trombone, **3–12**
Trumbauer, Frank, 1–221, **7–296**
Tucker, Ben, 6–28
Tucker, Orrin, **7–297**
Tucker, Tommy, **7–298**
Turner, Joe, 3–10, 9–11
Turnock, Brian, **7–299**
"Tuxedo Junction" (composition), 1–227
Tyner, McCoy, 1–42, 1–210, 1–219, 4–32, 9–13, 9–24

United States Armed Forces Radio Service. See Armed Forces Radio Service *and* service bands

Vaché, Warren Jr., 1–210, 4–13
Valentine, Kid Thomas, 6–35, 9–7
Van Gelder, Rudy, 1–219
van Veltzen, Eelco, 7–78
Varro, Johnny, 4–39
Vaughan, Sarah, **1–171**, 1–182, 1–183, 1–186, 1–193, 1–200, 1–215, 1–218, 4–18, **7–300**, 9–1, 9–8, 9–11
Venuti, Joe, 4–39, **7–301**
Vesala, Edward, 4–41
Vestre Jazzværk, **7–302**
Vian, Boris, **11–8**
Village Vanguard (club), 6–45
Vogue (record company), **7–327**

Wagner, Ollie, 6–16
Waldo, Terry, 1–187

Waldron, Mal, 1–208, 9–23
Walker, T-Bone, 1–212
Wallace, Sippie, 6–51
Waller, Fats, 1–129, 1–141, 1–183, 1–195, 1–199, 1–217, 1–218, 3–10, 4–11, 4–20, 4–43, **7–303**
Wallis, Bob, **7–304**
Warren, Fran, 1–197
Washington, Dinah, 1–215, 4–42, 9–10
Washington, Grover Jr., 2–36
Washington, Kenny, 3–6
Waters, Benny, 1–188
Watkins, Earl, 9–2
Watkins, Joe, 6–35
Watrous, Bill, 1–190
Watts, Ernie, 9–12
Weather Report, 1–179
Webb, Chick, 3–4, 3–6, **7–305**
Webb, Lawrence "Speed," 1–191
Webster, Ben, **7–306**, 9–4, 9–6, 9–15
Webster, Freddie, 6–48
Weems, Ted, **7–307**
Wein, George, 1–210
Weintraub Syncopators, 6–8
Wellstood, Dick, **1–172**, 3–10, 4–39, 9–11
Welsh, Alex, **7–308**
West Coast jazz, 1–193, 2–6, 2–28, **6–20**. See also cool jazz
West Jesmond Rhythm Kings. See Durham, Mike
Western swing, **6–21**
Weston, Randy, 1–222
"When a Man Loves a Woman" (composition), 1–230
White, Brian, **7–309**
White, Slap Rags, 6–16
Whiteman, Paul, 2–1
Wiener Musik Galerie, 4–41
Wiggins, Gerald, 6–22
Wiggs, Johnny, 6–36
Wilber, Bob, 4–42
Wilder, Joe, 1–185
Wiley, Lee, 1–194, 1–223, **7–310**
Williams, Alfred, 6–35
Williams, Fess, 9–9
Williams, Joe, 1–199, 1–215, 9–6, 9–11

Williams, Mary Lou, **1–173**, 1–218, 4–20, 4–32, 6–39, 6–48, 9–1, 9–4, 9–18
Williams, Roy, **7–311**
Williams, Tony, 1–211, 1–216, 1–219, 1–222, 2–36
Wilson, Cassandra, 9–6
Wilson, Gerald, 6–22
Wilson, Nancy, 6–46, 9–18
Wilson, Teddy, **1–174**, 1–197, 1–201
Witherspoon, Jimmy, 1–215
WNEW (radio station), 11–8
women and jazz, 2–25, 6–43
Wooding, Sam, 1–188
Woodman, Britt, 6–22
Woodman, Brother Jr., 6–22
Woodman, Coney, 6–22

Woods, Phil, 1–213
Wormworth, Tracy, 1–231

Young, Al, **1–175**
"Young at Heart" (composition), 7–251
Young, Lee, 6–22
Young, Lester, **1–176**, **1–177**, **1–178**, 1–183, 1–186, 1–214, 1–218, 2–1, 2–22, 3–11, 4–6, 4–12, 4–19, 4–21, 4–24, 6–39, **7–312**, **7–313**, **9–2**, 9–11, 9–14, 9–20
Young, Marl, 6–22, 6–23
Young, Trummy, 9–15

Zeitlin, Denny, 1–219
Zenith Hot Stompers, **7–314**
Zentner, Si, 4–4

Author Index

Note: The numbers following each author indicate the chapter and entry listing; for example, "Abe, K. (Katsuji), 9–1" indicates chapter 9, entry number 1. Boldfaced numbers indicate principal authorship.

Abe, K. (Katsuji), 9–1, 9–2
Adams, Simon, 2–1
Adler, Larry, 1–1
Albert, Margaret, 6–43
Alexander, Charles, 3–7
Alkyer, Frank, 4–1
Ambrosetti, Flavio, 1–228
Ansermet, Ernst-Alexandre, 4–20
Armstrong, Doug, 1–56
Armstrong, Louis, 1–5, 1–6, 4–20, 4–29, 4–40
Arnaud, Gérald, 1–179
Arts Foundation of Olde Towne [Columbus, OH], 6–46
Asher, Don, 1–14
Asman, James, 7–218
Astrup, Arne, 7–67
Atkins, Clarence, 6–20
Atkins, Jerry, 11–4
Avakian, George, 2–40
Avery, Ray, 9–3
Axelrod, Alan, 2–2

Bacon, Tony, 3–1
Badger, R. Reid, 1–72, 4–5

Bailey, Sid, 7–226
Baker, Carol, 1–15
Baker, Chet, 1–15
Baker, David N., 6–20, 6–43, 11–1
Balkind, Frankfurt Gips, 1–102
Ballanta-Taylor, Nicholas G. J., 4–40
Ballantine, Christopher, 6–1
Balliett, Whitney, 1–159, 1–178, 1–180, 2–40, 4–2, 4–20, 9–7
Baquet, George, 4–14
Baraka, Amiri [Leroi Jones], 2–40, 4–20, 4–29, 4–31, 4–40, 6–20, 11–1
Barker, Danny, 1–24, 2–40
Barnett, Anthony, 1–163, 7–275, 7–276, 7–279
Barrett, Richard, 1–28
Bartels, Carol O., 1–146
Basquiat, Jean-Michel, 4–14
Bastien, David T., 4–5
Bastin, Bruce, 1–49
Batchelor, Christian, 2–20
Bechet, Sidney, 4–14, 4–20, 4–29, 4–40
Behncke, Bernhard H., 7–221, 7–223
Bennett, Richard Rodney, 4–33
Bennett, Tony, 1–19

Berendt, Joachim E., 2–3, 3–8
Berger, Edward, 1–60, 1–142
Berger, Harris M., 6–47
Berger, Morroe, 4–38
Bergerot, Frank, 2–28
Bergh, Johs, 7–318
Bergmeier, Horst [J. P.], 6–7, 7–95, 7–110
Bergreen, Laurence, 1–7
Berlin, Edward A., 1–103
Berliner, Paul F., 5–1
Bernstein, Leonard, 4–20
Berrett, Joshua, 1–8, 1–101
Bied, Dan, 4–3, 4–4
Bielderman, Gerard, 7–2, 7–4, 7–6, 7–8,
    7–10, 7–11, 7–12, 7–13, 7–15, 7–16,
    7–21, 7–23, 7–27, 7–31, 7–33, 7–34,
    7–35, 7–41, 7–43, 7–44, 7–45, 7–47,
    7–51, 7–55, 7–57, 7–59, 7–63, 7–64,
    7–70, 7–71, 7–78, 7–80, 7–81, 7–92,
    7–94, 7–96, 7–97, 7–98, 7–99, 7–100,
    7–107, 7–109, 7–115, 7–120, 7–121,
    7–122, 7–123, 7–124, 7–133, 7–135,
    7–140, 7–142, 7–148, 7–149, 7–152,
    7–159, 7–161, 7–163, 7–167, 7–168,
    7–170, 7–171, 7–173, 7–174, 7–175,
    7–176, 7–182, 7–184, 7–188, 7–189,
    7–192, 7–193, 7–199, 7–200, 7–201,
    7–203, 7–209, 7–211, 7–218, 7–225,
    7–231, 7–234, 7–235, 7–236, 7–237,
    7–239, 7–243, 7–245, 7–247, 7–248,
    7–252, 7–253, 7–258, 7–260, 7–263,
    7–264, 7–265, 7–268, 7–273, 7–274,
    2–283, 7–285, 7–290, 7–292, 7–302,
    7–304, 7–308, 7–309, 7–311, 7–314
Bird, Christiane, 6–19
Bissonnette, Big Bill, 6–31
Blass, Charles, 1–149
Blumenthal, Bob, 6–20
Bockemuehl, Eugene, 1–23
Boggs, Vernon W., 2–4
Bogle, Donald, 1–11
Borei, Sven H. E., 1–100
Boujut, Michel, 1–9
Boulton, David, 4–6
Bourgois, Louis G., 1–101
Boyd, Brian G., 7–255
Boyd, Jean A., 6–21
Boyer, Richard O., 1–61

Brand, Jack, 7–186
Brard, Olivier, 7–319
Brask, Ole, 9–4
Braxton, Anthony, 4–20
Breakey, Basil, 6–2
Bredigkeit, B., 2–3
Bredigkeit, H., 2–3
Bregman, Robert, 7–228
Brethour, Ross, 7–190, 7–215
Britt, Stan, 1–152
Broadbent, Peter, 7–50
Broome, P. J., 6–50
Brothers, Thomas, 1–5
Brower, W. A., 6–20
Brown, Denis, 7–82, 7–127, 7–198, 7–300
Brown, James, 1–120
Bruff, Larry, 1–121
Bruyninckx, Walter, 7–315
Bryant, Clora, 6–22
Büchmann-Møller, Frank, 1–176, 1–178,
    7–312
Buckner, Reginald T., 4–5
Budds, Michael J., 2–32
Bukowski, Leonard, 7–228
Bushell, Garvin, 1–32
Butler, George, 11–1
Byrd, Veronica, 1–61

Callingham, Glyn, 9–22, 9–23
Calloway, Cab, 4–20
Campbell, James, 4–6
Campbell, Robert L., 1–167, 7–288, 7–289
Cangany, Harry, 3–2
Capes, John S., -7–166
Carlin, Richard, 2–5
Carmichael, Hoagy, 4–28
Carner, Gary, 1–50, 10–1
Carr, Ian, 1–99, 10–4
Carr, Peter, 1–4
Carr, Roy, 2–6
Carruth, Hayden, 4–7
Carter, Benny, 1–60
Carter, William, 6–32
Carver, Reginald, 1–181
Caujolle, Christian, 1–16
Cave, Mark, 1–146
Cerchiari, Luca, 1–51
Chambers, Jack, 1–52

Chambers, Leland H., 4–17
Cheatham, Adolphus "Doc," 1–34
Cherrett, Ted, 1–143
Chesnel, Jacques, 1–179
Chevan, David, 1–60
Chevigny, Paul, 6–44
Chilton, John, 1–86, 1–105, 7–252, 10–1
Chiswick, Linton, 2–7
Clancy, William D., 1–88
Clare, John, 6–3
Clarke, Donald, 1–153
Claxton, William, 1–16, 6–24, 9–5, 9–6
Clayton, Buck, 4–20
Cliffe, Peter, 2–17
Clooney, Rosemary, 1–35
Clute, Peter, 6–25
Clutten, Michael N., 7–48
Cohen, Frederick, 11–4
Coleman, Bill, 1–38
Coleman, Ornette, 2–40
Coleman, Ray, 1–154
Coller, Derek, 7–282
Collette, Buddy, 6–22
Collier, James Lincoln, 4–6, 4–8
Collins, R., 6–33
Coltrane, John, 4–1
Condon, Eddie, 4–20
Connor, D. Russell, 7–111
Constant, Denis, 1–116
Cook, Richard, 8–1
Cooke, Jack, 1–28
Cooke, Mervyn, 2–8
Coolidge, Clark, 4–9
Corbett, John, 4–16
Cortázar, Julio, 4–28
Coss, Bill, 1–131
Cox, Bette Yarbrough, 6–23
Cox, Bill, 1–168
Craker, Chris, 2–9
Crawford, Richard, 7–328
Creeley, Robert, 4–28
Crosby, Bing, 1–46
Crosby, Robert G., 1–18
Crouch, Stanley, 1–32, 1–45, 1–61, 1–70, 1–131, 2–40, 4–14, 4–20, 11–1
Crow, Bill, 4–10, 4–11
Crowther, Bruce, 1–182
Crumpacker, Bunny, 1–183

Crumpacker, Chick, 1–183
Curtis, Susan, 1–104
Cutler, Chris, 7–289

Dahl, Linda, 1–173
Dance, Stanley, 1–61, 1–70, 2–40, 4–1, 6–45
Dankworth, John, 1–48
Darrell, R. D., 1–70
Davis, Angela Y., 1–230
Davis, Francis, 1–131, 1–184, 4–12, 4–13
Davis, Margaret, 1–149
Davis, Miles, 4–20, 4–29
Dawson, Jim, 1–118
Dean, Roger T., 5–2
de Barros, Paul, 6–52
de Beauvoir, Simone, 4–28
Decaens, Jean-Loup, 7–256
Deffaa, Chip, 1–185, 1–186, 1–187, 1–188
de Jager, Marjolijn, 2–28
Delannoy, Luc, 1–177
Desmond, Paul, 4–20
de Toledano, Ralph. See Toledano, Ralph de
DeVeaux, Scott, 2–29
Dewe, Michael, 2–10
De Wilde, Laurent, 1–123
Dexter, Dave Jr., 4–1
Dibango, Manu, 1–58
Dickinson, Jonathan, 1–123
Dickinson, Peter, 1–115
Dietrich, Kurt, 1–189
Dobbin, Robert, 1–124
Dodds, Baby, 1–59
Dodge, Roger Pryor, 4–20, 4–38
Doran, James M., 7–49
Dorsey, Jimmy, 4–20
Dorsey, Tommy, 4–20
Drew, Paul Redmond, 2–10
Duany, Jorge, 2–4
Dupuis, Robert, 1–21
Dürr, Klaus-Uwe, 7–5, 7–217, 7–221, 7–223, 7–267, 7–272
Duval-Harrison, Daphne, 6–43

Ehrlich, Marty, 1–28
Ellington, Duke, 1–61, 1–70, 2–40
Elliott, Nancy Miller, 1–186

Ellison, Ralph, 1–61, 4–6, 4–20, 4–29
Elmore, Charles, 6–27
Elvers, Erwin, 7–15, 7–27, 7–36, 7–135, 7–142, 7–152, 7–163, 7–175, 7–182, 7–234, 7–292, 7–302
Elworth, Steven B., 4–16
Ennekari, Risto, 7–259
Enstice, Wayne, 1–190, 3–8
Epstein, Daniel Mark, 1–36
Erenberg, Lewis A., 2–21
Erlewine, Michael, 8–11
Erskine, Peter, 1–228
Europe, James Reese, 4–33, 4–40
Evans, Bill, 1–138, 2–40, 4–31
Evans, Linda K., 7–17, 7–219
Evans, Nicholas M., 11–2
Evans, Philip R., 7–17, 7–219, 7–296
Evensmo, Jan, 7–318, 7–329
Ewens, Graeme, 1–77

Fairweather, Digby, 7–218, 8–5,, 10–4
Fanø, Mette, 6–5
Feather, Leonard, 1–131, 1–159, 2–40, 3–8, 4–1, 4–40, 7–67, 10–5
Fell, John L., 3–10
Ferguson, Otis, 4–20
Fernett, Gene, 1–191
Ferri, Daniel, 9–14
Festival de Jazz de San Sebastián [Spain], 6–13
Fidelman, Geoffrey Mark, 1–75
Figi, J. B., 2–40
Fini, Francesco, 7–326
Firestone, Ross, 1–83
Fischer, Klaus Gotthard, 1–31, 7–325
Fisher, M. Eleanor, 1–202
Fitterling, Thomas, 1–124
Floyd, Samuel Jr., 4–29, 4–40
Folley-Cooper, Marquette, 4–14
Ford, Alun, 1–26
Fordham, John, 1–148, 1–192, 3–7, 4–15, 8–2
Fox, Jo Brooks, 1–193
Fox, Jules, 1–193
Franklin, Benjamin V, 4–5
Frazier, George, 2–40
Friedlander, Lee, 9–7
Friedman, Carol, 9–8

Friedwald, Will, 1–19, 1–155, 1–159, 1–194, 4–41
Fujioka, Yasuhiro, 7–58

Gabbard, Krin, 2–39, 4–5, 4–16, 4–17
Gabel, Edward F., 1–107
Gallichan, Syd R., 7–48
Gara, Larry, 1–59
Garber, Frederick, 4–17
Gardner, Mark, 7–240, 8–5
Garrod, Charles, 7–1, 7–3, 7–7, 7–9, 7–14, 7–18, 7–20, 7–26, 7–29, 7–30, 7–32, 7–38, 7–39, 7–40, 7–46, 7–52, 7–53, 7–60, 7–61, 7–62, 7–66, 7–68, 7–73, 7–74, 7–75, 7–79, 7–83, 7–84, 7–91, 7–93, 7–101, 7–102, 7–103, 7–104, 7–105, 7–108, 7–112, 7–113, 7–118, 7–125, 7–127, 7–129, 7–131, 7–132, 7–134, 7–136, 7–137, 7–143, 7–145, 7–146, 7–147, 7–150, 7–151, 7–154, 7–155, 7–156, 7–157, 7–158, 7–160, 7–162, 7–164, 7–165, 7–169, 7–172, 7–177, 7–178, 7–179, 7–180, 7–183, 7–185, 7–187, 7–190, 7–191, 7–194, 7–196, 7–197, 7–202, 7–204, 7–205, 7–206, 7–207, 7–210, 7–213, 7–216, 7–220, 7–224, 7–227, 7–232, 7–233, 7–241, 7–242, 7–244, 7–246, 7–249, 7–261, 7–262, 7–266, 7–269, 7–271, 7–281, 7–284, 7–287, 7–293, 7–294, 7–297, 7–298, 7–301, 7–305, 7–307
Gaut, Greg, 4–5
Gavin, James, 9–5
Gayford, Martin, 8–3
Gazdar, Coover, 7–114, 7–238
Geerken, Hartmut, 7–289
Geist, Gabi, 7–289
Gelly, Dave, 3–7
Gendron, Bernard, 4–16, 11–2
Gerard, Charley, 5–7
Gervais, Raymond, 7–278
Giddins, Gary, 1–10, 1–46, 1–50, 1–70, 1–195, 4–18, 4–20, 11–1, 11–2
Gifford, Barry, 1–119
Gignoux, Danny, 2–7
Gilbert, Henry F., 4–33
Gillespie, Dizzy, 4–6, 4–20, 4–29, 4–40
Gioia, Ted, 2–11, 6–24

Giovanni, Nikki, 4–29
Gitler, Ira, 1–45, 1–131, 2–40, 4–1, 4–19, 9–18, 10–5
Gleason, Ralph J., 1–45, 1–159, 1–178, 4–1, 4–19, 4–20
Gleeson, Scoop, 4–33
Godbolt, Jim, 11–3
Goggin, Jim, 1–128, 6–25
Goldberg, Joe, 1–45
Goldenberg, David, 11–4
Goldson, Elizabeth, 4–14
Golson, Benny, 1–205, 4–31
Gordon, Claire P., 1–165
Gordon, Steve, 6–2
Gottlieb, Robert, 4–20, 7–52
Gottlieb, William, 2–7, 4–1, 4–14, 9–9, 9–14
Gourse, Leslie, 1–113, 1–125, 1–171, 1–231
Granata, Charles L., 1–156
Gray, Herman, 1–28
Gray, John, 10–2
Green, Benny, 1–50, 2–40, 4–20, 4–21
Green, Sharony Andrews, 1–84
Green, William, 6–22
Greer, Sonny, 4–20
Griffiths, David, 1–196, 7–144, 7–291
Groves, Alan, 1–137
Grudens, Richard, 1–197, 1–198, 1–199, 1–232
Gruyters, Sjef, 7–133

Hadler, Mona, 4–17
Hager, Andrew G., 1–200
Hair, Raymond, 7–165
Hajdu, David, 1–166
Hall, Fred M., 1–30, 1–201
Hall, George, 7–261
Hall, William, 1–1
Hamada, Yoh-ichi, 7–58
Hammond, John, 1–178, 4–1, 4–20
Hampton, Lionel, 4–20
Handy, D. Antoinette, 1–112, 1–233, 4–1
Hansen, Chadwick, 1–93
Hargrove, Rich, 1–202
Harlos, Christopher, 4–17
Harris, Kenny, 1–110
Harrison, Max, 1–53, 1–70, 3–7, 4–20

Hartley, Jack, 7–251
Hartman, Charles O., 11–5
Harvey, Mark S., 4–5
Hasse, John Edward, 1–62, 1–66
Hatchett, Louis, 7–277
Hauff, Sigrid, 7–289
Hawes, Hampton, 4–20
Hazeldine, Mike, 6–36, 7–138
Hazell, Edward, 2–13, 2–38
Heath, Moira, 1–203
Hefele, Bernhard, 7–289
Heffley, Mike, 1–27
Henderson, Leora, 4–20
Hennessey, Mike, 1–33
Hennessey, Thomas J., 2–18, 5–8
Hentoff, Nat, 1–45, 1–50, 1–131, 1–178, 2–40, 4–1, 4–6, 4–20, 4–22
Herman, Woody, 1–89
Hester, Karlton Edward, 1–41
Hester, Stanley, 7–219
Hester, Stephen, 7–219
Hilbert, Robert, 1–147, 7–257, 11–4
Hill, Dick, 1–2
Himmelstein, David, 2–40
Hinton, Milt, 9–4, 9–10
Hintze, Clarence C., 7–250
Hobsbawm, Eric J., 4–23
Hoctor, Michelle, 6–15
Hodeir, André, 1–53, 1–70, 4–20
Hodes, Art, 1–93, 2–40, 4–20
Hoefsmit, Sjef, 7–85
Hoffman, Matthew, 1–20
Holden, Stephen, 1–159
Holiday, Billie, 4–20, 4–29, 4–40
Holley, Eugene Jr., 1–61
Holtje, Steve, 8–4
Hopkins, Claude, 1–94
Horn, Paul, 1–95
Hornstein, Julius, 6–28
Hosiasson, José, 11–2
Hostager, Todd J., 4–5
House, Son, 4–29
Howlett, Felicity, 2–40
Hubbard, Roy, 7–291, 7–314
Huesmann, Günther, 2–3
Huggard, Dennis O., 7–320, 7–321
Hughes, Dick, 1–96
Hughes, Langston, 4–29

Hughes, Ralph, 9–11
Hultin, Randi, 1–228
Hunt, Laird, 9–12
Hurston, Zora Neale, 4–31

Ingless, Steve, 6–14
Irwin, Lew, 1–157
Isoardi, Steven, 6–22

Jackson, Richard, 1–146
James, Burnett, 4–24
James, Etta, 1–97
James, Michael, 1–61
Jarrett, Michael, 11–6
Jenkins, Leroy, 7–279
Jenkins, Willard, 6–20
Johnsen, Andreas, 1–186
Johnsen, John, 1–186
Johnston, Peter, 7–143
Jones, Harold, 7–117
Jones, LeRoi. See Baraka, Amiri
Jones, Patti, 1–3
Jones, Quincy, 4–1
Jordan, Steve, 1–106
Jost, Ekkehard, 2–33, 8–5
Judge, Philip, 1–1

Kaliss, Jeff, 1–81
Kansas City Jazz Museum, 6–40
Kaplan, Lloyd S., 6–49
Kater, Michael H., 6–8
Keepnews, Orrin, 2–40, 4–20
Keepnews, Peter, 1–53
Keller, David, 1–136
Kelson, Jack, 6–22
Kempton, Murray, 4–20
Kennedy, Don, 1–204
Kennedy, William, 6–30
Kenney, William H. III, 4–5, 4–16, 6–29
Kenton, Audree Coke, 1–88
Kernfeld, Barry, 5–3, 8–5, 10–6
Kessler, Karl Heinz, 7–289
Khair, Emilie Eklin, 1–92
Kiner, Larry F., 7–296, 7–330
King, Jonny, 2–12
Kington, Miles, 4–25
Kinze, Charles, 1–5

Kirchner, Bill, 1–53
Kjellberg, Erik, 1–100
Klauber, Bruce H., 1–109
Klinkowitz, Jerome, 7–214
Kluck, Henk, 7–24
Knight, Arthur, 4–17
Knopper, Steve, 8–6
Koenig, Karl, 3–3, 6 34
Kofsky, Frank, 1–42, 1–45, 2–40, 5–9
Komara, Edward M., 7–229, 11–2
Korall, Burt, 3–4
Korst, Bill, 7–1, 7–7, 7–26, 7–30, 7–32, 7–40, 7–46, 7–73, 7–74, 7–79, 7–91, 7–113, 7–118, 7–136, 7–158, 7–177, 7–186, 7–216, 7–241, 7–244, 7–249, 7–266
Koster, Piet, 7–313
Kriebel, Robert C., 1–90
Krupa, Gene, 4–20
Kuehn, John, 7–67
Kuhlman, Gus, 7–310
Kukla, Barbara J., 6–41
Kukla, Jon, 1–146
Kunert, Wolfgang, 4–41

Lábska, Yvetta, 6–11
Lacy, Steve, 1–124
Laird, Ross, 7–331
Lake, Steve, 4–41
Lambert, Dan, 3–8
Lambert, Eddie, 1–63, 7–85
Lancaster, Byard, 4–26
Lane, G. B., 3–12
Lange, Art, 1–228, 4–1
Langhorn, Peter, 7–306
Larkin, Colin, 10–7
Larkin, Philip, 4–27, 4–28
Lasa, Jesús, 6–13
Latham, John, 7–33, 7–96, 7–116
Latxague, Robert, 9–12
Lax, Robert, 7–289
Lee, Nancy Ann, 8–4
Lee, Raymond, 7–22, 7–25, 7–28, 7–37, 7–54, 7–106, 7–116, 7–119, 7–124, 7–138, 7–139, 7–153, 7–192, 7–212, 7–243, 7–254, 7–299
Lee, William F., 1–74
Lees, Gene, 1–91, 1–134, 1–159, 1–205

LeFevre, M. Theresa, 1–146
Lemmon, Alfred E., 1–146
Leonard, Herman, 9–14
Lester, James, 1–169
Levin, Floyd, 7–226
Levinson, Peter J., 1–98
Lewis, Furry, 4–29
Lewis, Laurie, 1–133
Liebman, David, 1–206, 11–7
Ligthart, Arie, 1–174
Lindemeyer, Paul, 3–11
Lipsitz, George, 1–111
Litchfield, Jack, 6–17
Litweiler, John, 1–39, 4–6
Livingston, Alan, 7–195
Lock, Graham, 1–28, 1–207, 1–208
Løgager, Eva, 1–163
Lohmann, Jan, 1–51, 7–65
Long, Richard A., 1–11
Lord, Tom, 7–316
Lorrai, Marcello, 1–229
Lott, Eric, 4–16, 4–31
Lotz, Rainer E., 6–7, 7–95
Love, Preston, 1–111
Lowe, Jacques, 9–13
Loza, Steven, 1–140
Lucas, Nick, 3–8
Lyons, Jimmy, 11–1
Lyttkens, Bertil, 7–181

Macanic, Deborah, 4–14
MacDonald, Ian, 1–47
MacKenzie, Harry, 7–330, 7–332, 7–333
Mackey, Nathaniel, 1–28
Mackintosh, Robert, 1–151
Magee, Jeffrey, 7–328
Maggin, Donald L., 1–79
Magill, John, 1–146
Mailer, Norman, 4–28
Male, Melinda, 1–229
Mandel, Howard, 2–34
Man Ray, 4–14
Marcellin-Rice, Louis, 1–179
Marchand-Kiss, Christophe, 9–12
Marquis, Donald M., 1–25
Marsalis, Wynton, 1–61, 1–114
Marsh, Graham, 9–21, 9–22, 9–23
Martin, Henry, 5–4

Martinelli, Francesco, 7–230
Martyn, Barry, 6–35, 6–36
Masotti, Roberto, 1–229
Massagli, Luciano, 7–86
Mathieson, Kenny, 1–209, 3–7
Matisse, Henri, 4–14
McBride, Christian, 2–12
McDonough, John, 4–6
McGregor, Maxine, 1–116
McLeod, Jim, 1–210
McNeil, Janice, 4–14
McNeil, W. K., 7–277
McPartland, Marian, 4–1, 4–6, 4–20
Meadows, Eddie S., 10–3
Meltzer, David, 4–28, 4–29
Meriwether, Doug, 7–250
Merlin, Arnaud, 2–28
Merod, Jim, 4–31
Meyer, Arnvid, 6–5
Meyer, Edward N., 1–172
Mezzrow, Mezz, 1–119
Middlebrook, Diane Wood, 1–170
Milkowski, Bill, 1–132, 1–211, 1–212, 4–1
Miller, Marc H., 1–11
Miller, Mark, 6–16
Miller, William F., 3–6
Mingus, Charles, 2–40, 4–1, 4–6
Minor, William, 6–12, 6–26
Mirtle, Jack, 7–195
Mobach, Harm, 7–313
Monet, Rubye, 1–138
Monson, Ingrid, 5–5
Moody, Bill, 1–213
Moorhouse, Barry, 3–1
Morgenstern, Dan, 1–6, 1–11, 1–50, 1–70, 1–142, 1–178, 1–191, 2–3, 2–40, 4–1, 4–20, 6–43, 7–85, 9–15, 11–1
Morrill, Dexter, 7–130
Morton, Brian, 8–1
Morton, Jelly Roll, 4–20, 4–38, 4–40
Mosbrook, Joe, 6–48
Motion, Tim, 9–14
Moulé, François-Xavier, 7–87
Muikku, Jari, 6–6
Murray, Albert, 1–61, 4–29, 4–31
Mustazza, Leonard, 1–158, 1–159
Myers, Eric, 6–4

Nakao, Yoichi, 1–84
Nelson, Don, 4–1
Nevers, Daniel, 7–319
Nevill, Tim, 2–3
Nicholson, Stuart, 1–64, 1–76, 2–35, 2–36
Nielsen, Ole, 7–88
Nisenson, Eric, 1–43, 1–54, 4–30
Nketia, J. H. Kwabena, 6–43

Obrecht, Jas, 3–8
O'Brien, Ed, 1–160, 7–270
Odio, Elena B., 1–177
Ogren, Kathy, 4–5
Oliphant, Dave, 6–51, 11–2
O'Meally, Robert G., 1–61, 4–31
Oppong-Wife, Jonathan, 9–14
Owens, Thomas, 2–30
Oxtot, Dick, 1–128

Palmer, Richard F., 4–27, 7–83, 7–84
Palmer, Robert, 2–40
Panassié, Hugues, 1–70
Panish, Jon, 5–10
Parker, Chan, 1–129
Parker, Douglass, 11–2
Parker, Tony, 1–87
Parks, Gordon, 4–14
Parnell, Jack, 1–18
Pasich, Kirk, 1–91
Pasternak, Judith, 2–19
Paudras, Francis, 1–138
Pegg, Bev, 7–291
Penwarden, Charles, 1–9
Pepper, Art, 4–28
Peretti, Burton H., 5–11
Pernet, Robert, 7–322
Perry, David, 1–214
Persson, Jan, 9–15
Peterson, Oscar, 4–1
Petkov, Steven, 1–159
Petteruti, Robert, 6–49
Pettinger, Peter, 1–73
Peyton, Dave, 4–40
Piazza, Tom, 2–40, 4–32, 8–7
Pinfold, Mike, 1–182
Polomski, Lothar, 7–333
Porter, Lewis, 1–44, 1–45, 1–176, 1–178, 2–13, 4–33, 7–58, 7–312

Porter, Roy, 1–136
Powell, Neil, 10–8
Preiss, Cliff, 9–13
Price, Michael H., 3–8
Price, Sammy, 1–139
Priestley, Brian, 3–7, 10–4
Purser, Julian, 7–11, 7–99, 7–218

Raben, Erik, 7–317
Radano, Ronald M., 1–29
Ragab, Salah, 7–289
Raps, Beth G., 1–58
Rasmussen, Lars, 7–141
Rasula, Jed, 4–16
Rattenbury, Ken, 1–65
Raymond, Al, 1–224
Redfern, David, 9–16
Reed, Ishmael, 4–29
Reese, Gregory, 6–20
Reig, Teddy, 1–142
Rentsch, Christian, 1–228
Richmond, Caroline, 1–139
Riley, Herlin, 3–5
Ripmaster, Terence M., 1–135, 6–42
Ritz, David, 1–97
Roberts, John Storm, 2–4, 2–37
Roland, Paul, 1–215
Rosenkrantz, Timme, 1–163
Rosenthal, David H., 2–31
Rosenthall, Rap, 6–18
Ross, Courtney Sole, 1–102
Ross, Dan B., 1–146
Rouard, Danielle, 1–58
Rowland, Mark, 1–216
Rubin, Paul, 1–190, 3–8
Ruck, Nancy, 1–146
Ruff, Willie, 1–145
Ruppli, Michel, 7–327
Russell, Bill, 6–36
Russell, Ross, 4–38, 11–2
Russell, William, 1–126, 4–38
Rust, Brian, 1–2, 4–34
Ryan, Tim, 1–37
Rye, Howard, 1–34, 1–93

Saks, Norman, 7–228
Salazar, Max, 2–4
Salemann, Dieter, 7–208

Author Index

Sallis, James, 3–8
Sanchez, Sonia, 4–29
Sandmel, Ben, 6–38
Santoro, Gene, 4–20, 4–35, 4–36
Sargeant, Winthrop, 4–33
Sartre, Jean-Paul, 4–20
Sayers, Scott P. Jr., 1–160
Scanlan, Tom, 1–106, 2–22
Schaap, Phil, 1–76, 1–131, 1–178
Scherman, Tony, 1–216
Schiedt, Duncan, 1–217, 2–7
Schlouch, Claude, 7–295
Schoenberg, Loren, 1–178, 2–40
Schuller, Gunther, 1–70, 2–40, 4–20, 4–40, 4–41, 11–1
Schwartz, Barbara, 7–126
Schwartz, Jonathan, 1–159
Selchow, Manfred, 7–69
Selk, Len, 7–310
Shadwick, Keith, 1–218, 2–14
Shaw, Arnold, 1–159, 2–23
Shaw, Artie, 4–28
Shipton, Alyn, 1–24, 1–34, 1–80, 1–137
Shor, Russ, 11–4
Short, Bobby, 1–151
Sidran, Ben, 1–219
Simon, Bill, 3–8
Simon, George T., 1–131
Simon, Géza Gábor, 6–9, 7–19
Simosko, Vladimir, 7–42
Simpson, Norman, 7–13, 7–97, 7–100, 7–122, 7–140, 7–171, 7–263, 7–286, 7–308, 7–311
Sinatra, Nancy, 1–161
Singer, Barry, 1–141
Sinisalo, Susan, 6–6
Smith, Bill, 1–28
Smith, Carl, 7–240
Smith, Charles Edward, 2–40
Smith, Michael P., 6–37, 6–38
Smith, Paul, 1–229
Smith, Stuff, 1–163
Smith, W. O., 1–164
Smith, Willie "The Lion," 4–20, 4–29
Smits, Guus, 7–37
Snow, Michael, 7–278
Souchon, Edmond, 4–20
Southern, Eileen, 4–29

Soyinka, Wole, 4–29
Spady, James G., 6–20
Spagnardi, Ronald, 3–6
Spilka, Bill, 9–17
Spitzer, David D., 9–18
Stagg, Mike, 3–3
Stanley, Ray, 7–265
Stansby, Ray, 7–245
Starr, S. Frederick, 4–6
Stearns, Marshall W., 4–40
Steed, Janna Tull, 1–66
Stewart, Chuck, 2–7
Stewart, Frank, 1–114
Stewart, Rex, 1–165
Stewart, Thomas W., 1–227
Stockdale, Robert L., 7–76, 7–77
Stokes, W. Royal, 6–45
Storb, Ilse, 1–31
Stowe, David W., 2–24
Stratemann, Klaus, 1–12, 1–67
Stroff, Stephen M., 1–127, 8–8
Stuart, David, 2–40
Stump, Paul, 1–117
Sturm, Fred, 5–6
Such, David G., 1–220
Sudhalter, Richard M., 1–221
Summerfield, Maurice J., 3–9
Sutro, Dirk, 2–15
Suzuki, Naoki, 7–323
Swanson, Bill, 4–37
Swanzy, David, 1–112
Swenson, John, 8–9
Szwed, John F., 1–167

Tanner, Lee, 9–19
Tanner, Paul O., 1–168
Tapscott, Horace, 6–22
Taylor, Arthur, 1–222
Taylor, Billy, 4–14, 4–33, 6–43, 11–1
Taylor, Cecil, 4–20
Teubig, Klaus, 7–56
Thomas, Lorenzo, 11–2
Thompson, G. Bertram, 1–31
Thorbjørn, Sjøgren, 7–306
Thornbury, Will, 1–129
Thress, Dan, 3–5
Timner, W. E., 7–89
Toledano, Ralph de, 4–38

Tormé, Mel, 1–144, 1–223, 3–4, 4–1
Touchet, Leo, 6–39
Tracy, Sheila, 1–225
Travis, Dempsey J., 1–13, 1–68
Troup, Stuart, 1–89
Troxler, Niklaus, 9–24
Trumbauer, William, 7–296
Tschannen, Lance, 1–228
Tucker, Clay, 6–50
Tucker, Mark, 1–32, 1–69, 1–70
Tucker, Michael, 1–78
Tynan, John, 4–1
Tyner, McCoy, 4–32

Ulanov, Barry, 1–131
Ullman, Michael, 2–13
Umphred, Neal, 8–10
Underwood, Lee, 1–95

Vaché, Warren W. Sr., 1–22, 1–94, 4–39
Vail, Ken, 1–71, 1–82, 2–16
Valburn, Jerry, 7–90
van de Munt, Aart, 7–209, 7–225, 7–235, 7–236
van der Elsken, Ed, 9–20
Van Horn, Rick, 3–2
van Loo, Humphrey, 1–174
Vare, Ethlie Ann, 1–162
Vian, Boris, 11–8
Vidacovich, Johnny, 3–5
Vinding, Terkild, 3–10
Vogel, Eric, 4–6
Vuorela, Jari-Pekka, 6–6

Walser, Robert, 4–40
Ward, Tyrone, 1–85
Waters, Ethel, 4–29
Watrous, Peter, 1–45
Way, Chris, 2–25
Weiland, Steven, 4–5
Weiler, Uwe, 7–324
Weir, Bob, 1–139
Wellstood, Dick, 2–40
Westerberg, Hans, 7–259
Wheeler, Geoffrey, 7–334
White, Andrew, 2–40

White, Booker, 4–29
White, John, 1–150, 4–27
Whitehead, Kevin, 6–10
Whyatt, Bert, 7–280
Widerøe, Arild, 7–41
Wiener Musik Galerie [Vienna], 4–41
Wild, David, 1–45
Willard, Bill, 4–23
Willard, Hal, 1–57
Williams, Alan, 1–108
Williams, Berneice, 6–20
Williams, K. Leander, 6–20
Williams, Martin T., 1–45, 1–70, 2–40, 4–20, 4–42
Williams, Mary Lou, 4–20
Williams, Richard, 1–55
Williams, William Carlos, 4–28
Wilmer, Val, 1–28, 3–5
Wilson, Gerald, 6–22
Wilson, John S., 4–1, 4–20
Wilson, Olly, 11–1
Wilson, Peter Niklas, 1–40, 4–41
Wilson, Teddy, 1–174
Woideck, Carl, 1–45, 1–130, 1–131
Wolfe, Bernard, 1–119
Wölfer, Jürgen, 7–222, 7–251
Wood, Brian, 7–25, 7–37, 7–54, 7–254
Wood, Ean, 1–226, 2–26
Woods, Bernie, 2–27
Wright, David G., 1–122
Wright, Laurie, 7–303
Wright, Richard, 4–29
Wulff, Ingo, 1–17
Wyndham, Tex, 4–43
Wynn, Ron, 8–11

Yancy, Youseff, 4–26
Yoshida, George, 5–12
Young, Al, 1–175
Young, Ben, 7–72
Young, Matt, 6–22

Zaradin, John, 3–7
Zwerin, Mike, 1–228

Title Index

Note: The numbers following each title indicate the chapter and entry listing; for example, "Abbi Hübner Discography, 7–135" indicates chapter 7, entry number 135.

Abbi Hübner Discography, 7–135
Abdullah Ibrahim, 7–141
Abe Lyman and His Orchestra, 7–183
Acker Bilk Discography, 7–21
Al Donahue and His Orchestra: Plus Van Alexander and His Orchestra, 7–1, 7–73
Al Fairweather Discography, 7–96
Alain Marquet Discography, 7–189
Alan Elsdon Discography, 7–92
Alex Welsh Discography, 7–308
All Music Guide to Jazz, 8–11
All or Nothing at All, 1–153
All That Savannah Jazz, 6–27
Alvino Rey and His Orchestra, Plus the King Sisters 1939–1958, 7–158, 7–249
American Musicians II, 1–180
The Andrews Sisters, 7–3
Anita O'Day, 7–222
Annie Hawkins Discography, 7–124
Anthony Braxton, 1–26
Archie Semple Discography, 7–26
Art Kassel and His Orchestra; Plus: Johnny Mesner and His Orchestra, 7–150, 7–202
Art of Recording, 11–7

Arthur and the Nights at the Turntable, 1–133
Artie Shaw, 1–150
As Though I Had Wings, 1–15
Ascension, 1–43
Assessing, Insuring, and Disposing of Jazz Record Collections, 11–4
Australian Jazz Directory 1998, 6–4
Avant-garde Jazz Musicians, 1–220

Baby Dodds Story, 1–59
Back Beats and Rim Shots, 1–22
Barrelhouse Jazzband Discography, 7–15
Basic Musical Library, "P" Series, 1–1000, 7–330
Bass Book, 3–1
Bassically Speaking, 1–60
Bebop, 2–30
Bebop and Nothingness, 4–12
Bebop Revolution in Words and Music, 11–2
Belgian Jazz Discography, 7–322
Ben, 7–306
Ben Bernie and His Orchestra, 7–20
Benkó Dixieland Band, 7–19
Benny Goodman, 7–111

Berklee, 2–34
Bernard Etté, A Biodiscography, 7–95
Beryl Bryden Discography, 7–35
Best Damn Trumpet Player, 1–197
Best of Jazz, 8–3
Beyond the Blues, 6–2
Beyond Category, 1–62
Big Band Jump Personality Interviews, 1–204
Big Bands Go to War, 2–25
Big Jim, 7–254
Bill Evans, 1–73
Billy Eckstine, 7–82
Billy May and His Orchestra, 7–194
Biographical Encyclopedia of Jazz, 10–5
Birth of Bebop, 2–29
Bix, 7–17
Black and Blue, 1–141
Black Gypsy, 7–279
Black Music, White Business, 5–9
Black Women in American Bands and Orchestras, 1–233
Blackwell Guide to Recorded Jazz, 8–5
Bley Play, 7–24
Blue, 4–30
Blue Flame, 1–90
Blue Note, 9–21
Blue Note 2, 9–22
Blues Legacies and Black Feminism, 1–230
Blues Up and Down, 4–32
Blutopia, 1–207
Bob Chester and His Orchestra, 7–46
Bob Crosby and His Orchestra, 7–61
Bob Wallis Discography, 7–304
Bobby Byrne and His Orchestra; Plus: Dean Hudson and His Orchestra, 7–40, 7–136
Bobby Hackett, 7–117
Bobby Sherwood and His Orchestra; Plus: Randy Brooks and His Orchestra, 7–32, 7–266
Bobby Short, 1–151
Bobby Timmons, 7–295
Bodgie Dada and the Cult of Cool, 6–3
Book of Hungarian Jazz, 6–9
Born to Swing, 1–226, 2–26

Bouncing with Bud, 7–240
Boy Meets Horn, 1–165
Boyd Raeburn and His Orchestra; Plus: Johnny Bothwell and George Handy, 7–26, 7–118, 7–244
Brian Lemon Discography, 7–171
Brian Turnock Discography, 7–299
Brian White Discography, 7–309
Buddy Bolden and the Last Days of Storyville, 1–24
Buddy Clark, 7–52
Buddy DeFranco, 7–67
Buddy Morrow and His Orchestra, 7–213
Bunny Berigan, 1–21

Call Me Lucky, 1–46
Call to Assembly, 1–145
Campiana, 1–33
Carmen McRae, 7–198
Catalogue of the National Jazz Festival Recordings, Tauranga, 7–320
Cats of Any Color, 1–205
Celebrating the Duke, 4–19
Celebrating the Saxophone, 3–11
Central Avenue, 6–23
Central Avenue Sounds, 6–22
Century of Jazz, 2–6
Chan Parker, 1–129
Changes Over Time, 5–6
Charlie Barnet and His Orchestra 1933–1973, 7–14
Charlie Christian, 7–50
Charlie Parker, 1–130
Charlie Parker Companion, 1–131
Charlie Parker Discography, 7–228
Charlie Parker and Thematic Improvisation, 5–4
Charlie Spivak and His Orchestra, 7–281
Charly Antolini Discography, 7–4
Charquet & Co., 7–209
Chasing the Vibration, 1–208
Chet Baker in Europe, 1975–1988, 1–17
Chicago Jazz, 6–29
Chick Webb and His Orchestra, Including: Ella Fitzgerald and Her Orchestra, 7–102, 7–305
Chops, 9–17

Chris Barber Discography, 7–11
Chris Blount Discography, 7–25
Chris McGregor and the Brotherhood of Breath, 1–116
Chuck Foster and His Orchestra, 7–105
Clarinet Wizard, 7–37
Claude Luter Discography, 7–182
Claude Thornhill and His Orchestra, 7–294
Claxography, 9–5
Cleveland Jazz History, 6–48
Clyde Lucas and His Orchestra; Plus: Al Kavelin and His Orchestra; Carl Ravazza and His Orchestra; Ted Straeter and His Orchestra, 7–151, 7–179, 7–246, 7–284
Colin Bowden Discography, 7–28
Color of Jazz, 5–10
Command Performance, USA!, 7–332
Complete Idiot's Guide to Jazz, 2–2
Congo Colossus, 1–77
Crazy Fingers, 1–94
Creation of Jazz, 5–11
Cuff Billett Discography, 7–22
Cy Laurie Discography, 7–167

Dan Bied's Jazz Reader, 4–3
Dance of the Infidels, 1–138
Dancing in Your Head, 4–35
Dancing to a Black Man's Tune, 1–104
Daniel Barda Discography, 7–12
Dave Brennan Discography, 7–31
Dave Brubeck, 1–31
Dave Shepherd Discography, 7–265
Day Before Yesterday, 6–14
Debut Label, 7–324
Del Courtney and His Orchestra; Plus: Gray Gordon and His Orchestra, 7–60, 7–112
Desert Sands, 7–275
Dial Recordings of Charlie Parker, 7–229
Dick Hawdon Discography, 7–123
Dick Haymes and His Orchestra, 7–127
Dick Jurgens and His Orchestra, 7–147
Different Drummers, 6–8
Digby Fairweather Discography, 7–97
Dill Jones Discography, 7–144

Ding! Ding! A Bio-Discographical Scrapbook on Vic Dickenson, 7–69
Directory of Jazz Festivals and Related Major Jazz Events, Part One: Europe, 6–5
Directory of Musicians in Ireland, 6–15
Discographical Listing of Jazz Recordings of New Zealand, 1930–1980, 7–321
Discography of British Traditional Jazz Bands/Musicians, vol. 1: Avon Cities Skiffle Group 1956–1958; Avon Cities [Jazz Band] 1956–1997; Dick Charlesworth 1957–1994; Clyde Valley Stompers 1956–1983; Saints Jazz Band 1956–1983, 7–8, 7–44, 7–200, 7–258
Discography of British Traditional Jazz Bands/Musicians, vol. 2: Black Bottom Stompers 1971–1982; Bill Brunskill's Jazzmen 1972–1986; Brian Green 1965–1968, 1994–1996; Colin Kingwell's Jazz Bandits 1964–1995, 7–23, 7–34, 7–115, 7–159
Discography of British Traditional Jazz Bands/Musicians, vol. 3: Denise Lawrence & Storyville Tickle 1984–1997; The Savannah Jazz Band 1988–1997; Jim Shelley's (Frisco) Jazz Band 1976–1997, 7–168, 7–260, 7–264
Discography of British Traditional Jazz Bands, vol. 4: Chez Chesterman 1960–1998; Mike Daniels' Delta Jazz Band 1948–1995; Roy Kirby Paragon Jazz Band; John Maddocks 1971–1998, 7–47, 7–63, 7–161, 7–184
Discography of Danish Traditional Jazz Bands, vol. 1: Bourbon Street Jazzband 1975–1998; Gentlemen of Jazz 1989–1998; Pee Dee Jazzband 1988–1999; Vestre Jazzværk 1979–1997, 7–27, 7–109, 7–234, 7–302
Discography of Dutch Traditional Jazz Bands, vol. 1: Eric Krans' Dixieland Pipers 1950–1963; Bert de Kort's Dixieland Pipers 1977–1985; Harbour Jazz Band 1967–1996; Reunion Jazz

Band 1966–1998; Revival Jassband 1977–1993, 7–71, 7–120, 7–247, 7–248
Discography of Dutch Traditional Jazz Bands, vol. 2: Circus Square Jazz Band 1968–1995; Storyville Jassband 1968–1995; Freetime Old Dixie Jassband 1975–1995; Charlestown Jazzband 1971–1998, 7–43, 7–51, 7–107, 7–283
Discography of Gerhard "Doggy" Hund and the Maryland Jazz Band of Cologne, 7–139
Discography of the Down Town Band Leaders, 7–78
Discography of Mike Durham and West Jesmond Rhythm Kings, 7–80
Discography Peruna Jazzmen, 7–236
Discography Swiss Dixie Stompers, 7–292
Discovering Great Jazz, 8–8
Dixieland, 2–19
Dixonia, 7–72
Dizzy, 1–81
Dizzy Gillespie, 1–82
Doc Houlind Discography, 7–133
Donostiako Jazzaldia, 6–13
Don't You Sing, 1–96
Doris Day, 7–66
Dorsey Brothers and Their Orchestra, 7–75
Down Beat, 4–1
Drifting on a Read, 11–6
Drowning in the Sea of Love, 1–175
Drummin' Men, 3–4
Duke Ellington (Lambert), 1–63, 7–85
Duke Ellington (Rattenbury), 1–65
Duke Ellington (Steed), 1–66
Duke Ellington (Stratemann), 1–67
Duke Ellington on Compact Disc, 7–90
Duke Ellington Primer, 1–68
Duke Ellington Reader, 1–70
Duke's Bones, 1–189
Duke's Diary, Part One, 1–71
Duncan Swift Discography, 7–291
Dutch Swing College Band Discography, 7–81

Earthly Recordings of Sun Ra, 7–288
Easy Swing, 7–114
Eddy Howard and His Orchestra, 7–134
Eggy Ley Discography, 7–173
Ella Fitzgerald, 1–76
Ellington, 1–69
Ellingtonia, 1923–1974, 7–89
Elliot Lawrence and His Orchestra, 7–169
Erskine Hawkins and His Orchestra, 7–125
Essays on Jazz, 4–24
Evan Parker Discography, 7–230
Every Night Was New Year's Eve, 1–168

Faces in the Crowd, 4–18
Fall from Grace, 1–108
Fascinating Rhythm, 2–17
"Fats" in Fact, 7–303
Fessor Discography, 7–175
Festival International de Jazz de Montréal, 6–18
50 Jazz Greats from Heaven, 9–1
Fire Music, 10–2
First Bass, 7–238
First Call Drummer Don Lamond, 1–110
First Fifty Years, 2–38
First Lady of Song, 1–75
Frank Roberscheuten Discography, 7–253
Frank Rosolino, 7–256
Frank Sinatra (Britt), 1–152
Frank Sinatra (Sinatra), 1–161
Frank Sinatra, 1952–1981, 7–269
Frank Sinatra Reader, 1–159
Fred Hunt Discography, 7–140
Freddy Martin and His Orchestra, 7–191
Freddy Randall Discography, 7–245
Free Jazz, 2–33
Frits Kaatee Discography, 7–148
From Birdland to Broadway, 4–10
From Jazz to Swing, 2–18, 5–8
Frontiers of Jazz, 4–38
Future Jazz, 2–34

Gene Krupa and His Orchestra, 7–164
Genius That Was Django, 1–143
Geoff Cole Discography, 7–55
George Chisholm Discography, 7–48

George Kaatee Discography, Incorporating the New Orleans Syncopators, 7–149
George Melly Discography, Incorporating Mick Mulligan's Jazz Band, 7–199
Georgie Auld and His Orchestra, 7–7
Get Into Jazz, 2–9
Giant Steps, 1–209
Giant Strides, 1–172
Gigs, 6–44
Girl Singer, 1–35
Glass Enclosure, 1–137
Glen Gray & the Casa Loma Orchestra, 7–113
Glenn Miller, 1–121
Glenn Miller and His Orchestra, 7–204
Gloucester Gabriel, 1–1
Go Ahead, John, 1–117
Golden Age of Jazz, 9–9
Goldmine's Price Guide to Collectible Jazz Albums, 1949–1969, 8–10
Good Life, 1–19
Goodbyes and Other Messages, 4–2
Grant Green, 1–84
Great American Drums and the Companies That Made Them, 1920–1969, 3–2
Great College Jazz Orchestras, 1–227
Great Jazz Drummers, 3–6
Great Jazz Revival, 6–25
"Greatest Slideman Ever Born": A Discography of Edward "Kid" Ory, 7–226
Greatest Swing Band in the World, 1–87
Groovin' High, 1–80
Guide to Classic Recorded Jazz, 8–7
Guide to the Duke Ellington Recorded Legacy on LPs and CDs, vol. 1, 7–87
Guinness Who's Who of Jazz, 10–7
Guitar in Jazz, 3–8

Hal McIntyre and His Orchestra, 7–197
Hard Bop, 2–31
Harlem Ramblers Discography, 7–121
Harry James and His Orchestra, vols. 1–3, 7–143
Helen Forrest, 7–104
Henri Chaix Discography, 7–41

Henry Busse and His Orchestra; Plus: Clyde McCoy and His Orchestra, 7–39, 7–196
Henry King and His Orchestra, 7–156
Herman Chittison: A Bio-Discography, 7–49
History of Jazz, 2–11
History of Jazz in Paterson, 6–42
History of Jazz Tenor Saxophone: Black Artists, 7–329
Hitler's Airwaves, 6–7
Horace Heidt and His Orchestra, 7–128
Horn Works, 4–26
Hot Jazz, 1–196
Hot Man, 1–93

I Guess I'll Get the Papers and Go Home, 1–34
I Haven't Said Thanks, 1–203
Illustrated Story of Jazz, 2–14
In the Mainstream, 1–185
In the Moment, 4–13
In Search of Buddy Bolden, 1–25
Incident in Jazz, 4–41
Inside Paul Horn, 1–95
Isham Jones and His Orchestra, 7–145
Italian Instabile Orchestra, 1–229
It's About Time, 1–30

Jack Fallon Discography, 7–98
Jack Teagarden and His Orchestra, 7–293
Jackson Street After Hours, 6–52
Jaco, 1–132
Jammin' at the Margins, 2–39
Jan Garbarek, 1–78
Jan Garber and His Orchestra, 7–108
Jan Johansson, 1–100
Jan Morks Discography, 7–211
Jan Savitt and His Orchestra, 7–261
Jazz (Carlin), 2–5
Jazz (Cooke), 2–8
Jazz (van der Elsken), 9–20
Jazz: The American Theme Song, 4–8
Jazz: A Century of Change, 4–33
Jazz: A Crash Course, 2–1
Jazz: From Its Origins to the Present, 2–13
Jazz: Legends of Style, 1–218
Jazz: The 1980s Resurgence, 2–35

Jazz: La Photographie, 9–12
Jazz: Photographs, 9–18
Jazz: Photographs of the Masters, 9–13
Jazz: The Rough Guide, 10–4
Jazz Address Book, 9–19
Jazz Among the Discourses, 4–16
Jazz and Blues Lover's Guide to the U.S., 6–19
Jazz and the Cabaret Laws in New York City, 6–38
Jazz Anecdotes, 4–11
Jazz Anthology, 4–25
Jazz Book, 2–3
Jazz by Mail, 1936 to 1958, 7–334
Jazz Cadence of American Culture, 4–31
Jazz Changes, 4–42
Jazz Crusade, 6–31
Jazz Discography, 7–316
Jazz Duets, 1–200
Le Jazz en France, 7–319
Jazz Exiles, 1–213
Jazz Family Album, 9–11
Jazz for Dummies, 2–15
Jazz from the Beginning, 1–32
Jazz Gentry, 4–39
Jazz Greats, 1–214
Jazz Guitar, 3–9
Jazz Heroes, 1–192
Jazz in Black and White, 5–7
Jazz in Mind, 4–5
Jazz in Paris, 11–8
Jazz in Revolution, 1–48
Jazz in the Sixties, 2–32
Jazz Legends, 1–183
Jazz Man, 1–148
Jazz Man's Journey, 1–112
Jazz Map of New Orleans, 6–34
Jazz Memories, 4–4
Jazz Milestones, 2–16
Jazz Musician, 1–216
Jazz of the Southwest, 6–21
Jazz on CD, 8–2
Jazz on Japanese TV, 7–323
Jazz People of New Orleans, 9–7
Jazz Performers, 10–1
Jazz Pictures, 9–8
Jazz Portraits (Motion), 9–14

Jazz Portraits (Persson), 9–15
Jazz Profiles, 1–181
Jazz Records 1942–80, A Discography: Vol. 5, Dav–El, 7–317; Vol. 6, Duke Ellington, 7–88; Vol. 7 Ell–Fra, 7–317.
Jazz Research and Performance Materials, 10–3
Jazz Rock, 2–36
Jazz Scene, 4–23
Jazz Scrapbook (Historic New Orleans Collection), 1–146
Jazz Scrapbook (Oxtot), 1–128
Jazz Seen, 9–6
Jazz Singers, 1–215
Jazz Singing, 1–194
Jazz Spoken Here, 1–190
Jazz Standards on Record, 1900–1942, 7–328
Jazz Street, 9–2
Jazz Tenor Saxophone in Norway, 1917–1959, 7–318
Jazz Text, 11–5
Jazz Veterans, 1–186
Jazzin' the Black Forest, 7–325
Jazzplakate/Jazz Posters/Affiches de jazz, 9–24
Jean-Pierre Morel Discography, 7–209
Jelly Roll, Bix, and Hoagy, 6–30
Jess Stacy, 7–282
Jim McLeod's JazzTrack, 1–210
Jimmie Lunceford and His Orchestra, 7–180
Jimmie Lunceford Legacy on Records, 7–181
Jimmie Noone, 7–221
Jimmy Archey, 1–4
Jimmy Dorsey, 7–76
Joe Mooney, 1911–1975, 7–208
Joe Venuti and His Orchestra, 7–301
John Barnes Discography, 7–13
John Beecham Discography, 7–16
John Coltrane (Fujioka), 7–58
John Coltrane (Porter), 1–44
John Coltrane and the Jazz Revolution of the 1960s, 1–42
John Coltrane Companion, 1–45

John Kirby and His Orchestra; Plus Andy Kirk and His Orchestra, 7–160, 7–162
John Petters Discography, 7–237
John R. T. Davies Discography, 7–64
Johnny Long and His Orchestra, 7–177
Johnny Parker Discography, 7–231
Johnny Richards, 7–251
Joy of Jazz, 2–22
Joyful Noise, 6–37
Jukebox Saturday Night, 1–198
Jump for Joy, 1–61

Kansas City and All That Jazz, 6–40
Kay Kyser and His Orchestra, 7–165
Keeping Time, 4–40
Keith Ingham Discography, 7–142
Keith Jarrett, 1–99
Keith Nichols Discography, 7–218
Keith Smith Discography, 7–273
Ken Colyer Discography, 7–59
Ken Sims Discography, 7–268
Kenny Baker, 1–18
Kenny Ball Discography, 7–10
King of Ragtime, 1–103

Language of Jazz, 10–8
Larry Clinton and His Orchestra, 7–53
Lars Erstrand Discography, 7–94
Latin Jazz, 2–37
Laurie Chescoe Discography, 7–45
Leader of the Band, 1–91
Lee Wiley, 7–310
Legend, 1–162
Lennie Felix Discography, 7–100
Lennie Hastings Discography, 7–122
Les & Larry Elgart and Their Orchestras, 7–83, 7–84
Lester Young Reader, 1–178
Lestorian Notes, 7–313
Let the Good Times Roll, 1–105
Let's Dance, 2–23
Life in Ragtime, 1–72
Listen for the Jazz, 6–46
Listen: Gerry Mulligan, 7–214
Listen to the Stories, 4–22
Listen Up, 1–102
Little Red Book of Jazz Definitions, 4–37

Lost Chords, 1–221
Lost Jazz Shrines, 6–20
Louis Armstrong (Bergreen), 1–7
Louis Armstrong (Boujut), 1–9
Louis Armstrong (Miller), 1–11
Louis Armstrong, in His Own Words, 1–5
Louis Armstrong Companion, 1–8
Louis Armstrong 1923–1932, 7–5
Louis Armstrong Odyssey, 1–13
Louis Armstrong on the Screen, 1–12
Louis Jordan and His Orchestra, 7–146
Louis Prima and His Orchestra, 7–242
Lud Gluskin, 7–110
Lush Life, 1–166

M F Horn, 1–74
Madame Jazz, 1–231
Marabi Nights, 6–1
Marigold, 1–115
Martin Litton Discography, 7–176
Masters of Jazz, 1–179
Masters of Jazz Guitar, 3–7
Max Collie Discography, 7–57
Me and My Big Mouth, 1–1
Mel Bay Presents Bucky Pizzarelli, 1–135
Melodic and Polyrhythmic Development of John Coltrane's Spontaneous Composition in a Racist Society, 1–41
Melody Lingers On, 1–193
Merseysippi Jazz Band Discography, 7–201
Metal, Rock, and Jazz, 6–47
Mickey Ashman Discography, 7–6
Mike Pointon Discography, 7–239
Miles Davis (Cerchiari), 1–51
Miles Davis (Williams), 1–55
Miles Davis and David Liebman, 1–206
Miles Davis Companion, 1–50
Miles Davis Reader, 1–53
Milestones, 1–52
Milestones of Jazz, 2–7
Millergate, 1–122
Mills Brothers, 7–206
Mister, I Am the Band!, 7–250
Mitchell Ayres and His Orchestra, 7–9
Mixtery, 1–28
Monk, 1–123

Title Index

Monterey Jazz Festival, 6–26
Monty Sunshine Discography, 7–290
More Dialogues in Swing, 1–201
Morning Glory, 1–173
Muggsy Spanier, the Lonesome Road, 7–280
Music Men, 1–199
Music of Anthony Braxton, 1–27
Music of Billy May, 7–195
Music/Sound, 1948–1993, 7–278
Musical World of J.J. Johnson, 1–101
MusicHound Jazz, 8–4
MusicHound Swing!, 8–6
My Kind of Jazz, 4–34
My Singing Teachers, 1–223

Nat King Cole, 1–36
Nervous, Man, Nervous, 1–118
Never Sell a Copyright, 1–49
Neville Dickie Discography, 7–70
New Desor, an Updated Edition of Duke Ellington's Story on Records, 1924–1974, 7–86
New Dutch Swing, 6–10
New Grove Dictionary of Jazz, 10–6
New Musical Figurations, 1–29
New Orleans Clarinet, 7–138
New Orleans Jazz (Collins), 6–31
New Orleans Jazz (Martyn), 6–35
New Orleans Jazz and Second Line Drumming, 3–5
New Orleans Jazz Fest, 6–38
New Orleans Style, 6–36
New Orleans Syncopators, 7–147
New Perspectives on Jazz, 11–1
New Structures in Jazz and Improvised Music Since 1960, 5–2
New York Hot, 9–23
Notes and Tones, 1–222
Notes from a Battered Grand, 1–14
Now It's Jazz, 4–9

"Oh, Mister Jelly," 1–126
Ol' Blue Eyes, 1–158
Ole Brask, 9–4
Omniverse Sun Ra, 7–289

On the Road with the Jimmy Dorsey Aggravation, 1947–1949, 1–23
100 Years of Jazz & Blues, 6–43
One Man's Blues, 1–3
One Night Stand Series, 1–1001, 7–333
Orange Kellin Discography, 7–153
Ornette Coleman (Litweiler), 1–39
Ornette Coleman (Wilson), 1–40
Orrin Tucker and His Orchestra, 7–297
Oscar Klein Discography, 7–163
Oscar Peterson, 1–134
Other Music City, 6–50
Outcats, 1–184
Over the Waves, 7–119
Overtime, 9–10
Ozzie Nelson and His Orchestra, 7–216

Papa Bue Discography 1954–1998, 7–36
Passion's Piano, 1–92
Paul Strandberg Discography, 7–285
Pee Wee Russell, 1–147
Pee Wee Speaks, 7–257
Penguin Guide to Jazz on CD, 8–1
Pete Allen Discography, 7–2
Pete Lay Discography, 7–170
Pete Strange Discography, 7–286
Peter "Banjo" Meyer Discography, 7–203
Phil Mason Discography, 7–192
Picador Book of Blues and Jazz, 4–6
Pres, 1–177
Preservation Hall, 6–32
Pure at Heart, 1–163

Rage to Survive, 1–97
Ralph Flanagan and His Orchestra, 7–103
Ralph Marterie and His Orchestra, 7–190
Ray Foxley Discography, 7–106
Ray Noble and His Orchestra, 7–220
Ray Smith Discography, 7–274
Raymond Scott and His Orchestra, 7–262
Reading Jazz (Gottlieb), 4–20
Reading Jazz (Meltzer), 4–28
Really the Blues, 1–119
Red Head, 1–127
Recordings of Bob Shoffner, 7–267
Recordings of Jabbo Smith, 7–272

Recordings of Joe "King" Oliver, 7–223
Red Nichols Story, 7–219
Reference Back, 4–27
Rejoice When You Die, 6–39
Reluctant Art, 4–21
Reminiscing in Swingtime, 5–12
Reminiscing in Tempo (Nicholson), 1–64
Reminiscing in Tempo (Reig), 1–142
Representing Jazz, 4–17
Rhythm Man, 1–106
Richard Himber and His Orchestra, 7–132
Richard Maltby and His Orchestra, 7–185
Rockers, Jazzbos and Visionaries, 1–211
Rod Mason Discography, 7–193
Roger Marks Discography, 7–188
Rolling Stone Jazz and Blues Album Guide, 8–9
Rose Murphy Discography, 7–215
'Round About Midnight, 1–54
Roy Williams Discography, 1956–1997, 7–311
Russ Morgan and His Orchestra, 7–207

Salsiology, 2–4
Sam Donahue and His Orchestra, 7–74
Sammy Rimington Discography, 7–252
Sandy Brown Discography, 7–33
Sarah Vaughan, 7–300
Sassy, 1–171
Satchmo, 1–10
Satchmo, Duke, Rabbit, and Me, 1–202
Saying Something, 5–5
Seeing Jazz, 4–14
Serge Chaloff, 7–42
Sessions with Sinatra, 1–156
Setting the Tempo, 2–40
70 Years of Recorded Jazz, 7–315
Sheik's Blues, 7–54
Shelly Manne, 7–186
Shep Fields and His Orchestra, 7–101
Shooting from the Hip, 4–15
Sideman, 1–164
Sinatra (Britt), 1–139
Sinatra (Coleman), 1–154
Sinatra (Irwin), 1–157
Sinatra (Sayers), 1–160, 7–270

Sinatra! The Song is You, 1–155
Singing Jazz, 1–182
Sites and Sounds of Savannah Jazz, 6–28
Sitting In, 4–7
Skiffle Craze, 2–10
Slovak Popular Music and Jazz, 6–11
Song of the Hawk, 1–86
Song Stars, 1–232
Sonic Boom, 3–3
Sonny Burke and His Orchestra; Plus: Skinnay Ennis and His Orchestra, 7–38, 7–93
Sonny Dunham and His Orchestra; Plus: Ziggy Elman and His Orchestra, 7–79, 7–91
Sonny Morris Discography, 7–212
Sound of Miles Davis, 7–65
Space Is the Place, 1–167
Splasc(h) Records, 7–326
Stan Getz, 1–79
Stan Greig Discography, 7–116
Stan Kenton, 1–107
Stan Kenton and His Orchestra, vol. 1: 1940–1951, 7–154
Stan Kenton and His Orchestra, vol. 3: 1960–1979, 7–155
Stars of Jazz, 9–3
Steve Lane Discography, Incorporating the Famous Southern Stompers, 7–166
Stir It Up, 4–36
Story of Jazz, 2–28
Straight, No Chaser, 1–125
Straighten Up and Fly Right, 7–56
Stride!, 3–10
Stuff Smith Discography, 7–277
Such Melodious Racket, 6–16
Suits Me, 1–170
Sweet Butterfingers, 1–149
Sweet Swing Blues on the Road, 1–114
Swing Changes, 2–24
Swing City, 6–41
Swing Era, New York, 6–45
Swing It, 1–212
Swing Out, 1–191
Swing, Swing, Swing, 1–83
Swing That Music, 1–6

Swingin' the Dream, 2–21
Swinging Beginning, 7–259
Swinging Big Bands Into the 90s, 1–224
Sy Oliver and His Orchestra, 7–224
Sylvester Ahola, 1–2

Tadd, 1–47
Talking Jazz, 1–219
Talking Swing, 1–225
Tantalizing Tingles, 7–331
Ted Lewis and His Orchestra, 7–172
Ted Weems and His Orchestra, 7–307
Teddy Powell and His Orchestra, 7–241
Teddy Wilson Talks Jazz, 1–174
Tell Roy Rogers I'm Not In, 1–37
Terry Lightfoot Discography, 7–174
Tex Beneke and His Orchestra, 7–18
Texan Jazz, 6–51
Texas Shout, 4–43
Thelonious Monk, 1–124
There and Back, 1–136
They Died Too Young, 1–120
Thinking in Jazz, 5–1
This Thing Called Swing, 2–20
Thousand Honey Creeks Later, 1–111
Three Kilos of Coffee, 1–58
Tiny Bradshaw and His Orchestra; Plus: Lucky Millinder and His Orchestra, 7–30, 7–205
Tiny Hill and His Orchestra; Plus: Ray Herbeck and His Orchestra, 7–129, 7–131
Tito Puente and the Making of Latin Music, 1–140
Tomas Örnberg/Bent Persson, 7–225, 7–235
Tommy Dorsey, 7–77
Tommy Tucker and His Orchestra, 7–298
Tony Bennett, 1–20
Tony Pastor and His Orchestra, 7–232
Tony Pringle Discography, Incorporating the New Black Eagle Jazz Band, 7–243
Too Marvelous for Words, 1–169
Toronto Jazz, 6–17
Traditionalists and Revivalists in Jazz, 1–187
Tram, 7–296

Traps, the Drum Wonder, 1–144
Trombone, 3–12
Trumpet Blues, 1–98
Trumpet Story, 1–38
Tubby Hayes, 7–126
Twelve Lives in Jazz, 1–217
25 Years, 1–228

Unclosed Eye, 9–16
Unzipped Souls, 6–12
Up Jumped the Devil, 7–276

Vaughn Monroe and His Orchestra, 7–207
Vincent Lopez and His Orchestra, 7–178
Visions of Jazz, 1–195
Vogue Productions, 7–327
Voices of the Jazz Age, 1–188

Wally Fawkes Discography, 7–99
Wayne King and His Orchestra, 7–157
Werner Keller—Tremble Kids Discography, 7–152
West Coast Jazz, 6–24
What About Jazz in Finland?, 6–6
What Do They Want?, 1–139
What Jazz Is, 2–12
What to Listen for in Jazz, 5–3
When Art Farmer Remembered Gigi Gryce, 1–85
When the Music Stopped, 2–27
Who's Who in Rhode Island Jazz c. 1925–1988, 6–49
Wild Bill Davison, 1–56
Wildest One, 1–57
Will Bradley and His Orchestra; Plus: Freddie Slack and His Orchestra, 7–29, 7–271
Will Hudson and His Orchestra; The Hudson-Delange Orchestra; Eddie Delange and His Orchestra; George Paxton and His Orchestra; Bob Strong and His Orchestra, 7–68, 7–137, 7–233, 7–287
Will Osborne and His Orchestra, 7–227
The Will to Swing, 1–122
Willard Robinson and His Piano, 7–255

Wingy Manone and His Orchestra, 7–187
The Woodchopper's Ball, 1–89
Woody Herman (Clancy), 1–88
Woody Herman (Morrill), 7–130
World of Gene Krupa, 1–109
World of Jazz, 11–3
Writing Jazz, 4–29
Wynton Marsalis, 1–113

Xavier Cugat and His Orchestra, 7–62

You Got to Be Original, Man!, 7–312
You Just Fight for Your Life, 1–176
Young Chet, 1–16

Zenith Hot Stompers Discography, 7–314

About the Author

Janice Greenberg is a graduate of Douglass College, and earned an MLS from Rutgers University. She is a senior librarian in the Technical Services Department of the Jersey City Free Public Library.

She researched and wrote the chapter "Collection Development: Bibliography" for the book *Library Services to Youth of Hispanic Heritage*, edited by Barbara Immroth and Kathleen de la Peña McCook (McFarland, 2000). Her previous bibliography, "Participative Leadership," was written for the Trejo Foster Foundation's Third Institute ("Leadership for the 21st Century," 1997), held at Rutgers University.

Breinigsville, PA USA
10 March 2010
233955BV00002B/1/P